interchange

FIFTH EDITION

2

Student's Book

Jack C. Richards

with Jonathan Hull and Susan Proctor

WITH ONLINE SELF-STUDY

CAMBRIDGE UNIVERSITY PRESS

CAMBRIDGE
UNIVERSITY PRESS

University Printing House, Cambridge CB2 8BS, United Kingdom

One Liberty Plaza, 20th Floor, New York, NY 10006, USA

477 Williamstown Road, Port Melbourne, VIC 3207, Australia

314–321, 3rd Floor, Plot 3, Splendor Forum, Jasola District Centre, New Delhi – 110025, India

79 Anson Road, #06–04/06, Singapore 079906

Cambridge University Press is part of the University of Cambridge.

It furthers the University's mission by disseminating knowledge in the pursuit of education, learning and research at the highest international levels of excellence.

www.cambridge.org
Information on this title: www.cambridge.org/9781316623992

First published 2005
Second edition 2013

20 19 18 17 16 15 14 13 12 11 10

Printed in Poland by Opolgraf

A catalogue record for this publication is available from the British Library

ISBN	9781316620236	Student's Book 2 with Online Self-Study
ISBN	9781316620250	Student's Book 2A with Online Self-Study
ISBN	9781316620328	Student's Book 2B with Online Self-Study
ISBN	9781316620342	Student's Book 2 with Online Self-Study and Online Workbook
ISBN	9781316620366	Student's Book 2A with Online Self-Study and Online Workbook
ISBN	9781316620373	Student's Book 2B with Online Self-Study and Online Workbook
ISBN	9781316622698	Workbook 2
ISBN	9781316622704	Workbook 2A
ISBN	9781316622711	Workbook 2B
ISBN	9781316622728	Teacher's Edition 2 with Complete Assessment Program
ISBN	9781316622285	Class Audio 2 CDs
ISBN	9781316623992	Full Contact 2 with Online Self-Study
ISBN	9781316624005	Full Contact 2A with Online Self-Study
ISBN	9781316624029	Full Contact 2B with Online Self-Study
ISBN	9781108403061	Presentation Plus 2

Additional resources for this publication at www.cambridge.org/interchange

Cambridge University Press has no responsibility for the persistence or accuracy of URLs for external or third-party internet websites referred to in this publication, and does not guarantee that any content on such websites is, or will remain, accurate or appropriate. Information regarding prices, travel timetables, and other factual information given in this work is correct at the time of first printing but Cambridge University Press does not guarantee the accuracy of such information thereafter.

Informed by teachers

Teachers from all over the world helped develop *Interchange Fifth Edition*. They looked at everything – from the color of the designs to the topics in the conversations – in order to make sure that this course will work in the classroom. We heard from 1,500 teachers in:

- Surveys
- Focus Groups
- In-Depth Reviews

We appreciate the help and input from everyone. In particular, we'd like to give the following people our special thanks:

Jader Franceschi, **Actúa Idiomas,** Bento Gonçalves, Rio Grande do Sul, Brazil

Juliana Dos Santos Voltan Costa, **Actus Idiomas,** São Paulo, Brazil

Ella Osorio, **Angelo State University,** San Angelo, TX, US

Mary Hunter, **Angelo State University,** San Angelo, TX, US

Mario César González, **Angloamericano de Monterrey, SC,** Monterrey, Mexico

Samantha Shipman, **Auburn High School,** Auburn, AL, US

Linda, **Bernick Language School,** Radford, VA, US

Dave Lowrance, **Bethesda University of California,** Yorba Linda, CA, US

Tajbakhsh Hosseini, **Bezmialem Vakif University,** Istanbul, Turkey

Dilek Gercek, **Bil English,** Izmir, Turkey

Erkan Kolat, **Biruni University, ELT,** Istanbul, Turkey

Nika Gutkowska, **Bluedata International,** New York, NY, US

Daniel Alcocer Gómez, **Cecati 92,** Guadalupe, Nuevo León, Mexico

Samantha Webb, **Central Middle School,** Milton-Freewater, OR, US

Verónica Salgado, **Centro Anglo Americano,** Cuernavaca, Mexico

Ana Rivadeneira Martínez and Georgia P. de Machuca, **Centro de Educación Continua – Universidad Politécnica del Ecuador,** Quito, Ecuador

Anderson Francisco Guimerães Maia, **Centro Cultural Brasil Estados Unidos,** Belém, Brazil

Rosana Mariano, **Centro Paula Souza,** São Paulo, Brazil

Carlos de la Paz Arroyo, Teresa Noemí Parra Alarcón, Gilberto Bastida Gaytan, Manuel Esquivel Román, and Rosa Cepeda Tapia, **Centro Universitario Angloamericano,** Cuernavaca, Morelos, Mexico

Antonio Almeida, **CETEC,** Morelos, Mexico

Cinthia Ferreira, **Cinthia Ferreira Languages Services,** Toronto, ON, Canada

Phil Thomas and Sérgio Sanchez, **CLS Canadian Language School,** São Paulo, Brazil

Celia Concannon, **Cochise College,** Nogales, AZ, US

Maria do Carmo Rocha and CAOP English team, **Colégio Arquidiocesano Ouro Preto – Unidade Cônego Paulo Dilascio,** Ouro Preto, Brazil

Kim Rodriguez, **College of Charleston North,** Charleston, SC, US

Jesús Leza Alvarado, **Coparmex English Institute,** Monterrey, Mexico

John Partain, **Cortazar,** Guanajuato, Mexico

Alexander Palencia Navas, **Cursos de Lenguas, Universidad del Atlántico,** Barranquilla, Colombia

Kenneth Johan Gerardo Steenhuisen Cera, Melfi Osvaldo Guzman Triana, and Carlos Alberto Algarín Jiminez, **Cursos de Lenguas Extranjeras Universidad del Atlantico,** Barranquilla, Colombia

Jane P Kerford, **East Los Angeles College,** Pasadena, CA, US

Daniela, **East Village,** Campinas, São Paulo, Brazil

Rosalva Camacho Orduño, **Easy English for Groups S.A. de C.V.,** Monterrey, Nuevo León, Mexico

Adonis Gimenez Fusetti, **Easy Way Idiomas,** Ibiúna, Brazil

Eileen Thompson, **Edison Community College,** Piqua, OH, US

Ahminne Handeri O.L Froede, **Englishhouse escola de idiomas,** Teófilo Otoni, Brazil

Ana Luz Delgado-Izazola, **Escuela Nacional Preparatoria 5, UNAM,** Mexico City, Mexico

Nancy Alarcón Mendoza, **Facultad de Estudios Superiores Zaragoza, UNAM,** Mexico City, Mexico

Marcilio N. Barros, **Fast English USA,** Campinas, São Paulo, Brazil

Greta Douthat, **FCI Ashland,** Ashland, KY, US

Carlos Lizárraga González, **Grupo Educativo Anglo Americano, S.C.,** Mexico City, Mexico

Hugo Fernando Alcántar Valle, **Instituto Politécnico Nacional, Escuela Superior de Comercio y Administración-Unidad Santotomás, Celex Esca Santo Tomás,** Mexico City, Mexico

Sueli Nascimento, **Instituto Superior de Educação do Rio de Janeiro,** Rio de Janeiro, Brazil

Elsa F Monteverde, **International Academic Services,** Miami, FL, US

Laura Anand, **Irvine Adult School,** Irvine, CA, US

Prof. Marli T. Fernandes (principal) and Prof. Dr. Jefferson J. Fernandes (pedagogue), **Jefferson Idiomass,** São Paulo, Brazil

Herman Bartelen, **Kanda Gaigo Gakuin,** Tokyo, Japan

Cassia Silva, **Key Languages,** Key Biscayne, FL, US

Sister Mary Hope, **Kyoto Notre Dame Joshi Gakuin,** Kyoto, Japan

Nate Freedman, **LAL Language Centres,** Boston, MA, US

Richard Janzen, **Langley Secondary School,** Abbotsford, BC, Canada

Christina Abel Gabardo, **Language House,** Campo Largo, Brazil

Ivonne Castro, **Learn English International,** Cali, Colombia

Julio Cesar Maciel Rodrigues, **Liberty Centro de Línguas,** São Paulo, Brazil

Ann Gibson, **Maynard High School,** Maynard, MA, US

Martin Darling, **Meiji Gakuin Daigaku,** Tokyo, Japan

Dax Thomas, **Meiji Gakuin Daigaku,** Yokohama, Kanagawa, Japan

Derya Budak, **Mevlana University,** Konya, Turkey

B Sullivan, **Miami Valley Career Technical Center International Program,** Dayton, OH, US

Julio Velazquez, **Milo Language Center,** Weston, FL, US

Daiane Siqueira da Silva, Luiz Carlos Buontempo, Marlete Avelina de Oliveira Cunha, Marcos Paulo Segatti, Morgana Eveline de Oliveira, Nadia Lia Gino Alo, and Paul Hyde Budgen, **New Interchange-Escola de Idiomas,** São Paulo, Brazil

Patrícia França Furtado da Costa, Juiz de Fora, Brazil

Patricia Servín

Chris Pollard, **North West Regional College SK,** North Battleford, SK, Canada

Olga Amy, **Notre Dame High School,** Red Deer, Canada

Amy Garrett, **Ouachita Baptist University,** Arkadelphia, AR, US

Mervin Curry, **Palm Beach State College,** Boca Raton, FL, US

Julie Barros, **Quality English Studio,** Guarulhos, São Paulo, Brazil

Teodoro González Saldaña and Jesús Monserrrta Mata Franco, **Race Idiomas,** Mexico City, Mexico

Autumn Westphal and Noga La`or, **Rennert International,** New York, NY, US

Antonio Gallo and Javy Palau, **Rigby Idiomas,** Monterrey, Mexico Tatiane Gabriela Sperb do Nascimento, **Right Way,** Igrejinha, Brazil

Mustafa Akgül, **Selahaddin Eyyubi Universitesi,** Diyarbakır, Turkey

James Drury M. Fonseca, **Senac Idiomas Fortaleza,** Fortaleza, Ceara, Brazil

Manoel Fialho S Neto, **Senac – PE,** Recife, Brazil

Jane Imber, **Small World,** Lawrence, KS, US

Tony Torres, **South Texas College,** McAllen, TX, US

Janet Rose, **Tennessee Foreign Language Institute,** College Grove, TN, US

Todd Enslen, **Tohoku University,** Sendai, Miyagi, Japan

Daniel Murray, **Torrance Adult School,** Torrance, CA, US

Juan Manuel Pulido Mendoza, **Universidad del Atlántico,** Barranquilla, Colombia

Juan Carlos Vargas Millán, **Universidad Libre Seccional Cali,** Cali (Valle del Cauca), Colombia

Carmen Cecilia Llanos Ospina, **Universidad Libre Seccional Cali,** Cali, Colombia

Jorge Noriega Zenteno, **Universidad Politécnica del Valle de México,** Estado de México, Mexico

Aimee Natasha Holguin S., **Universidad Politécnica del Valle de México UPVM,** Tultitlàn Estado de México, Mexico

Christian Selene Bernal Barraza, **UPVM Universidad Politécnica del Valle de México,** Ecatepec, Mexico

Lizeth Ramos Acosta, **Universidad Santiago de Cali,** Cali, Colombia

Silvana Dushku, **University of Illinois Champaign,** IL, US

Deirdre McMurtry, **University of Nebraska – Omaha,** Omaha, NE, US

Jason E Mower, **University of Utah,** Salt Lake City, UT, US

Paul Chugg, **Vanguard Taylor Language Institute,** Edmonton, Alberta, Canada

Henry Mulak, **Varsity Tutors,** Los Angeles, CA, US

Shirlei Strucker Calgaro and Hugo Guilherme Karrer, **VIP Centro de Idiomas,** Panambi, Rio Grande do Sul, Brazil

Eleanor Kelly, **Waseda Daigaku Extension Centre,** Tokyo, Japan

Sherry Ashworth, **Wichita State University,** Wichita, KS, US

Laine Bourdene, **William Carey University,** Hattiesburg, MS, US

Serap Aydın, Istanbul, Turkey

Liliana Covino, Guarulhos, Brazil

Yannuarys Jiménez, Barranquilla, Colombia

Juliana Morais Pazzini, Toronto, ON, Canada

Marlon Sanches, Montreal, Canada

Additional content contributed by Kenna Bourke, Inara Couto, Nic Harris, Greg Manin, Ashleigh Martinez, Laura McKenzie, Paul McIntyre, Clara Prado, Lynne Robertson, Mari Vargo, Theo Walker, and Maria Lucia Zaorob.

Classroom Language Student questions

Plan of Book 2

Titles/Topics	Speaking	Grammar
UNIT 1 PAGES 2–7		
Good memories People; childhood; memories	Introducing yourself; talking about yourself; exchanging personal information; remembering your childhood; asking about someone's childhood	Past tense; *used to* for habitual actions
UNIT 2 PAGES 8–13		
Life in the city Transportation; transportation problems; city services	Talking about transportation and transportation problems; evaluating city services; asking for and giving information	Expressions of quantity with count and noncount nouns: *too many, too much, fewer, less, more, not enough*; indirect questions from Wh-questions
PROGRESS CHECK PAGES 14–15		
UNIT 3 PAGES 16–21		
Making changes Houses and apartments; lifestyle changes; wishes	Describing positive and negative features; making comparisons; talking about lifestyle changes; expressing wishes	Evaluations and comparisons with adjectives: *not . . . enough, too, (not) as . . . as*; evaluations and comparisons with nouns: *not enough . . . , too much/many . . . , (not) as much/many . . . as; wish*
UNIT 4 PAGES 22–27		
Have you ever tried it? Food; recipes; cooking instructions; cooking methods	Talking about food; expressing likes and dislikes; describing a favorite snack; giving step-by-step instructions	Simple past vs. present perfect; sequence adverbs: *first, then, next, after that, finally*
PROGRESS CHECK PAGES 28–29		
UNIT 5 PAGES 30–35		
Hit the road! Travel; vacations; plans	Describing vacation plans; giving travel advice; planning a vacation	Future with *be going to* and *will*; modals for necessity and suggestion: *must, need to, (don't) have to, ought to, -'d better, should (not)*
UNIT 6 PAGES 36–41		
Sure! I'll do it. Complaints; household chores; requests; excuses; apologies	Making requests; agreeing to and refusing requests; complaining; apologizing; giving excuses	Two-part verbs; *will* for responding to requests; requests with modals and *Would you mind . . . ?*
PROGRESS CHECK PAGES 42–43		
UNIT 7 PAGES 44–49		
What do you use this for? Technology; instructions	Describing technology; giving instructions; giving suggestions	Infinitives and gerunds for uses and purposes; imperatives and infinitives for giving suggestions
UNIT 8 PAGES 50–55		
Time to celebrate! Holidays; festivals; customs; celebrations	Describing holidays, festivals, customs, and special events	Relative clauses of time; adverbial clauses of time: *when, after, before*
PROGRESS CHECK PAGES 56–57		

Pronunciation/Listening	Writing/Reading	Interchange Activity
Reduced form of *used to* Listening to people talk about their past	Writing a paragraph about your childhood "A Life in Paintings: The Frida Kahlo Story": Reading about the life of this Mexican painter	"We have a lot in common.": Finding out about a classmate's childhood **PAGE 114**
Syllable stress Listening to a description of a transportation system	Writing an online post on a community message board about a local issue "The World's Happiest Cities": Reading about the happiest cities in the world	"Top travel destinations": Suggesting ways to attract tourists to a city **PAGE 115**
Unpronounced vowels Listening to people talk about capsule hotels	Writing an email comparing two living spaces "The Man with No Money": Reading about living without money	"A dream come true": Finding out about a classmate's wishes **PAGE 116**
Consonant clusters Listening to descriptions of foods	Writing a recipe "Pizza: The World's Favorite Food?": Reading about the history of pizza	"Oh, really?": Surveying classmates about their experiences **PAGE 117**
Linked sounds with /w/ and /y/ Listening to travel advice	Writing an email with travel suggestions "Adventure Vacations": Reading about unusual vacations	"Fun trips": Deciding on a trip **PAGES 118, 120**
Stress in two-part verbs Listening to the results of a survey about family life	Writing a message making a request "Hotel Madness: The Crazy Things People Say!": Reading about unusual hotel requests	"I'm terribly sorry.": Apologizing and making amends **PAGE 119**
Syllable stress Listening to a radio program; listening to people give suggestions for using technology	Writing a message asking for specific favors "The Sharing Economy – Good for Everybody?": Reading about the sharing economy	"Free advice": Giving advice to classmates **PAGE 121**
Stress and rhythm Listening to a description of Carnival in Brazil	Writing an entry on a travel website about a cultural custom "Out with the Old, In with the New": Reading about interesting New Year's customs	"It's worth celebrating.": Finding out how classmates celebrate special events **PAGE 122**

Titles/Topics	Speaking	Grammar

Pronunciation/Listening	Writing/Reading	Interchange Activity
Intonation in statements with time phrases Listening to people talk about changes	Writing a paragraph describing a person's past, present, and possible future "Aquaviva: Fighting for a Future": Reading about a town's attempt to attract new residents	"Cause and effect": Agreeing and disagreeing with classmates **PAGE 123**
Unreleased and released /t/ and /d/ Listening to people talk about their job preferences	Writing a an online cover letter for a job application "Global Work Solutions": Reading about understanding cultural differences in an international company	"You're hired.": Interviewing for a job **PAGE 124**
The letter o Listening to descriptions of monuments; listening for information about a country	Writing an introduction to an online city guide Reading about unusual museums	"True or false?": Sharing information about famous works **PAGE 125**
Contrastive stress in responses Listening to stories about unexpected experiences	Writing a description of a recent experience "Breaking Down the Sound of Silence": Reading about an unusual rock band	"It's my life.": Playing a board game to share past experiences **PAGE 126**
Emphatic stress Listening for opinions; listening to a movie review	Writing a movie review "The Real Art of Acting": Reading about unpleasant experiences actors put themselves through	"It was hilarious!": Asking classmates' opinions about movies, TV shows, and celebrities **PAGE 127**
Pitch Listening to people talk about the meaning of signs	Writing a list of rules "Understanding Idioms": Reading about idioms and their meaning	"Casual observers": Interpreting body language **PAGE 128**
Reduction of have Listening to people talk about predicaments; listening to a call-in radio show	Writing a blog post asking for advice "TOPTIPS.COM": Reading an online advice forum	"Tough choices": Deciding what to do in a difficult situation **PAGE 130**
Reduction of had and would Listening for excuses	Writing a report about people's responses to a survey "A Good Excuse for a Day Off Work": Reading about taking a sick day	"Just a bunch of excuses": Discussing calendar conflicts and making up excuses **PAGES 129, 131**

1 Good memories

▸ **Ask questions to get to know people**
▸ **Discuss childhoods**

1 SNAPSHOT

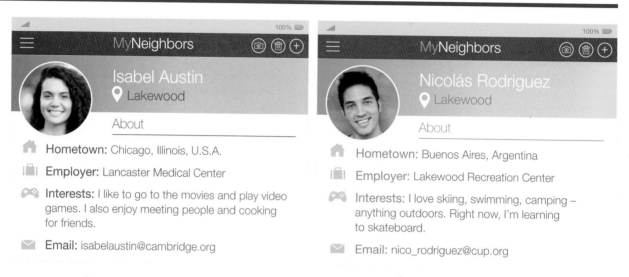

MyNeighbors 100%	**MyNeighbors** 100%
Isabel Austin ⦿ Lakewood	**Nicolás Rodriguez** ⦿ Lakewood
About	About
🏠 **Hometown:** Chicago, Illinois, U.S.A.	🏠 **Hometown:** Buenos Aires, Argentina
💼 **Employer:** Lancaster Medical Center	💼 **Employer:** Lakewood Recreation Center
🎮 **Interests:** I like to go to the movies and play video games. I also enjoy meeting people and cooking for friends.	🎮 **Interests:** I love skiing, swimming, camping – anything outdoors. Right now, I'm learning to skateboard.
✉ **Email:** isabelaustin@cambridge.org	✉ **Email:** nico_rodriguez@cup.org

Nicolás and Isabel are neighbors. Do you think they could be friends?

What social media sites do you belong to? Which one is your favorite?

Create your own online profile and share it with your classmates. What things do you have in common?

2 CONVERSATION Where did you learn to skateboard?

▶ **A** Listen and practice.

Isabel: Oh, I'm really sorry. Are you OK?

Nico: I'm fine. But I'm not very good at this.

Isabel: Neither am I . . . . Hey, I like your shirt. Are you from Argentina?

Nico: Yes, I am, originally. I was born there.

Isabel: Did you grow up there?

Nico: Yes, I did, but my family moved here 10 years ago, when I was in middle school.

Isabel: And where did you learn to skateboard?

Nico: Here in the park. I only started about a month ago.

Isabel: Well, it's my *first* time. Can you give me some lessons?

Nico: Sure. Just follow me.

Isabel: By the way, my name is Isabel.

Nico: And I'm Nico. Nice to meet you.

▶ **B** Listen to the rest of the conversation. What are two more things you learn about Isabel?

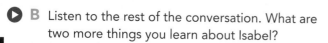

3 GRAMMAR FOCUS

▶ Past tense

Where **were** you born?

I **was** born in Argentina.

Were you born in Buenos Aires?

Yes, I **was**.

No, I **wasn't**. I **was** born in Córdoba.

When **did** you **move** to Los Angeles?

I **moved** here 10 years ago. I **didn't speak** English.

Did you **take** English classes in Argentina?

Yes, I **did**. I **took** classes for a year.

No, I **didn't**. My aunt **taught** me at home.

GRAMMAR PLUS *see page 132*

A Complete these conversations. Then practice with a partner.

1. A: Your English is very good. When _____ you begin to study English?

B: I _____ in middle school.

A: What _____ you think of English class at first?

B: I _____ it was a little difficult, but fun.

2. A: Where _____ you born?

B: I _____ born in Mexico.

A: _____ you grow up there?

B: No, I _____ . I _____ up in Canada.

3. A: Where _____ you meet your best friend?

B: We _____ in high school.

A: Do you still see each other?

B: Yes, but not very often. She _____ to South Korea two years ago.

4. A: _____ you have a favorite teacher when you _____ a child?

B: Yes, I _____ . I _____ a very good teacher named Mr. Potter.

A: What _____ he teach?

B: He _____ math.

B PAIR WORK Take turns asking the questions in part A. Give your own information when answering.

4 LISTENING Why did you move?

▶ A Listen to interviews with two immigrants to the United States. Why did they move to the U.S.A.?

▶ B Listen again and complete the chart.

	Enrique	Jessica
1. What were the most difficult changes?		
2. What do they miss the most?		

C GROUP WORK Enrique and Jessica talk about difficult changes. What could be some positive things about moving to a city like New York?

5 SPEAKING Tell me about yourself.

A PAIR WORK Check (✓) six questions below and add your own questions.
Then interview a classmate you don't know very well. Ask follow-up questions.

- ☐ Where were your grandparents born?
- ☐ Where did they grow up?
- ☐ Did you see them a lot when you were young?
- ☐ Who's your favorite relative?

- ☐ When did you first study English?
- ☐ Can you speak other languages?
- ☐ What were your best subjects in middle school?
- ☐ What subjects didn't you like?

A: Where were your grandparents born?
B: My grandfather was born in Brazil,
but my grandmother was born in Colombia.
A: Really? Where did they first meet?

useful expressions

Oh, that's interesting.
Really? Me, too!
Wow! Tell me more.

B GROUP WORK Tell the group what you learned about your partner. Then answer any questions.

"Vera's grandfather was born in Brazil, but her grandmother was born in . . ."

6 WORD POWER

A Complete the word map. Add two more words of your own to each category.
Then compare with a partner.

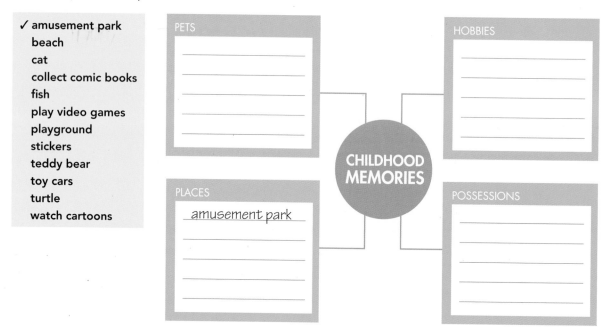

✓ amusement park
beach
cat
collect comic books
fish
play video games
playground
stickers
teddy bear
toy cars
turtle
watch cartoons

PETS

HOBBIES

CHILDHOOD MEMORIES

PLACES
  amusement park

POSSESSIONS

B PAIR WORK Choose three words from the word map and use them
to describe some of your childhood memories.

A: I loved to watch cartoons when I was a kid.
B: Me, too. What was your favorite?
A: I liked anything with superheroes in it. What about you?

7 PERSPECTIVES When I was a kid . . .

A Listen to these statements about changes. Check (✓) those that are true about you.

- [ ] **1.** "When I was a kid, I never used to play sports, but now I like to keep fit."
- [ ] **2.** "I used to go out with friends a lot, but now I don't have any free time."
- [ ] **3.** "When I was younger, I didn't use to collect anything, but now I do."
- [ ] **4.** "I didn't use to be a good student, but now I love to study and learn new things."
- [ ] **5.** "I never used to follow politics, but now I read the news online every morning."
- [ ] **6.** "I used to be really neat and organized, but now I'm very messy."
- [ ] **7.** "I used to care a lot about my appearance. Now, I'm too busy to care about how I look."

B **PAIR WORK** Look at the statements again. Which changes are positive? Which are negative?

"I think the first one is a positive change. It's good to exercise."

8 GRAMMAR FOCUS

Used to

Used to **refers to something that you regularly did in the past but don't do anymore.**

Did you **use to** collect things?

　Yes, I **used to** collect comic books.

　No, I **didn't use to** collect anything,
　but now I collect old records.

What sports **did** you **use to** play?

　I **used to play** baseball and volleyball.

　I **never used to** play sports,
　but now I play tennis.

GRAMMAR PLUS *see page 132*

A Complete these questions and answers. Then compare with a partner.

1. **A:** _____Did_____ you _____use to_____ have any pets when you were a kid?
   B: Yes, I _____ have a white cat named Snowball.

2. **A:** _____ you and your classmates _____ play together after school?
   B: No, we _____ play during the week. We _____ study a lot.

3. **A:** What music _____ you _____ listen to?
   B: I _____ listen to rock a lot. Actually, I still do.

4. **A:** What hobbies _____ you _____ have when you were little?
   B: I _____ have any hobbies, but now I play chess every week.

B How have you changed? Write sentences about yourself using *used to* or *didn't use to*. Then compare with a partner. Who has changed the most?

your hairstyle　　　your taste in music
your hobbies　　　　the way you dress

> I used to wear my hair much longer.
> I didn't use to have a beard.

9 PRONUNCIATION *Used to*

▶ **A** Listen and practice. Notice that the pronunciation of **used to** and **use to** is the same.

When I was a child, I **used to** play the guitar.
I **used to** have a nickname.
I didn't **use to** like scary movies.
I didn't **use to** study very hard at school.

B **PAIR WORK** Practice the sentences you wrote in Exercise 8, part B. Pay attention to the pronunciation of **used to** and **use to**.

10 SPEAKING Memories

A **PAIR WORK** Add three questions to this list. Then take turns asking and answering the questions. Ask follow-up questions.

1. What's your favorite childhood memory?
2. What sports or games did you use to play when you were younger?
3. Did you use to have a nickname?
4. Where did you use to spend your vacations?
5. Is your taste in food different now?
6. _____
7. _____
8. _____

B **CLASS ACTIVITY** Tell the class two interesting things about your partner.

11 WRITING We used to have a lot of fun.

A Write a paragraph about things you used to do as a child. Use some of your ideas from Exercise 10.

> I grew up in a small town, and my friends and I used to
> play outside a lot. We used to play all kinds of games.
> My favorite was hide-and-seek. We also used to ride
> our bikes to a beautiful lake near our school . . .

B **GROUP WORK** Share your paragraphs and answer any questions. Did you and your classmates use to do the same things? Do kids today do the same things you used to do?

12 INTERCHANGE 1 We have a lot in common.

Find out more about your classmates. Go to Interchange 1 on page 114.

A Scan the article. Where was Kahlo from? What happened when she was 18? Who did she marry?

A Life in Paintings:
The Frida Kahlo Story

Mexican painter Frida Kahlo (1907–1954) was both a talented artist and a woman of great courage. Her paintings tell an amazing story of tragedy and hope.

At the age of six, Kahlo developed polio, and she spent nine months in bed. The illness damaged her right leg forever. Most girls didn't use to play sports back then, but Kahlo played soccer and took up boxing. Exercising helped Kahlo get stronger. Kahlo even dreamed of becoming a doctor one day.

At 18, Kahlo was in a terrible bus crash, and her destiny changed. She wore a full body cast for months because her injuries were so bad. But again, Kahlo refused to give up. She entertained herself by painting self-portraits. She said, "I paint myself because I'm often alone, and because I am the subject I know best."

Kahlo suffered from very bad health the rest of her life, but she continued to paint. Other artists began to recognize her talent – an unusual achievement for a woman at the time. In 1929, she married famous Mexican painter Diego Rivera, but their marriage was troubled. Kahlo once said, "There have been two great accidents in my life . . . Diego was by far the worst."

Kahlo became pregnant three times. Unfortunately, because of her injuries from the bus accident and her generally poor health, none of her babies survived childbirth. This sadness almost destroyed Kahlo. Her paintings often show a broken woman, both in heart and body.

When she traveled, Kahlo always attracted attention. She dressed in long traditional Mexican skirts, wore her hair in long braids, and let her thick eyebrows grow naturally. She chose to look different, and people noticed her beauty everywhere she went.

Kahlo died at the age of 47 in the house where she was born. Her life was short, but extraordinary. Her paintings still amaze people with their honesty and originality.

B Read the article. Then circle the following words in the article and match them to the definitions below.

1. courage _____
2. tragedy _____
3. destiny _____
4. cast _____
5. recognize _____
6. injury _____

a. ability to control your fear in a difficult situation
b. accept that something is good or valuable
c. damage to a person's body
d. a special hard case that protects a broken bone
e. the things that will happen in the future
f. very sad event or situation

C Answer the questions.

1. What did Kahlo do to get healthier after her childhood illness?
2. Why did Kahlo start painting?
3. Why did Kahlo often do self-portraits?
4. What did Kahlo compare her marriage to?
5. Why couldn't Kahlo have children?
6. What was unusual about Kahlo's appearance?

D **GROUP WORK** What was unusual about Kahlo's life?
When do you think it's good to be different from what people expect?

Good memories **7**

2 Life in the city

▸ Discuss transportation and public services
▸ Ask questions about visiting cities

1 WORD POWER Compound nouns

A Match the words in columns A and B to make compound nouns.
(More than one combination may be possible.)

subway + station = subway station

A		B
bicycle	LANE	center
bus	STOP	garage
green	SPACE	jam
parking	GARAGE	lane
recycling	CENTER	light
street	LIGHT	space
subway	SYSTEM	stand
taxi	STAND	station
traffic	JAM	stop
train	STATION	system

traffic jam

green space

B PAIR WORK Which of these things can you find where you live?

A: There are a lot of bus lanes.   **B:** Yes. But there isn't a subway system.

2 PERSPECTIVES City services

▶ **A** Listen to these opinions about city services. Match them to the correct pictures.

YOUR VOICE COUNTS!

_____ 1. The streets are dark and dangerous. I don't think there are enough police officers. And we need more streetlights.

_____ 2. There's too much pollution from cars, motorcycles, and old buses. In cities with less pollution, people are healthier.

_____ 3. There should be fewer cars, but I think that the biggest problem is parking. There just isn't enough parking.

B PAIR WORK Does your city or town have similar problems? What do you think is the biggest problem?

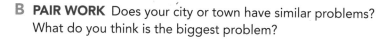

3 GRAMMAR FOCUS

Expressions of quantity

With count nouns	With noncount nouns
There are **too many** cars.	There is **too much** pollution.
There should be **fewer** cars.	There should be **less** pollution.
We need **more** streetlights.	We need **more** public transportation.
There aren't **enough** police officers.	There isn't **enough** parking.

GRAMMAR PLUS *see page 133*

A Complete these statements about city problems. Then compare with a partner. (More than one answer may be possible.)

1. We need _____MORE_____ public schools.
2. There are _____TOO MANY_____ accidents.
3. There are _____FEWER_____ public parks.
4. There is _____LESS_____ noise all the time.
5. There is _____NOT ENOUGHT_____ recycling in our city.
6. The government should build _____MORE_____ affordable housing.
7. The city needs _____MORE_____ bicycle lanes.
8. There are _____FEWER_____ free Wi-Fi hotspots.

B **PAIR WORK** Write sentences about the city or town you are living in. Then compare with another pair.

1. The city should provide more . . .
2. We have too many . . .
3. There's too much . . .
4. There isn't enough . . .
5. There should be fewer . . .
6. We don't have enough . . .
7. There should be less . . .
8. We need more . . .

4 LISTENING It'll take forever.

A Listen to a city resident talk to her new neighbor about the city. Check (✓) True or False for each statement.

	True	False	
1. Jacob already started his new job downtown.	☐	✓	He starts his new job tomorrow.
2. The city needs more buses.	☐	✓	
3. There aren't enough tourists in the city.	☐	☐	
4. Not many people ride bikes in the city.	☐	✓	THERE ARE 125.000 peoples rides
5. Sophia offers to lend Jacob her bike.	☐	☐	

B Listen again. For the false statements, write the correct information.

C **PAIR WORK** What things can a city do to improve the problems that Sophia mentions? Does your city have similar problems?

5 DISCUSSION Rate your city.

A GROUP WORK Which of these services are available in your city or town?
Discuss what is good and bad about each one.

_____ recycling system   _____ parks and green spaces   _____ affordable housing
_____ transportation system   _____ Wi-Fi service   _____ recreational and sports facilities

B GROUP WORK How would you rate the services where you live?
Give each item a rating from 1 to 5.

1 = terrible   2 = needs improvement   3 = average   4 = good   5 = excellent

A: I'd give the parks a 4. There are enough parks, but they aren't always clean.
B: I think a rating of 4 is too high. There aren't enough green spaces
in many areas of the city . . .

6 WRITING A social media post

A Read this post about traffic in the city
on a social networking page.

B Use your statements from Exercise 3,
part B, and any new ideas to write a
post about a local issue.

C GROUP WORK Take turns reading
your messages. Do you have any of
the same concerns?

> Posted by Michelle K
> Today at 5:30   ♡ ⌐
>
> I'm tired of this city. There's too much traffic, and
> it's getting worse. It used to take me 15 minutes to
> get to class. Today it took me more than 30 minutes
> during rush hour! There should be more subway lines.
> I think people want to use public transportation, but
> we need more . . .
>
> comment

7 SNAPSHOT

Common Tourist Questions

☐ What's the best way to see the city?   ☐ Where can I buy a SIM card for my phone?
☐ How much do taxis cost?   ☐ Where's a good place to meet friends?
☐ Which hotel is closest to the airport?   ☐ Where can I get a city guide?
☐ Where should I go shopping?   ☐ What museums should I see?
☐ What festivals or events are taking place?   ☐ What are some family-friendly activities?

Check (✓) the questions you can answer about your city.
What other questions could a visitor ask about your city?
Talk to your classmates. Find answers to the questions you didn't check.

8 CONVERSATION Do you know where . . . ?

▶ **A** Listen and practice.

Rachel: Excuse me. Do you know where the nearest ATM is?

Clerk: There's one down the street, across from the café.

Rachel: Great. And do you know where I can catch a bus downtown?

Clerk: Sure. Just look for the signs for "Public Transportation."

Rachel: OK. And can you tell me how often they run?

Clerk: They run every 10 minutes or so.

Rachel: And just one more thing. Could you tell me where the restrooms are?

Clerk: Right inside. Do you see where that sign is?

Rachel: Oh. Thanks a lot.

▶ **B** Listen to the rest of the conversation. Check (✓) the information that Rachel asks for.

☐ the cost of the bus fare   ☐ the location of a taxi stand

☐ the cost of a city guide   ☐ the location of a bookstore

9 GRAMMAR FOCUS

▶ **Indirect questions from Wh-questions**

Wh-questions with *be*	Indirect questions
Where is the nearest ATM?	Could you tell me **where the nearest ATM is**?
Where are the restrooms?	Do you know **where the restrooms are**?
Wh-questions with *do*	**Indirect questions**
How often do the buses run?	Can you tell me **how often the buses run**?
What time does the bookstore open?	Do you know **what time the bookstore opens**?
Wh-questions with *can*	**Indirect questions**
Where can I catch the bus?	Do you know **where I can catch the bus**?

GRAMMAR PLUS *see page 133*

A Write indirect questions using these Wh-questions. Then compare with a partner.

1. Where can I rent a car?
2. How much does a city tour cost?
3. How early do the stores open?
4. Where's the nearest Wi-Fi hotspot?
5. How much does a taxi to the airport cost?
6. What time does the post office open?
7. Where's an inexpensive hotel in this area?
8. How late do the nightclubs stay open?

B PAIR WORK Take turns asking and answering the questions you wrote in part A.

A: Do you know where I can rent a car?
B: You can rent one at the airport.

10 PRONUNCIATION Syllable stress

▶ **A** Listen and practice. Notice which syllable has the main stress in these two-syllable words.

● ●
subway

● ●
garage

traffic

police

▶ **B** Listen to the stress in these words. Write them in the correct columns. Then compare with a partner.

buses	improve	● ●	● ●
bookstore	provide	_____	_____
event	public	_____	_____
hotel	taxis	_____	_____
		_____	_____

11 SPEAKING The best of our town

A Complete the chart with indirect questions.

	Name:
1. Where's the best area to stay? *"Do you know where the best area to stay is* ?"	
2. What's the best way to see the city? " ?"	
3. How late do the buses run? " ?"	
4. How much do people tip in a restaurant? " ?"	
5. What's a good restaurant to try the local food? " ?"	
6. What are the most popular attractions? " ?"	
7. Where can I hear live music? " ?"	

B **PAIR WORK** Use the indirect questions in the chart to interview a classmate about the city or town where you live. Take notes.

A: Do you know where the best area to stay is?
B: It depends. You can stay near . . .

C **CLASS ACTIVITY** Share your answers with the class. Who knows the most about your city or town?

12 INTERCHANGE 2 Top travel destinations

Discuss ways to attract tourists to a city. Go to Interchange 2 on page 115.

A Skim the article. Which of the following things does it mention?

transportation   natural areas   safety   entertainment   schools   housing

The World's Happiest Cities ☺

Search 🔍

Home   About   Articles   Community   Traveling   Food   Booking

When author Dan Buettner went looking for the world's happiest people on four different continents, he found some really great places to live!

_____ a. Singapore

With a population of 5.1 million, Singapore is really crowded, and people work very long hours. Yet 95 percent of Singapore residents say they are happy. Subway trains almost always arrive on time. The police are good at their jobs and always ready to help. People in Singapore love that their city is so clean and safe.

_____ b. Aarhus, Denmark

Although people pay an incredible 68 percent of their salaries in taxes here, they get lots of services for free: healthcare, education, and daycare for young children. The city has lots of entertainment options too, like museums, shopping, and nightlife. For those who love nature, it's only a 15-minute bike ride to incredible beaches and forests.

_____ c. San Luis Obispo, California, U.S.A.

People here smile and feel happy more than in any other American city. Most people travel less than 10 minutes to work, and there are lots of bike lanes, so commuting is easy. Residents share their joy with others, too. Almost 25 percent of people in San Luis Obispo volunteer to help people in their free time.

_____ d. Monterrey, Mexico

Although many of its people don't earn high salaries, they still feel rich. People in Monterrey have strong family relationships and very busy social lives. They also have a positive attitude about life – they laugh and stay strong even in times of trouble.

Adapted from http://www.rd.com/advice/travel/the-4-happiest-cities-on-earth

B Read the article. Match the paragraphs (a–d) to the pictures (1–4).

C Read the comments from residents of these four cities. Which city do you think they live in? Write the letter.

1. "I spend a lot of time with my relatives." _____
2. "A lot of what I earn goes to the government, but I don't mind." _____
3. "I can see great art in my city." _____
4. "I often have to spend eleven hours or more in the office." _____
5. "I help children with their homework after school for free." _____
6. "I try to be cheerful, even when things are going badly." _____
7. "I take the train to work, and I'm never late." _____
8. "On weekends, I can get out of the city without taking the car." _____

D **PAIR WORK** Which sentences in part C are true for you and your city or town? How would you improve the place where you live?

Units 1–2 Progress check

SELF-ASSESSMENT

How well can you do these things? Check (✓) the boxes.

I can . . .	Very well	OK	A little
Understand descriptions of childhood (Ex. 1)	☐	☐	☐
Ask and answer questions about childhood and past times (Ex. 1, 2)	☐	☐	☐
Express opinions about cities and towns; agree and disagree (Ex. 3)	☐	☐	☐
Ask for and give information about a city or town (Ex. 4)	☐	☐	☐

1 LISTENING What was that like?

▶ **A** Listen to an interview with Charlotte, a fashion designer. Answer the questions in complete sentences.

  1. Where did she grow up? What is her hometown like?
  2. What did she want to do when she grew up?
  3. What were her hobbies as a child?
  4. What sport did she use to play?
  5. What was her favorite place? What did she use to do there?

B **PAIR WORK** Use the questions in part A to interview a partner about his or her childhood. Ask follow-up questions to get more information.

2 DISCUSSION In the past, . . .

A **PAIR WORK** Talk about how life in your country has changed in the last 50 years. Ask questions like these:

What kinds of homes did people live in?
How did people use to communicate?
What did people use to do in their free time?
How did people use to dress?
How were schools different?
What kinds of jobs did men have? women?

  A: What kinds of homes did people live in?
  B: Houses used to be bigger. Now most people live in small apartments.

B **GROUP WORK** Compare your answers. Do you think life was better in the past? Why or why not?

3 SURVEY Are there enough parks?

A What do you think about these things in your city or town? Complete the survey.

	Not enough	OK	Too many/Too much
free shows and concerts	☐	☐	☐
places to go dancing	☐	☐	☐
parks and green spaces	☐	☐	☐
places to go shopping	☐	☐	☐
noise	☐	☐	☐
places to sit and have coffee	☐	☐	☐
public transportation	☐	☐	☐
places to meet new people	☐	☐	☐

B **GROUP WORK** Compare your opinions and suggest ways to make your city or town better. Then agree on three improvements.

A: How would you make our city better?

B: There should be more shows and concerts. There aren't enough free activities for young people.

C: I disagree. There should be more schools. We don't need more entertainment.

4 ROLE PLAY Can I help you?

Student A: Imagine you are a visitor in your city or town. Write five indirect questions about these categories. Then ask your questions to the hotel front-desk clerk.

Transportation   Sightseeing
Hotels   Shopping
Restaurants   Entertainment

Student B: You are a hotel front-desk clerk. Answer the guest's questions.

A: Excuse me.

B: Can I help you?

Change roles and try the role play again.

---

useful expressions

Let me think. Oh, yes, . . .
I'm not really sure, but I think . . .
Sorry, I don't know.

WHAT'S NEXT?

Look at your Self-assessment again. Do you need to review anything?

3 Making changes

▸ **Compare houses and apartments**
▸ **Discuss life changes**

1 WORD POWER Homes

A These words are used to describe houses and apartments.
Which are positive (**P**)? Which are negative (**N**)?

bright	P	dingy	N	private	P
comfortable	P	expensive	N	quiet	P
convenient	P	huge	P/N	run-down	N
cramped	N	inconvenient	N	safe	P
dangerous	N	modern	P	small	N/P
dark	N	noisy	N	spacious	P

cramped

B **PAIR WORK** Tell your partner two positive and two negative
features of your house or apartment.

"I live in a nice neighborhood. It's safe and very convenient.
However, the apartment is a little cramped and kind of expensive."

2 PERSPECTIVES How's your new apartment?

▶ **A** Listen to a family talk about their new apartment. Which opinions are about
the building or the neighborhood? Which are about the apartment?

APT

BUILDING

APT

APT

NEIGHBORHOODS

1. I don't like living in an apartment.
We don't have as much privacy
as we had in our old place.

2. I just can't sleep at night. The
neighbors make too much noise.
The building isn't as quiet as our
old one.

3. The new apartment is too dark
and too hot. There aren't enough
windows.

4. Our new apartment isn't big
enough for our family. We don't
have a big kitchen anymore, so
cooking is difficult.

5. The location is just as convenient
as the old one, but there aren't
as many good restaurants
around.

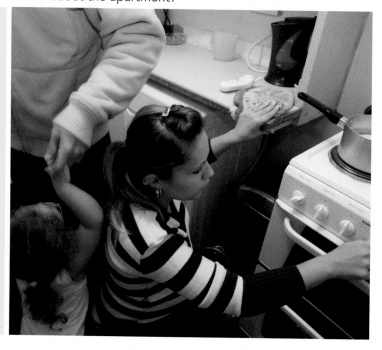

B **PAIR WORK** Look at the opinions again. Talk about similar problems you have.

A: My next-door neighbors make too much noise. They have parties every Saturday.
B: My brother has the same problem. His neighbor's band practices all weekend!

3 GRAMMAR FOCUS

▶ Evaluations and comparisons

Evaluations with adjectives	**Evaluations with nouns**
Our apartment is**n't** big **enough** for our family.	There are**n't enough** windows.
This apartment is **too** hot.	The neighbors make **too much** noise.
Comparisons with adjectives	**Comparisons with nouns**
The building is**n't as** quiet **as** our old one.	We do**n't** have **as many** bedrooms **as** we used to.
The location is **just as** convenient **as** the old one.	We do**n't** have **as much** privacy **as** we had.

GRAMMAR PLUS *see page 134*

A Imagine you are looking for a house or an apartment to rent. Read the two ads. Then rewrite the opinions using the words in parentheses. Compare with a partner.

Spacious, modern house ⌂

3 bedrooms, 1 bathroom; in quiet suburb 20 miles from downtown; 2-car garage; $1500 per month.

Comfortable apartment

2 bedrooms, 1 bathroom; downtown, near subway; 1 parking space; built in 1920; $900 per month.

1. The house is 20 miles from downtown. (too)
2. It's not convenient enough. (too)
3. It has only one bathroom. (not enough)
4. The rent is very high. (too)

It's too far from downtown.

5. The apartment is too old. (not enough)
6. There are only two bedrooms. (not enough)
7. It's not spacious enough. (too)
8. There's only one parking space. (not enough)

B Write comparisons of the house and the apartment using these words and *as . . . as*. Then compare with a partner.

big	noisy
bedrooms	expensive
bathrooms	modern
spacious	convenient
private	parking spaces

The apartment isn't as big as the house.

The apartment doesn't have as many bedrooms as the house.

C GROUP WORK Which would you prefer to rent: the house or the apartment? Why?

A: I'd choose the apartment. The house isn't close enough to public transportation.

B: I'd rent the house because the apartment is too small.

4 PRONUNCIATION Unpronounced vowels

A Listen and practice. The vowel immediately after a stressed syllable is sometimes not pronounced.

● ●   ● ● ●

average   comfortable
different   interesting
separate   vegetable

B Write four sentences using some of the words in part A. Then read them with a partner. Pay attention to unpronounced vowels.

> Today, the average house is much smaller than 50 years ago.

5 LISTENING A home away from home

A Listen to Josh describe a "capsule hotel." Check (✓) True or False for each statement.

	True	False	
1. Tokyo sometimes feels too noisy.	☐	✓	Sometimes it feels too big.
2. A capsule hotel is not as convenient as a regular hotel.	☐	☑	JUST AS CONVENIENT
3. Inside every capsule there is a TV, a radio, and an alarm clock.	☑	☐	
4. The capsule is a good option if you're busy and tired.	☑	☐	
5. Josh would recommend a capsule hotel to anyone.	☐	☑	CLAUSTROPHOBIA

B Listen again. For the false statements, write the correct information.

C GROUP WORK Where else do you think a capsule hotel would be popular? Why?

6 WRITING My new home

A Imagine you've just moved to this apartment. Write an email to a friend comparing your old home to your new one.

Hi Chloe,

How's everything? I have some great news. We just moved to a new apartment! Do you remember our old apartment? It was too small, and I didn't have enough space for my things. My new bedroom is spacious, and I have a separate area to study in. The apartment also has a balcony. It isn't very big, but now we can have breakfast outdoors on Sundays. The . . .

Reply Forward

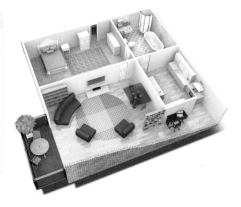

B PAIR WORK Read each other's emails. How are your descriptions similar? different?

SNAPSHOT

MAKE A WISH

☐ Have a healthier lifestyle

☐ Go back to school

☐ Start my own business

☐ Improve my personality

☐ Enjoy life more

☐ Move to a new home

☐ Add more hours to the day

☐ Make new friends

☐ Do volunteer work

☐ Spend more time with my family

Check (✓) some of the things you would like to do. Then tell a partner why.
Which of these wishes would be easy to achieve? Which would be difficult or impossible?
What other things would you like to change about your life? Why?

8 **CONVERSATION** I wish I could.

▶ **A** Listen and practice.

Harry: So, are you still living with your parents, Dylan?

Dylan: Yes, I am. But sometimes I wish I had my own apartment.

Harry: Why? Don't you like living at home?

Dylan: It's OK, but my parents are always asking me to come home early. I wish they'd stop worrying about me.

Harry: Yeah, parents are like that!

Dylan: Plus, they don't like my friends, and they won't stop criticizing them. I wish life weren't so difficult.

Harry: So, why don't you move out?

Dylan: Hey, I wish I could, but where else can I get free room and board?

▶ **B** Listen to the rest of the conversation. What changes would Harry like to make in his life?

Making changes **19**

9 GRAMMAR FOCUS

▶ Wish

Use wish + past tense to refer to present wishes.

I **live** with my parents.

   I wish I **didn't live** with my parents.

   I wish I **had** my own apartment.

I **can't move** out.

   I wish I **could move** out.

Life **is** difficult.

   I wish it **were*** easier.

   I wish it **weren't** so difficult.

My parents **won't stop** worrying about me.

   I wish they **would stop** worrying about me.

***For the verb be, were is used with all pronouns after wish.**

GRAMMAR PLUS *see page 134*

A Read these other comments that Dylan makes. Then rewrite the sentences using *wish*. (More than one answer is possible.)

1. My mother doesn't like my girlfriend.   *I wish she liked my girlfriend.*
2. My girlfriend is too short to be a model.   *She wishes she were taller.*
3. My classes are really boring.
4. I'm not on vacation right now.
5. My family can't afford a bigger house.
6. The neighbors won't stop making noise.
7. Harry doesn't like his job.

B **PAIR WORK** Think of five things you wish you could change. Then discuss them with your partner.

A: What do you wish you could change?

B: Well, I don't have much free time. I wish I had time to . . .

10 SPEAKING Make it happen.

A If you could wish for three things, what would they be? Write down your wishes.

B **GROUP WORK** How can you make your wishes come true? Get suggestions from your classmates.

A: I wish I had more money.

B: Why don't you look for another job?

A: I don't have enough experience. I wish I had a diploma.

C: You can go back to school or take an online course.

11 INTERCHANGE 3 A dream come true

Find out more about your classmates' wishes. Go to Interchange 3 on page 116.

A Skim the article. Which of these sentences is true?

Boyle decided that a life without money was impossible to live.

Boyle wanted to give people the chance to live a different lifestyle.

THE MAN WITH
NO MONEY

A Can you imagine your life without any money? Not even a cent, a real, or a peso? One man decided to try it out.

B Mark Boyle was a successful manager of an organic food company in Ireland. He had a good life. But he worried about the damage humans were doing to the environment. He also believed people bought more things than they needed. Boyle wished we grew our own food and made our own furniture, so we wouldn't waste as much as we do today. So one day, he left his job and started an experiment – could he live for a year without buying anything?

C He sold his houseboat and moved into an old mobile home. He got it for free from a website where people give away things they don't want. It wasn't as comfortable as his old place at first, but he soon made it feel like home. He parked it on a farm near Bristol, England. Instead of paying rent, he worked on the farm. He burned wood from the forest to heat his home, so he didn't pay electricity or gas bills.

D Boyle didn't go shopping, either. He grew his own fruit and vegetables. He also looked for food in the trash cans of supermarkets and cooked it on a wood stove. He made his own toothpaste from fish bones and seeds. To wash his clothes, he used a special type of nut to make soap. Boyle even built his own toilet and used old newspapers from the farm for toilet paper.

E He began using money again after eighteen months. He says his life change made him feel healthier, happier, and closer to nature. He wrote two books about his experience and used the money to start "The Free House," a farm in Ireland where people can live without money.

B Read the article. Then circle the correct word or words.

1. Before the experiment, Mark Boyle was **good at / unhappy with** his job.
2. Boyle thought that people **spent too much / discussed money too often**.
3. Boyle worked on a farm **to earn money to pay rent / so he didn't have to pay rent**.
4. Boyle made cleaning products from things he found in **trash cans / the forest**.
5. Boyle generally felt **worse / better** after living without money.

C Match the sentences to the paragraphs they describe. Write the letter.

____ 1. Describes a big change that happened in the person's life

____ 2. Describes the way the person's everyday habits changed

____ 3. Asks a question to make the reader think about the topic

____ 4. Gives general information about the past of the main person in the story

____ 5. Explains how the person felt about the whole experiment

D **PAIR WORK** Discuss Boyle's experience. Would you like to try it?

Do you think people today spend too much money on things they don't need?

4 Have you ever tried it?

▶ **Describe past personal experiences**
▶ **Discuss food, recipes, and cooking methods**

1 SNAPSHOT

TRADITIONAL DISHES FROM AROUND THE WORLD

Lebanon
Kibbeh Labanieh
Lamb or beef meatballs cooked in yogurt with spices

South Korea
Galbi
Korean-style barbecued meat

Singapore
Gulai Kepala Ikan
A dish made from a fish head cooked in a rich curry sauce

Brazil
Moqueca
Fish and shellfish stew cooked in coconut milk in a clay pot

Which dishes are made with meat? with fish?
Have you ever tried any of these dishes? Which ones would you like to try?
What traditional foods are popular in your country?

2 CONVERSATION I've never heard of that!

▶ **A** Listen and practice.

Aiden Hey, this sounds strange – frog legs with butter and garlic sauce. Have you ever eaten frog legs?

Claire Yes, I have. I had them here just last week.

Aiden Did you like them?

Claire Yes, I did. They were delicious! Why don't you try some?

Aiden No, I don't think so. I'm a little scared of them.

Server Have you decided on an appetizer yet?

Claire Yes. I'll have a small order of frog legs, please.

Server And you, sir?

Aiden I think I'll have the snails.

Claire Snails? That's adventurous of you!

▶ **B** Listen to the rest of the conversation. How did Aiden like the snails? What else did he order?

3 PRONUNCIATION Consonant clusters

▶ **A** Listen and practice. Notice how the two consonants at the beginning of a word are pronounced together.

/k/	/t/	/m/	/n/	/p/	/r/	/l/
scan	start	smart	snack	spare	brown	blue
skim	step	smile	snow	speak	gray	play

B **PAIR WORK** Find one more word on page 22 for each consonant cluster in part A. Then practice saying the words.

4 GRAMMAR FOCUS

▶ **Simple past vs. present perfect**

Use the simple past for experiences at a definite time in the past.
Use the present perfect for experiences within a time period up to the present.

Have you ever **eaten** frog legs?

Yes, I **have**. I **tried** them last month.

Did you **like** them?

Yes, I **did**. They **were** delicious.

Have you ever **been** to a Vietnamese restaurant?

No, I **haven't**. But I **ate** at a Thai restaurant last night.

Did you **go** alone?

No, I **went** with some friends.

GRAMMAR PLUS *see page 135*

A Complete these conversations. Then practice with a partner.

1. **A:** Have you ever _____eaten_____ (eat) sushi?
   B: Yes, I _____. In fact, I _____ (eat) some just last week.

2. **A:** Have you ever _____ (try) Moroccan food?
   B: No, I _____, but I'd like to.

3. **A:** Did you _____ (have) breakfast today?
   B: Yes, I _____. I _____ (eat) a huge breakfast.

4. **A:** Have you ever _____ (be) to a picnic at the beach?
   B: Yes, I _____. My family and I _____ (have) a picnic on the beach last month. We _____ (cook) hamburgers.

5. **A:** Did you _____ (cook) dinner last night?
   B: Yes, I _____. I _____ (make) spaghetti with tomato sauce.

B **PAIR WORK** Ask and answer the questions in part A. Give your own information.

5 LISTENING Have you tried this before?

▶ **A** Listen to six people ask questions in a restaurant. Are they talking about these items? Write **Y** (yes) or **N** (no).

1. _N_ plate
   ___juice___

2. ___ the check

3. ___ cake
   _____

4. ___ meat
   _____

5. ___ water
   _____

6. ___ the menu
   _____

▶ **B** Listen again. For the no (**N**) items, write what they might be talking about instead.

6 SPEAKING How did you like it?

PAIR WORK Ask your partner these questions and four more of your own. Then ask follow-up questions.

Have you ever drunk fresh sugar cane juice?
Have you ever been to a vegetarian restaurant?
Have you ever had an unusual ice cream flavor?
Have you ever eaten something you didn't like?

A: Have you ever drunk fresh sugar cane juice?
B: Yes, I have. I drank it in Egypt once.
A: How did you like it?
B: I loved it, actually.

7 INTERCHANGE 4 Oh, really?

Find out some interesting facts about your classmates. Go to Interchange 4 on page 117.

8 WORD POWER Cooking methods

A How do you cook the foods below? Check (✓) the methods that are most common.

bake   boil   fry   grill   roast   steam

Methods	Foods								
	fish	shrimp	eggs	chicken	beef	potatoes	onions	corn	bananas
bake	☐	☐	☐	☐	☐	☐	☐	☐	☐
boil	☐	☐	☐	☐	☐	☐	☐	☐	☐
fry	☐	☐	☐	☐	☐	☐	☐	☐	☐
grill	☐	☐	☐	☐	☐	☐	☐	☐	☐
roast	☐	☐	☐	☐	☐	☐	☐	☐	☐
steam	☐	☐	☐	☐	☐	☐	☐	☐	☐

B PAIR WORK What's your favorite way to cook or eat the foods in part A?

A: Have you ever fried bananas?
B: No, I haven't. But sometimes I grill them.

▶ **A** Listen to this recipe for macaroni and cheese. Do you think this is a healthy dish?

Baked Macaroni and Cheese

🍝 1 package elbow macaroni

🧈 4 tablespoons butter

🍦 2 cups heavy cream

🧀 4 cups cheddar cheese, shredded

First, boil the macaroni in a large pot for 5 minutes.
Then melt the butter on medium heat and add the cream.
Stir for about 2 minutes. Next, add the cheese. Stir until the cheese is melted. Season with salt and pepper.
After that, add the cooked macaroni and mix well. Finally, bake for 20 minutes.

B **PAIR WORK** Look at the steps in the recipe again. Number the pictures from 1 to 5. Would you like to try this traditional American dish?

10 GRAMMAR FOCUS

▶ **Sequence adverbs**

First, boil the macaroni in a large pot.
Then melt the butter on medium heat.
Next, add the cheese.
After that, add the cooked macaroni.
Finally, bake for 20 minutes.

GRAMMAR PLUS see page 135

A Here's a recipe for a couscous salad. Look at the pictures and number the steps from 1 to 5. Then add a sequence adverb to each step.

☐ _____ drain the couscous and let it cool.

1 *First,* _____ chop some olives, parsley, and cheese.

☐ _____ toss the cooked couscous with the olives, parsley, and cheese.

☐ _____ pour some couscous into the hot water and let it sit for 10 minutes.

☐ _____ boil a pot of water.

B **PAIR WORK** Cover the recipe and look only at the pictures. Explain each step of the recipe to your partner.

Have you ever tried it? **25**

11 LISTENING How do you make it?

A Listen to people explain how to make these snacks. Which snack are they talking about? Number the photos from 1 to 4. (There is one extra photo.)

□
spaghetti

□
chocolate chip cookies

□
salsa

□
French toast

□
popcorn

B Listen again. Check (✓) the steps you hear for each recipe.

1. ✓ add
   ✓ chop
   □ heat

2. □ cut
   □ heat
   □ pour

3. □ stir
   □ cook
   □ cover

4. □ mix
   □ bake
   □ mash

C PAIR WORK Tell your partner how to make one of the snacks above. Your partner will guess which snack it is.

12 SPEAKING It's my favorite food.

GROUP WORK Discuss these questions.

What's your favorite food?

Is it easy to make?

What's in it?

How often do you eat it?

Where do you usually eat it?

How healthy is it?

"My favorite food is pizza. It's not difficult to make. First, . . ."

13 WRITING My cookbook

A Read this recipe. Is this an easy recipe to make?

Guacamole

First, chop the tomato, onion, chili pepper, and cilantro. Then scoop out the flesh of the avocados and mash it with a fork. Next, squeeze the lime and mix the juice with the avocado. Finally, combine all the ingredients, mix well, and season with salt to taste.

1 tomato
half a red onion
3 avocados
1 lime
1 fresh green chili pepper
2 tablespoons cilantro

B Now think of something you know how to make. First, write down the things you need. Then describe how to make it.

C GROUP WORK Read and discuss each recipe. Then choose one to share with the class. Explain why you chose it.

A Scan the article. Which city does pizza come from? When did pizza arrive in New York? What do people in Japan like on their pizzas?

PIZZA:

The World's Favorite Food?

Food, and the way we eat it, is always changing. As society develops, we learn new ways of growing, processing, and cooking food. _[a]_ Also, when people travel to live in other countries, they take their knowledge of cooking with them. And food must fit modern lifestyles and local tastes, too. One food that has done this successfully is the pizza.

The pizza we recognize today first appeared in Italy in 1889. A famous baker from Naples made a special pizza for the Italian royal family. _[b]_ Queen Margherita loved the dish so much, the baker named it after her. Since then, this simple meal of bread, cheese, and tomato has traveled the world, and it has adapted to local cultures.

Pizza began its journey in the 1890s, when many Italians moved to New York in search of a better life. There they continued to make pizzas, and the first pizzeria opened in 1905.

At first it was only popular with Italians, but by the late 1940s, Americans discovered a taste for it. Today, they spend an incredible $37 billion a year on pizzas. _[c]_

Pizza continued its travels around the world, adapting all the time. In Sweden, for example, it is not unusual to have peanuts and bananas on your pizza. _[d]_ Japan is a nation of seafood lovers, so not surprisingly, they love octopus and squid, as well as roasted seaweed, toppings. Australians sometimes choose kangaroo or crocodile, and in the Philippines they like mango on their pizza.

The popularity of the pizza is also related to our changing lifestyles. In today's super-fast society, people often don't have the time or energy to cook. So, they order takeout – and very often, it's a pizza. _[e]_ If you don't even have time to sit down, buy a single slice and eat it standing up!

The pizza has come a long way. From its beginnings in an Italian city, it has grown to become one of the world's favorite foods.

·LOMBARDI'S in 1905·

B Read the article. Where do these sentences belong? Write the letters a–e.

_____ **1.** That's more than $100 per American!

_____ **2.** What we ate 200 years ago was very different from what we eat today.

_____ **3.** In Belgium, people eat chocolate pizzas with marshmallows on top.

_____ **4.** Sometimes you don't even have to pick it up; it's delivered to your home.

_____ **5.** He was very worried they wouldn't like it, but they did.

C How has local food changed in your country in the last 50 years? What new foods do you eat now that you didn't eat before?

Units 3–4 Progress check

SELF-ASSESSMENT

How well can you do these things? Check (✓) the boxes.

I can . . .	Very well	OK	A little
Evaluate a house or apartment (Ex. 1)	☐	☐	☐
Express opinions about houses or apartments; agree and disagree (Ex. 1)	☐	☐	☐
Discuss life changes (Ex. 2)	☐	☐	☐
Describe past personal experiences (Ex. 3)	☐	☐	☐
Describe recipes (Ex. 4)	☐	☐	☐

1 SPEAKING For rent

A PAIR WORK Use the topics in the box to write an ad for an apartment.
Use this ad as a model. Make the apartment sound as good as possible.

FOR RENT
Comfortable 1-bedroom apartment

Spacious, bright; located downtown; convenient to public transportation; 1 bathroom, modern kitchen; 1-car garage

$1200 a month

age	windows	parking
size	bathroom(s)	cost
location	bedroom(s)	noise

B GROUP WORK Join another pair. Evaluate and compare the apartments.
Which would you prefer to rent? Why?

A: There aren't enough bedrooms in your apartment.
B: But it's convenient.
C: Yes, but our apartment is just as convenient!

2 LISTENING Making changes

A Listen to three people talk about things they wish they could change.
Check (✓) the topic each person is talking about.

1. ☐ city ☐ travel _____
2. ☐ school ☐ skills _____
3. ☐ free time ☐ money _____

B Listen again. Write one change each person would like to make.

C PAIR WORK Use the topics in part A to express your own wishes.

3 SURVEY Memorable meals

A Complete the survey with your food opinions and experiences.
Then use your information to write questions.

Me	Name
1. I've eaten _____. I liked it.	
Have you ever eaten ? _Did you like it_ ?	?
2. I've eaten _____. I hated it.	
_____ ?	?
3. I've never tried _____. But I want to.	
	?
4. I've been to the restaurant _____ I enjoyed it.	
	?
5. I've made _____ for my friends. They loved it.	
	?

B **CLASS ACTIVITY** Go around the class and ask
your questions. Find people who have had the
same experiences as you. Write a classmate's
name only once.

A: Have you ever eaten a sloppy joe sandwich?
B: Yes, I have.
A: Did you like it?
B: Yes . . . but it was too messy.

4 ROLE PLAY Reality cooking competition

GROUP WORK Work in groups of four. Two students
are the judges. Two students are the chefs.

Judges: Make a list of three ingredients for the chefs
to use. You will decide which chef creates the
best recipe.

Chefs: Think of a recipe using the three ingredients the
judges give you and other basic ingredients.
Name the recipe and describe how to make it.
"My recipe is called . . . . To make it, first . . . .
Then . . . . Next, ..."

Change roles and try the role play again.

WHAT'S NEXT?

Look at your Self-assessment again. Do you need to review anything?

5 Hit the road!

▸ Discuss vacation and travel plans
▸ Give travel advice

1 SNAPSHOT

What do you like to do on vacation?

take a fun trip　　discover something new　　stay home　　enjoy nature

☐ visit a foreign country
☐ travel in my own country

☐ go to a music festival
☐ take a photography course

☐ hang out with friends
☐ host a family reunion

☐ go camping
☐ relax at the beach

Which activities do you like to do on vacation? Check (✓) the activities.
Which activities would you like to do on your next vacation?
Make a list of other activities you like to do on vacation. Then compare with a partner.

2 CONVERSATION I guess I'll just stay home.

▶ **A** Listen and practice.

Nora: I'm so excited! We have two weeks off! What are you going to do?

Lily: I'm not sure. I guess I'll just stay home. Maybe I'll hang out with some friends and watch my favorite series. What about you? Any plans?

Nora: Yeah, I'm going to relax at the beach with my cousin. We're going to go surfing every day. And my cousin likes to snorkel, so maybe we'll go snorkeling one day.

Lily: Sounds like fun.

Nora: Hey, why don't you come with us?

Lily: Do you mean it? I'd love to! I'll bring my surfboard!

Nora: That's great! The more the merrier!

▶ **B** Listen to the rest of the conversation. Where are they going to stay? How will they get there?

3 GRAMMAR FOCUS

▶ **Future with *be going to* and *will***

Use *be going to* + verb for plans you've decided on.

What **are** you **going to do**?

I'm going to relax at the beach.

We're **going to go** surfing every day.

I'm not **going to do** anything special.

Use *will* + verb for possible plans before you've made a decision.

What **are** you **going to do**?

I'm not sure. I **guess I'll** just **stay** home.

Maybe I'll take a course.

I don't know. I **think I'll go** camping.

I **probably won't go** anywhere.

GRAMMAR PLUS *see page 136*

A Complete the conversation with appropriate forms of *be going to* or *will*. Then compare with a partner.

1. A: Have you made any vacation plans?

B: Well, I've decided on one thing – I _____ take a bike tour.

A: That's great! For how long?

B: I _____ be away for about a week. I need to take some time off.

A: So, when are you leaving?

B: I'm not sure. I _____ probably leave around the end of next month.

A: And where _____ you _____ go?

B: I haven't thought about that yet. I guess I _____ go down south.

A: That sounds like fun. _____ you _____ buy a new bicycle?

B: I'm not sure. Actually, I probably _____ buy one – I don't have enough money right now. I guess I _____ rent one.

A: _____ you _____ go with anyone?

B: No. I need some time alone. I _____ travel by myself.

2. A: What are your plans for the holiday weekend?

B: I _____ visit my parents.

A: What _____ you _____ do there?

B: Nothing much. I _____ hang out with some old school friends. And we _____ probably have a barbecue on Sunday.

A: That sounds like fun. When _____ you _____ leave?

B: I'm not sure yet. I _____ probably leave on Friday night if I don't need to work on Saturday.

A: _____ you _____ fly there?

B: I wish I could, but it's too expensive. I guess I _____ take the train.

A: _____ you _____ go alone?

B: Maybe my brother _____ go, too. He hasn't decided yet.

A: Do you know when you are coming back?

B: I think I _____ come back on Monday.

A: Good. Then we can have dinner together on Monday.

B Have you thought about your next vacation? Write answers to these questions. (If you already have plans, use *be going to*. If you don't have fixed plans, use *will*.)

1. How are you going to spend your next vacation?
2. Where are you going to go?
3. When are you going to take your vacation?
4. How long are you going to be on vacation?
5. Is anyone going to travel with you?

I'm going to spend my next vacation . . .
OR I'm not sure. Maybe I'll . . .

C GROUP WORK Take turns telling the group about your vacation plans. Use your information from part B.

4 WORD POWER Travel preparations

A Complete the chart. Then add one more word to each category.

ATM card	cash	medication	plane ticket	swimsuit
backpack	first-aid kit	money belt	sandals	travel insurance
carry-on bag	hiking boots	passport	suitcase	vaccination

Clothing	Money	Health	Documents	Luggage

B **PAIR WORK** What are the five most important items you need for these vacations?

a beach vacation   a rafting trip   a trip to a foreign country

5 INTERCHANGE 5 Fun trips

Decide between two vacations. Student A, go to Interchange 5A
on page 118; Student B, go to Interchange 5B on page 120.

6 PERSPECTIVES Travel advisor

A Listen to these pieces of advice from experienced travelers.
What topic is each person talking about?

"You must have a valid passport to travel overseas. You ought to make a copy of your passport and keep it in a secure place."

"When you fly, you should keep important things in your carry-on bag, such as your medication and ATM card. You shouldn't pack them in your checked luggage."

"You should try some of the local specialties, but you'd better avoid the stalls on the street. You shouldn't drink tap water."

"In most countries, you don't have to have an international driver's license, but you have to carry a license from your own country. You also need to be 21 or over."

"You'd better buy travel insurance before you leave your country."

"You'd better keep a copy of your credit card numbers at the hotel. And you shouldn't carry a lot of cash when you go out."

B **PAIR WORK** Look at the advice again. Do you think this is all good advice? Why or why not?

7 GRAMMAR FOCUS

Modals for necessity and suggestion

Describing necessity

You **must** have health insurance.

You **need to** be 21 or over.

You **have to** get a passport.

You **don't have to** get vaccinations.

Giving suggestions

You**'d better** avoid the stalls on the street.

You **ought to** make a copy of your passport.

You **should** try some local specialties.

You **shouldn't** carry a lot of cash.

GRAMMAR PLUS *see page 136*

A Choose the best advice for someone who is going on vacation. Then compare with a partner.

1. You _____ pack too many clothes. You won't have room to bring back any gifts. (don't have to / shouldn't)

2. You _____ carry identification with you. It's the law! (must / should)

3. You _____ buy a money belt to carry your passport, ATM card, and cash. (have to / ought to)

4. You _____ make hotel reservations in advance. It might be difficult to find a room after you get there. (have to / 'd better)

5. You _____ buy a round-trip plane ticket because it's cheaper. (must / should)

6. You _____ check out of most hotel rooms by noon if you don't want to pay for another night. (need to / ought to)

B **PAIR WORK** Imagine you're going to travel abroad. Take turns giving each other advice.

"You must take enough medication for your entire trip."

1. You . . . take enough medication for your entire trip.

2. You . . . take your ATM card with you.

3. You . . . get the necessary vaccinations.

4. You . . . forget to pack your camera.

5. You . . . have a visa to enter some foreign countries.

6. You . . . change money before you go. You can do it when you arrive.

8 PRONUNCIATION Linked sounds with /w/ and /y/

Listen and practice. Notice how some words are linked by a /w/ sound, and other words are linked by a /y/ sound.

/w/
You should know about local conditions.

/y/
You shouldn't carry a lot of cash.

/w/
You ought to do it right away.

/y/
You must be at least 21 years old.

9 LISTENING A pleasant trip

▶ **A** Listen to an interview with a spokeswoman from the London Visitor Center.
Number the topics she discusses in the correct order from 1 to 4.

a. ☐ money _____
b. ☐ public transportation _____
c. ☐ safety _____
d. ☐ planning a trip _____

▶ **B** Listen again. Write one piece of advice that she gives for each topic.

C GROUP WORK Which pieces of advice for London apply to your city or town?
Which don't? Why and why not?

10 WRITING Have a safe trip.

A Imagine someone is going to visit your town, city, or country.
Write an email giving some suggestions for sightseeing activities.

Reply Forward

Dear Michael,

I'm so glad you're coming to visit me in Valparaiso.
There are lots of things to see here, and we are going
to walk a lot, so bring some comfortable shoes. Don't
forget your swimsuit, because I'm planning to take
you to Vina del Mar for a day at the beach. It will be
warm, so you don't need to pack . . .

Valparaiso, Chile

B PAIR WORK Exchange emails. Is there anything else the visitor
needs to know about (food, money, business hours, etc.)?

11 DISCUSSION Around the world

A PAIR WORK You just won a free 30-day trip around
the world. Discuss the following questions.

When will you leave and return?
Which direction will you go (east, west, north, or south)?
Where will you choose to stop? Why?
How will you get from place to place?
How long will you stay in each place?

B PAIR WORK What do you need to do before you go?
Discuss these topics.

shopping   documents   reservations
packing   money   vaccinations

A: I think we'd better buy new suitcases.
B: Good idea. And we should check the weather before we pack.

A Skim the article. Match paragraphs A, B, and C to the photos.

ADVENTURE  VACATIONS

⦿ Home ⦿ About ⦿ Vacations ⦿ Hot spots ⦿ Discounts

A good vacation, for many people, means comfortable accommodations, a great atmosphere, and tasty food. It's a pleasant, relaxing experience. But for some, this type of vacation just isn't enough!

In today's world, many of us have safe, sometimes boring lives. We work, sleep, eat, and watch TV. So more and more people are looking for adventure. They want excitement and danger. They might even want to feel a little afraid!

____ **A** How about staying on a desert island in the middle of the Indian Ocean? If you want, you can spend your whole vacation completely alone. You'll sleep in a tent and go fishing for your food. Your only company will be the monkeys and lizards. But don't worry. If you get bored, just call the travel company and they'll send a boat to pick you up!

____ **B** Or how about spending a week in the sub-zero temperatures of the North? You will fly to the Arctic, and the local Sami people will teach you to survive in this very difficult environment. You'll learn how to keep yourself warm and make special snowshoes. You can also go ice-fishing and look after reindeer. You'll even learn how to tell when it is going to snow.

____ **C** But if the Arctic's too cold, you could try the heat of the jungle instead. Deep in the Amazon rain forest, you'll sleep in the open air. At first, you'll spend a week with local guides. They will train you to do many things, like find food and water or light fires with stones. They will even teach you to pick the tastiest insects for dinner! Then you'll spend a week by yourself with no tent, no extra clothes, and no cell phone. You'll be completely alone – except for the crocodiles and snakes, of course!

B Read the article. Then complete the summary using words from the article.

Nowadays, life can sometimes be a little boring. So, many people are searching for an exciting or dangerous **1)** _____ during their vacations. Some people like the idea of visiting a desert island. There, they spend nights in a **2)** _____ and look for fruit and other plants to eat. If they decide to go to the Arctic instead, they will walk around with unusual **3)** _____ on their feet, and they'll have the experience of taking care of **4)** _____. If they decide to choose a trip to the rain forest, they'll learn many things from **5)** _____, and afterward, they'll live for a whole **6)** _____ completely alone.

C Read the comments of people who are on one of these three trips. Which vacation are they on? Write the letter.

____ 1. "I know what the weather will be like tomorrow."
____ 2. "I haven't seen anybody since the moment I arrived."
____ 3. "My whole body is absolutely freezing!"
____ 4. "I've learned so much these first seven days."
____ 5. "I've had enough now! I'm going to call for help."
____ 6. "I haven't eaten anything like this before!"

D GROUP WORK Which of these three vacations would you be prepared to try? Which would you refuse to go on? Why?

6 Sure! I'll do it.

▶ **Discuss common complaints**
▶ **Make and respond to requests**
▶ **Apologize**

1 SNAPSHOT

FAMILY COMPLAINTS

☐ We never have dinner together as a family.
☐ Everybody is always arguing about housework.
☐ My daughter never takes her headphones off.
☐ My father criticizes everything I do.
☐ My husband never helps around the house.
☐ My kids are always texting their friends.
☐ My mother often calls me late at night.
☐ My parents don't respect my privacy.
☐ My brother never puts his phone away.
☐ My wife always brings work home on weekends.

Which complaints seem reasonable? Which ones seem unreasonable? Why?
Do you have similar complaints about anyone in your family? Check (✔) the complaints.
What other complaints do people sometimes have about family members?

2 CONVERSATION I'll turn it off.

▶ **A** Listen and practice.

Nolan Please turn down the TV. I have to study.

Ken I'm sorry. I'll turn it down.

Nolan It's still too loud.

Ken All right. I'll turn it off. I'll go watch this show in my room.

Nolan Thanks.

Ken No problem.

Nolan This place is such a mess. Rodrigo, your clothes are all over the place.

Rodrigo They're not mine. . . . And these books are yours, actually. Why don't you put them away?

Nolan I'm sorry. I guess I'm kind of nervous about my exam tomorrow.

Rodrigo That's OK. I know how you feel. Those exams drive me crazy, too.

▶ **B** Listen to the rest of the conversation. What complaints do Nolan and Rodrigo have about Ken?

3 GRAMMAR FOCUS

> **Two-part verbs; *will* for responding to requests**

With nouns	With pronouns	Requests and responses
Turn down the TV.	**Turn** it **down**.	Please turn down the music.
Turn the TV **down**.	(NOT: ~~Turn down it.~~)	OK. I**'ll** turn it down.
Put away your books.	**Put** them **away**.	Put away your books, please.
Put your books **away**.	(NOT: ~~Put away them.~~)	All right. I**'ll** put them away.

GRAMMAR PLUS *see page 137*

A Complete the requests with these words. Then compare with a partner.

your boots	your socks	your jacket	the cat	the trash
the TV	✓ the lights	the magazines	the music	the yard

1. Turn ___the lights___ off, please.
2. Turn _____ on, please.
3. Please turn _____ down.
4. Pick up _____, please.
5. Please put _____ away.

6. Hang _____ up, please.
7. Please take _____ off.
8. Clean _____ up, please.
9. Please take _____ out.
10. Please let _____ out.

B **PAIR WORK** Take turns making the requests above. Respond with pronouns.

A: Turn the lights off, please.
B: No problem. I'll turn them off.

4 PRONUNCIATION Stress in two-part verbs

A Listen and practice. Both words in a two-part verb receive equal stress.

●	●	●	●		●	●	●	●		●	●	●
Pick	up	your	things.		Pick	your	things	up.		Pick	them	up.
Turn	off	the	light.		Turn	the	light	off.		Turn	it	off.

B Write four more requests using the verbs in Exercise 3.
Then practice with a partner. Pay attention to stress.

5 WORD POWER Housework

A Find a phrase that is usually paired with each two-part verb. (Some phrases go with more than one verb.) Then add one more phrase for each verb.

the garbage	the magazines	the microwave	your coat
the groceries	the mess	the towels	your laptop

clean up _____ _____   take out _____ _____

hang up _____ _____   throw out _____ _____

pick up _____ _____   turn off _____ _____

put away _____ _____   turn on _____ _____

B What requests can you make in each of these rooms? Write four requests and four excuses. Use two-part verbs.

the kitchen   the living room

the bathroom   the bedroom

C **PAIR WORK** Take turns making the requests you wrote in part B. Respond by giving an excuse.

A: Marabel, please pick up the wet towel you left on your bed.

B: Sorry, I can't pick it up right now. I have to put my new clothes away.

6 LISTENING Helping around the house

A Listen to the results of a survey about family life. Check (✔) the answer to each question. Sometimes more than one answer is possible.

	Men	Women	Boys	Girls
1. Who is the messiest in the house?				
2. Who does most of the work in the kitchen?				
3. Who does the general chores inside and outside the house?				
4. Who worries most about expenses?				

B Listen again. According to the survey, what specific chores do men, women, boys, and girls usually do? Take notes.

C **GROUP WORK** How does your family compare to the survey results? Who helps the most with general chores around the house? Who helps the least?

A Match the sentences. Then listen and check your answers. Are all the requests reasonable?

1. "Would you take your garbage out, please? ____

2. "Would you mind not parking your car in my parking space? ____

3. "Would you mind turning the music down, please? ____

4. "Could you close the door behind you and make sure it locks? ____

5. "Can you keep your cat inside, please? ____

a. We don't want strangers to enter the building."

b. It often comes into my apartment through the balcony."

c. It can attract insects."

d. The walls are really thin, so the sound goes through to my apartment."

e. I need to park mine there."

B Look at the requests again. Have you ever made similar requests? Has anyone ever asked you to do similar things?

8 GRAMMAR FOCUS

Requests with modals and *Would you mind . . . ?*

Modal + simple form of verb	*Would you mind . . .* + gerund
Can you **keep** your cat inside, please?	**Would you mind keeping** your cat inside?
Could you **turn** the music **down**, please?	**Would you mind turning** the music **down**, please?
Would you please **park** your car in your space?	**Would you mind not parking** your car in my space?

GRAMMAR PLUS *see page 137*

A Match the requests in column A with the appropriate responses in column B. Then compare with a partner and practice them. (More than one answer may be possible.)

A

1. Would you mind not using your phone in class? ____
2. Would you mind speaking more quietly? ____
3. Would you please turn on the air conditioner? ____
4. Can you make me a sandwich? ____
5. Can you help me with my homework? ____
6. Could you lend me twenty dollars, please? ____

B

a. Sure, no problem. I'd be glad to.
b. Sorry. We didn't know we were so loud.
c. Sure. Do you want anything to drink?
d. Sorry. I had to talk to my boss.
e. I'm sorry, I can't. I don't have any cash.
f. I'm really sorry, but I'm busy.

B PAIR WORK Take turns making the requests in part A. Give your own responses.

C CLASS ACTIVITY Think of five unusual requests. Go around the class and make your requests. How many people accept? How many refuse?

A: Would you please lend me your car for the weekend?

B: Oh, I'm sorry. I'm going to wash it.

9 SPEAKING Apologies

Choose one of the situations below. Take turns making a request to your "neighbor." The "neighbor" should apologize by giving an excuse, admitting a mistake, or making an offer or a promise.

A: Would you mind not making so much noise? It's very late.
B: Oh, I'm sorry. I didn't realize it bothered you.

Different ways to apologize

give an excuse	"I'm sorry. I didn't realize . . ."
admit a mistake	"I forgot I left it there."
make an offer	"I'll take it out right now."
make a promise	"I promise I'll . . ./I'll make sure to . . ."

10 INTERCHANGE 6 I'm terribly sorry.

How good are you at apologizing? Go to Interchange 6 on page 119.

11 WRITING A public message

A Think of a problem that you could have with your neighbors. Write a message explaining the problem and making a request.

> To the person who left a big mess in the laundry room yesterday afternoon: Would you mind cleaning up after you finish your laundry? I fell down and almost broke my leg because the floor was all wet. Thank you.

B PAIR WORK Exchange messages with your classmates. Write a message apologizing for the problem you caused to your "neighbor."

> I'm sorry about the mess in the laundry room. My boss called me, and I had to go back to the office. I'll make sure to clean it up next time.

C GROUP WORK Take turns reading your messages aloud. Do you have similar problems with your neighbors? How do you solve them?

A Scan the text. How many of the requests and complaints are about food?

HOME   WORLD   CULTURE   TRAVEL   BUSINESS   SPORTS   FOOD

HOTEL MADNESS: THE CRAZY THINGS PEOPLE SAY!

There are about 500,000 hotels around the world. Every day, receptionists, servers, chefs, and managers work in these hotels looking after their guests. Guests often make special requests for things like an extra-large bed or a room with a view of the water. And sometimes people complain when something is not satisfactory. In the U.S., around two-thirds of these complaints are about the noise that other guests are making. Sometimes, guests' requests and complaints can make a hotel worker's job almost impossible!

Here are some very weird requests that hotel workers have actually heard:

"Would you mind lending me your suit tomorrow? I have a job interview to go to!"

"Could one of the staff give my daughter a hand with her homework?"

"Can you please fill my bath with chocolate milk?"

"I'd like chicken for dinner, please, but only the right leg."

"Can you make sure all the strawberries in my cereal are the same size?"

Some hotel guests are also very good at finding (or imagining) problems! These are some of their crazy complaints:

At a London hotel, 40 miles from the coast: "I can't see the ocean from my room."

At a Portuguese hotel: "My bed is way too comfortable. I keep oversleeping and missing the best part of the day!"

At a hotel in Spain: "There are too many tasty dishes on the restaurant buffet. I've gained more than 5 pounds!"

To a receptionist in the middle of the night: "I haven't been able to sleep at all! My wife won't stop snoring!"

After coming back from a day trip to a water park: "Nobody told us to bring our swimsuits and towels."

So the next time you're at a hotel and the staff look tired, be patient! Maybe they've had a stressful day!

B Read the article. Find the words in *italics* in the article. Then match each word with its meaning.

1. *give (somebody) a hand* ___
2. *satisfactory* ___
3. *weird* ___
4. *snoring* ___
5. *oversleep* ___

a. to breathe in a noisy way when asleep
b. help a person do something
c. good enough
d. not wake up early enough
e. very strange

C The sentences below are false. Correct each sentence to make it true.

1. It's common for guests to request a bigger room.
2. One hotel guest asked to borrow an employee's dress.
3. Another guest wanted the fruit at breakfast to be the same color.
4. One person wasn't happy because he kept getting up too early.
5. Someone complained about not taking the right things to go sightseeing.

D **PAIR WORK** Imagine you are the managers of a hotel. How would you respond to the requests and complaints above? Try to be as polite as you can!

Units 5–6 Progress check

SELF-ASSESSMENT

How well can you do these things? Check (✓) the boxes.

I can . . .	Very well	OK	A little
Understand descriptions of people's plans (Ex. 1)	☐	☐	☐
Discuss vacation plans (Ex. 2)	☐	☐	☐
Give travel advice (Ex. 2)	☐	☐	☐
Make and respond to requests (Ex. 3, 4)	☐	☐	☐
Apologize and give excuses (Ex. 3, 4)	☐	☐	☐

1 LISTENING What are your plans?

▶ **A** Listen to Lily, Tyler, and Abby describe their summer plans. What is each person going to do?

Summer plans	Reason
1. Lily _____	_____
2. Tyler _____	_____
3. Abby _____	_____

▶ **B** Listen again. What is the reason for each person's choice?

C PAIR WORK What did you do last summer? Listen to your partner and share with the class.

2 DISCUSSION Vacation plans

A GROUP WORK Imagine you are going to go on vacation. Take turns asking and answering these questions.

A: Where are you going to go on your next vacation?
B: I'm going to go to New York.
A: What are you going to do?
B: I'm going to visit the museums. Maybe I'll see a musical on Broadway.
A: Why did you choose that?
B: Well, I want to have a more cultural vacation this year.

B GROUP WORK What should each person do to prepare for his or her vacation? Give each other advice.

3 ROLE PLAY Making excuses

Student A: Your partner was supposed to do some things, but didn't. Look at the pictures and make a request about each one.

Student B: You were supposed to do some things, but didn't. Listen to your partner's requests. Apologize and either agree to the request or give an excuse.

A: Your room is a big mess. Please clean it up.

B: I'm sorry. I forgot about it. I'll clean it up after dinner.

Change roles and try the role play again.

4 GAME Can I ask you a favor?

A Write three requests on separate cards. Put an X on the back of two of the cards.

Can you help me with my homework?

Could you get me a cup of coffee?

Would you mind cooking dinner tonight?

B CLASS ACTIVITY Shuffle all the cards together. Take three new cards.

Go around the class and take turns making requests with the cards. Hold up each card so your classmate can see the back.

When answering:

X on the back = refuse the request and give an excuse

No X = agree to the request

Can you help me with my homework?

I'm sorry, I can't. I'm . . .

WHAT'S NEXT?

Look at your Self-assessment again. Do you need to review anything?

7 What do you use this for?

▶ Describe uses and purposes of technology
▶ Give suggestions

1 SNAPSHOT

Inventions We Can't Live Without

- [ ] smartphones
- [ ] digital cameras
- [ ] Internet
- [ ] e-readers
- [ ] tablet computers
- [ ] streaming TV
- [ ] robots
- [ ] 3-D printers
- [ ] driverless cars
- [ ] GPS technology
- [ ] drones
- [ ] Wi-Fi

How long have the inventions above been around in your country?
How was life different before them?
Check (✓) three inventions you couldn't live without. Compare with a partner.

2 PERSPECTIVES Smartphone usage

▶ **A** How do you use your smartphone? Listen and respond to the statements.

I use my smartphone . . .	Often	Sometimes	Hardly ever	Never
to send messages	[ ]	[ ]	[ ]	[ ]
for watching videos	[ ]	[ ]	[ ]	[ ]
to take photos	[ ]	[ ]	[ ]	[ ]
to post on social media sites	[ ]	[ ]	[ ]	[ ]
for doing school assignments	[ ]	[ ]	[ ]	[ ]
to send emails	[ ]	[ ]	[ ]	[ ]
to shop online	[ ]	[ ]	[ ]	[ ]
to check the weather	[ ]	[ ]	[ ]	[ ]
to read e-books	[ ]	[ ]	[ ]	[ ]
for listening to music	[ ]	[ ]	[ ]	[ ]

B **PAIR WORK** Compare your answers. Are your answers similar or different?

3 GRAMMAR FOCUS

> **Infinitives and gerunds for uses and purposes**

Infinitives	**Gerunds**
I use my cell phone **to send** messages.	I use my cell phone **for sending** messages.
Some people use their phones **to watch** videos.	Some people use their phones **for watching** videos.
People often use their phones **to take** photos.	People often use their phones **for taking** photos.

GRAMMAR PLUS *see page 138*

A **PAIR WORK** What do you know about this technology? Complete the sentences in column A with information from column B. Use infinitives and gerunds. (More than one combination is possible.)

A	B
1. Many people use tablet computers . . .	look for criminals.
2. You can use your smartphone . . .	perform dangerous tasks.
3. Engineers use 3-D printers . . .	get directions.
4. People can use the Internet . . .	make car parts.
5. Companies sometimes use robots . . .	make video calls.
6. The police use drones . . .	learn languages.

Many people use tablet computers to make video calls.
Many people use tablet computers for making video calls.

B **PAIR WORK** Think of one other use for the items in column A.

"Paparazzi use drones to spy on celebrities."

C **GROUP WORK** List some unexpected uses for these new and old items. Compare your answers with the whole class. Who came up with the most uses?

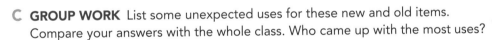

a smartphone   a paper clip   a webcam   a pencil   invisible tape   an old CD

"You can use your smartphone for driving your car."

4 PRONUNCIATION Syllable stress

A Listen and practice. Notice which syllable has the main stress.

● ● ●	● ● ●	● ● ●
Internet	invention	engineer
messages	assignment	DVD
digital	computer	recommend
_____	_____	_____
_____	_____	_____

B Where is the stress in these words? Add them to the columns in part A. Then listen and check.

directions   driverless   entertain   equipment   media   understand

5 WORD POWER Plugged in

A Complete the chart with words and phrases from the list. Add one more to each category. Then compare with a partner.

✓ computer whiz	hacker	check in for a flight	geek
computer crash	edit photos	download apps	software bugs
flash drive	identity theft	make international phone calls	frozen screen
smart devices	early adopter	solar-powered batteries	phone charger

Problems with technology	Gadgets and devices	People who are "into" technology	Things to do online
		computer whiz	

B **GROUP WORK** Discuss some of the positive and negative consequences of living in a connected world.

– Have you ever had any of the problems mentioned in part A? What happened? What did you do?

– Do you have any smart devices? Which ones? How do they help you? How much do you depend on them?

– Do you have any friends who never put their phone away? Is anyone in your family addicted to new technologies? Are you?

– What is one gadget you would really like to have? Why?

– Is identity theft a problem where you live? What about hackers? How do you protect against them?

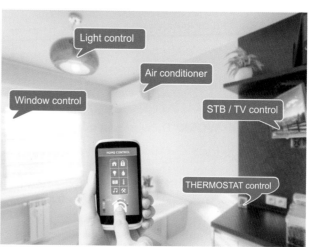

Light control
Air conditioner
Window control
STB / TV control
HOME CONTROL
THERMOSTAT control

6 LISTENING They've thought of everything!

A Listen to two people talk about the best apps for travel. Check (✓) the four app categories. (There are two extra categories.)

☐ safety _____

☐ packing _____

☐ music _____

☐ transportation _____

☐ attractions _____

☐ hotel _____

B Listen again. What can you use the apps for? Write the uses next to the categories you checked above.

C **PAIR WORK** What are your favorite apps? Discuss and share with the class.

7 CONVERSATION What do I do now?

▶ **A** Listen and practice.

Justin: I can't believe my phone's frozen again.

Allie: How long have you had it?

Justin: About a year. It's not that old.

Allie: Maybe someone hacked it.

Justin: Really? You think so?

Allie: No, I'm just kidding. It's probably just a virus.

Justin: Oh. So what do I do now?

Allie: First, you'd better install a good antivirus app. And be sure to update it.

Justin: OK, I'll download one now. What else should I do?

Allie: Well, don't forget to reset all your passwords.

Justin: That's a good idea. I never remember to change my passwords.

Allie: One more thing. Try not to use public Wi-Fi networks.

Justin: You're right. I have to learn to be more careful.

▶ **B** Listen to the rest of the conversation. What else does Justin want help with? What does Allie suggest?

8 GRAMMAR FOCUS

▶ **Imperatives and infinitives for giving suggestions**

Be sure to update the app.

Make sure to charge your phone.

Remember to back up your files.

Don't forget to reset your passwords.

Try not to use public Wi-Fi networks.

GRAMMAR PLUS *see page 138*

A Look at the suggestions. Rewrite them using these phrases. Then compare with a partner.

Make sure to . . .   Try to . . .   Remember to . . .

Be sure not to . . .   Try not to . . .   Don't forget to . . .

1. **a.** Before using an electronic safe, you have to reset the passcode.
   b. You should check if it's locked after you close it.
2. **a.** Don't get your phone wet or it might not work anymore.
   b. It's important to back up your contacts and other important information.
3. **a.** You must set your alarm system each time you leave home.
   b. Don't use your birthday as a code.
4. **a.** You ought to keep the lenses of your digital camera clean.
   b. It's important to keep the lens cap on when you're not taking photos.

B PAIR WORK Take turns giving other suggestions for using the items in part A.

What do you use this for? 47

9 LISTENING Smart suggestions

▶ **A** Listen to people give suggestions for using three of these things. Number them 1, 2, and 3. (There are two extra things.)

☐ portable speaker

☐ GPS system

☐ flash drive

☐ smartphone

☐ ATM card

▶ **B** Listen again. Write two suggestions you hear for each thing. Then compare with a partner.

1. _____   _____

2. _____   _____

3. _____   _____

C **PAIR WORK** What do you know about the other two things in part A? Give suggestions about them. "Be sure to buy one with lots of memory."

10 INTERCHANGE 7 Free advice

Give your classmates some advice. Go to Interchange 7 on page 121.

11 WRITING A message

A Imagine your brother is coming over for dinner, but you are going to be busy all day. Your roommate has agreed to help you. Think of three things you need help with. Then write a message with instructions.

B **GROUP WORK** Take turns reading your messages aloud. Did you ask for similar favors?

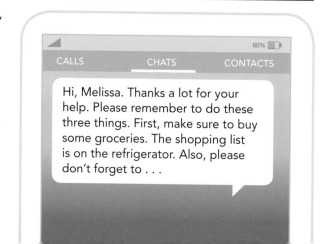

Hi, Melissa. Thanks a lot for your help. Please remember to do these three things. First, make sure to buy some groceries. The shopping list is on the refrigerator. Also, please don't forget to . . .

A Skim the article. What is the sharing economy? What three examples does the article give?

THE SHARING ECONOMY – GOOD FOR EVERYBODY?

Modern technology has made it easier for ordinary people to rent things or services to others. With the click of an app, we can find almost anything. It could be a new dress to wear on the weekend, or someone to clean your house. This is the sharing economy, and it is now a profitable $20 billion-a-year business. But some people are now asking: Just how good is it for society in general?

Not long ago, when people went on vacation, they usually stayed in a hotel. Today they have the choice of staying in someone's private house. They pay less, but what effect does this have on the hotel industry and the wider economy? Hotels receive fewer guests, but they still have to pay salaries to their employees and taxes to the government. Many people who rent out rooms do not. So the government gets less money, and some hotels might even close down.

Then there are car-sharing sites. Instead of using your own car for a long trip you can get a ride with someone for a small fee. Some people argue this is better for the environment, since fewer cars on the roads means less pollution. But how many people choose to use these sites rather than taking the bus or the train? Public transportation is, after all, much kinder to the environment than cars.

Many sites offer cooking services. Instead of going to a restaurant, you can use an app to order dishes from people in your neighborhood.

There is even a site where you can buy leftover food that people haven't eaten! This is sure to save you time and money. But is it risky? Can you trust the people cooking your food? Restaurants have to follow strict regulations to make sure their food is safe to eat.

There is no doubt that the sharing economy is growing. Some economists think it will be worth $335 billion by 2025. As new technology makes sharing food, accommodation, and transportation easier all the time, the question of "Is it fair?" will remain.

B Read the article. Find the words in *italics* below. Then circle the meaning of each word.

1. When a business is *profitable*, it **makes / loses** money.
2. *Taxes* are money that people **give to / receive from** the government.
3. If something is *risky*, it's **dangerous / safe**.
4. *Regulations* are **rules / people** that control how we do things.
5. When something is *fair*, everybody has **equal / different** opportunities.

C Answer the questions.

1. How much is the sharing economy worth nowadays?
2. What is the advantage of staying in a private house instead of a hotel?
3. Why is car sharing less damaging to the environment?
4. What is better for the environment than car sharing?
5. How can buying food from non-professionals be risky?

D Do you use any of these sharing-economy services? Are they ever risky? Do you think they are fair?

8 Time to celebrate!

▸ Discuss holidays and special occasions
▸ Describe celebrations, annual events, and customs

1 SNAPSHOT

HOLIDAYS AND FESTIVALS

Day of the Dead
November 2nd
Mexicans make playful skeleton sculptures and bake *pan de muerto* – bread of the dead.

Saint Patrick's Day
March 17th
People of Irish background wear green to celebrate their culture with parades, dancing, parties, and special foods.

Chinese New Year
January or February
Chinese people celebrate the lunar new year with fireworks and dragon dances.

Thanksgiving
November
In the United States, families get together, have a traditional meal, and give thanks for life and health.

Do you celebrate these or similar holidays in your country?
What other special days do you have?
What's your favorite holiday or festival?

2 WORD POWER Ways to celebrate

A Which word or phrase is not usually paired with each verb?
Put a line through it. Then compare with a partner.

1. **eat**	candy	sweets	~~a mask~~
2. **give**	presents	a celebration	money
3. **go to**	decorations	a wedding	a party
4. **have a**	picnic	beach	meal
5. **play**	games	candles	music
6. **send**	cards	flowers	a barbecue
7. **visit**	relatives	food	close friends
8. **watch**	a birthday	a parade	fireworks
9. **wear**	costumes	invitations	traditional clothes

B **PAIR WORK** Do you do any of the things in part A as part of a cultural or family celebration? When? Tell your partner.

3 PERSPECTIVES Favorite celebrations

▶ **A** Listen to these comments about special days of the year. Match them to the correct pictures.

____ **1.** "My favorite celebration is Mother's Day. It's a day when my husband and my kids make pancakes for me – just like I used to make for my mom – and I get to have breakfast in bed."

____ **2.** "February 14th is the day when people give cards and presents to the ones they love. I'm really looking forward to Valentine's Day! I already have a gift for my boyfriend."

____ **3.** "New Year's Eve is a night when I have fun with my friends. We usually have a big party. We stay up all night and then go out for breakfast in the morning."

B **PAIR WORK** What do you like about each celebration in part A?

4 GRAMMAR FOCUS

▶ **Relative clauses of time**

Mother's Day is **a day**	**when** my kids make pancakes for me.
February 14th is **the day**	**when** people give cards to the ones they love.
New Year's Eve is **a night**	**when** I have fun with my friends.

GRAMMAR PLUS *see page 139*

A How much do you know about these times? Complete the sentences in column A with information from column B. Then compare with a partner.

A
1. Mother's Day is a day when _____
2. New Year's Eve is a night when _____
3. April Fools' Day is a day when _____
4. Valentine's Day is a day when _____
5. Labor Day is a day when _____
6. Summer is a time when _____

B
a. people sometimes play tricks on friends.
b. people celebrate their mothers.
c. many people like to go to the beach.
d. people in many countries honor workers.
e. people express their love to someone.
f. people have parties with family and friends.

B Complete these sentences with your own information. Then compare with a partner.

Winter is the season . . .
Birthdays are days . . .
Spring is the time of year . . .

Children's Day is a day . . .
July and August are the months . . .
A wedding anniversary is a time . . .

5 LISTENING Time for Carnival!

Carnival in Brazil

▶ **A** Listen to Vanessa talk about her trip to Carnival in Brazil. Write three facts about Carnival that she mentions.

▶ **B** Listen again and answer these questions about Vanessa's experience.

Why did she have to book her hotel six months early?
What happened when Vanessa got lost?
What was her favorite thing about Carnival? Why?

C **PAIR WORK** Think of another famous celebration that is similar to Carnival. Describe it to the class. They will try to guess the celebration.

6 SPEAKING Favorite holidays

A **PAIR WORK** Choose your three favorite holidays. Tell your partner why you like each one.

A: I really like Independence Day.
B: What do you like about it?
A: It's a day when we watch parades and fireworks.
B: Do you do anything special?
A: We usually have a barbecue. My father makes burgers, and my mother makes her special potato salad.

B **CLASS ACTIVITY** Take a class vote. What are the most popular holidays in your class?

7 WRITING An online entry

A Write an entry for a travel website about a festival or celebration where you live. When is it? How do people celebrate it? What should a visitor see and do?

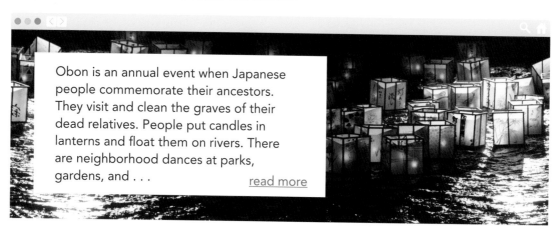

Obon is an annual event when Japanese people commemorate their ancestors. They visit and clean the graves of their dead relatives. People put candles in lanterns and float them on rivers. There are neighborhood dances at parks, gardens, and . . .

read more

B **PAIR WORK** Read your partner's entry. What do you like about it? Can you suggest anything to improve it?

8 CONVERSATION A traditional wedding

▶ **A** Listen and practice.

JULIA Is this a picture from your wedding, Anusha?

ANUSHA Yes. We had the ceremony in India.

JULIA And was this your wedding dress?

ANUSHA Yes. It's a sari, actually. In India, when women get married, they usually wear a brightly colored sari, not a white dress.

JULIA It's beautiful! So, what are weddings like in India?

ANUSHA Well, in some traditions, after the groom arrives, the bride and groom exchange garlands of flowers. We did that. But we didn't do some other traditional things.

JULIA Oh? Like what?

ANUSHA Well, before the wedding, the bride's female relatives usually have a party to celebrate. But I'm an only child, and I don't have any female cousins, so we skipped that.

JULIA That makes sense. You know, I have heard about this one tradition . . . When the groom takes off his shoes, the bride's sisters steal them! I guess you didn't do that, either?

ANUSHA Oh, no, we did that part. My mom stole them!

▶ **B** Listen to the rest of the conversation.
What does Anusha say about her wedding reception?

9 PRONUNCIATION Stress and rhythm

▶ **A** Listen and practice. Notice how stressed words and syllables occur with a regular rhythm.

●　　　●　　　●　　　●　　　●　　　●　　　●

When women get married, they usually wear a brightly colored sari.

▶ **B** Listen to the stress and rhythm in these sentences. Then practice them.

1. After the groom arrives, the bride and groom exchange garlands of flowers.
2. Before the wedding, the bride's female relatives usually have a party to celebrate.
3. When the groom takes off his shoes, the bride's sisters steal them.

10 GRAMMAR FOCUS

▶ **Adverbial clauses of time**

When women get married,	they usually wear a brightly colored sari.
After the groom arrives,	the bride and groom exchange garlands of flowers.
Before the wedding,	the bride's female relatives usually have a party to celebrate.

GRAMMAR PLUS see page 139

A What do you know about wedding customs in North America?
Complete these sentences with the information below.

1. Before a man and woman get married, they usually ____
2. When a couple gets engaged, the man often ____
3. Right after a couple gets engaged, they usually ____
4. When a woman gets married, she usually ____
5. When guests go to a wedding, they almost always ____
6. Right after a couple gets married, they usually ____

a. wears a long white dress and a veil.
b. go on a short trip called a "honeymoon."
c. give the bride and groom gifts or some money.
d. gives the woman an engagement ring.
e. begin to plan the wedding.
f. date each other for a year or more.

B PAIR WORK What happens when people get married in your country?
Tell your partner by completing the statements in part A with your own
information. Pay attention to stress and rhythm.

11 INTERCHANGE 8 It's worth celebrating.

How do your classmates celebrate special occasions? Go to Interchange 8 on page 122.

12 SPEAKING My personal traditions

A GROUP WORK How do you usually celebrate the dates below? Share your personal traditions with
your classmates.

your birthday   New Year's Eve   your country's national day   your favorite holiday

A: On my birthday, I always wear new
clothes, and I often have a party.
What about you?

B: I usually celebrate my birthday with my
family. We have a special meal and
some relatives come over.

C: I used to celebrate my birthday at home,
but now I usually go out with friends.

B CLASS ACTIVITY Tell the class the most
interesting traditions you talked about in
your group. Do you share any common
traditions? Did you use to celebrate those
dates the same way when you were younger?

A Skim the article. Which of these phrases could be a title for this article?

The best New Year's resolutions   New Year's traditions around the world

How to host a New Year's Eve party

Out with the Old, In with THE NEW

It's midnight on New Year's Eve. Clocks are striking twelve as people welcome in the coming year and say goodbye to the old. It's a time when people wish for good luck in the future and forget bad things in the past. Around the world, people do different things to help their wishes come true. Some of <u>them</u> might surprise you.

Food is often central to New Year's customs. In Ireland, they hit the walls and doors of their houses with loaves of bread. They hope <u>this</u> will make good luck enter the house and bad luck leave it. The Spanish and the Mexicans eat twelve grapes in twelve seconds – <u>one</u> for luck in each of the coming months. Eating grapes so fast isn't easy, but it's fun and often messy!

Colors are important, too. Brazilians, for example, choose their clothes very carefully – for peace they wear white, yellow might bring success, and red means love is in the air! The Chinese believe red brings good luck, so they like to dress in this color, too. They also give family members and friends red envelopes containing money.

Some people destroy things on New Year's Eve because they want to forget the past. In Ecuador and Colombia, people make a dummy and fill it with sawdust, newspaper, or old clothes. <u>They</u> dress it, put a mask on it, and name it after someone famous or a friend or family member. Then they burn it.

And some customs have no reason at all; <u>they</u> just develop over time. On New Year's Eve in Germany, several TV stations show a short black-and-white movie called *Dinner for One*. It's a comedy in English, starring English actors. Nobody knows why they do this, not even the Germans!

B Read the article. Check (✓) True or False for each statement about New Year's customs. Then correct each false statement.

	True	False	
1. In Ireland, people eat loaves of bread for good luck.	☐	☐	
2. They eat apples for good luck in Spain.	☐	☐	
3. In China, people change the color of their doors.	☐	☐	
4. In Colombia, they burn a doll with old things inside.	☐	☐	
5. In Germany, people watch *Dinner for One* because it's about New Year's Eve.	☐	☐	

C What do the underlined words in the article refer to? Write the correct word.

1. them _____   **3.** one _____   **5.** they _____

2. this _____   **4.** They _____

D What do people in your country do for the New Year? What is your favorite New Year's tradition?

Units 7–8 Progress check

SELF-ASSESSMENT

How well can you do these things? Check (✓) the boxes.

I can . . .	Very well	OK	A little
Describe uses and purposes of objects (Ex. 1)	☐	☐	☐
Give instructions and suggestions (Ex. 2)	☐	☐	☐
Describe holidays and special occasions (Ex. 3, 5)	☐	☐	☐
Understand descriptions of customs (Ex. 4, 5)	☐	☐	☐
Ask and answer questions about celebrations and customs (Ex. 5)	☐	☐	☐

1 GAME Guess my object.

A PAIR WORK Think of five familiar objects. Write a short description of each object's use and purpose. Don't write the name of the objects.

> It's electronic. It's small. It connects to the Internet.
>
> You wear it. It communicates with your phone.

B GROUP WORK Take turns reading your descriptions and guessing the objects. Keep score. Who guessed the most items correctly? Who wrote the best descriptions?

2 ROLE PLAY It's all under control.

Student A: Choose one situation below. Decide on the details and answer Student B's questions. Then get some suggestions.

Start like this: *I'm really nervous. I'm . . .*

giving a speech
What is it about?
Where is it?
How many people will be there?

going on a job interview
What's the job?
What are the responsibilities?
Who is interviewing you?

taking my driving test
When is it?
How long is it?
Have you prepared?

Student B: Student A is telling you about a situation. Ask the appropriate questions above. Then give some suggestions.

Change roles and try the role play again.

useful expressions

Try to . . .	Try not to . . .
Remember to . . .	Be sure to . . .
Don't forget to . . .	Make sure to . . .

3 SPEAKING Unofficial holidays

A PAIR WORK Choose one of these holidays or create your own.
Then write a description of the holiday. Answer the questions below.

Buy Nothing Day

National Day of Unplugging

World Smile Day

What is the name of the holiday? When is it?
How do you celebrate it?

B GROUP WORK Read your description to the
group. Then vote on the best holiday.

> Buy Nothing Day is a day when you can't buy
> anything. It's a day to think about what we consume,
> what we really need, and how much money we waste.

4 LISTENING Marriage customs around the world

▶ **A** Listen to two people discuss a book about marriage customs.
Match each country to the title that describes its marriage custom.

1. Sweden ___
2. China ___
3. Paraguay ___
4. Germany ___

a. *Fighting for Love*
b. *Dishes for Good Luck*
c. *Kisses for Guests*
d. *Tears of Happiness*

▶ **B** Listen again. Complete the sentences to describe the custom.

1. When the groom leaves the table, _____.
2. One month before the wedding, _____.
3. When they want to marry the same man, _____.
4. After the guests bring the dishes to the couple, _____.

C PAIR WORK Think of some marriage customs from your country.
How are they similar to these customs? How are they different?

5 DISCUSSION Just married

GROUP WORK Talk about marriage in your country.
Ask these questions and others of your own.

How old are people when they get married?
What happens after a couple gets engaged?
What happens during the ceremony?
What do the bride and groom wear?
What kinds of food is served at the reception?
What kinds of gifts do people usually give?

WHAT'S NEXT?

Look at your Self-assessment again. Do you need to review anything?

9 Only time will tell.

▶ Discuss life in different times
▶ Discuss consequences

1 SNAPSHOT

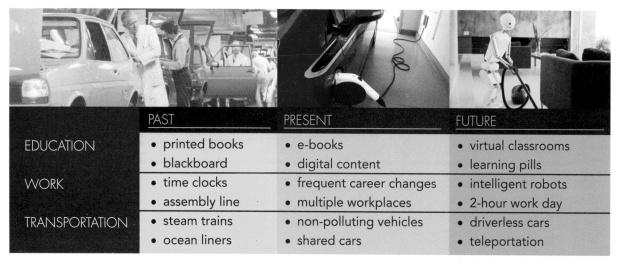

	PAST	PRESENT	FUTURE
EDUCATION	• printed books • blackboard	• e-books • digital content	• virtual classrooms • learning pills
WORK	• time clocks • assembly line	• frequent career changes • multiple workplaces	• intelligent robots • 2-hour work day
TRANSPORTATION	• steam trains • ocean liners	• non-polluting vehicles • shared cars	• driverless cars • teleportation

Which of these changes are the most important? How have they affected the way we live?
Do you think any of the future developments could happen in your lifetime?
Can you think of two other developments that could happen in the future?

2 CONVERSATION That's a thing of the past!

▶ **A** Listen and practice.

Tom: I hardly recognize our old neighborhood.
A few years ago, there were just houses
around here.

Mia: I know. They're building a lot of new apartments.
The whole neighborhood's different.

Tom: Remember the little burger restaurant we used to go
to after school, Hamburger Heaven?

Mia: Of course . . . Now it's another office tower. And I
hear they're tearing down our high school.
They're going to build a shopping mall.

Tom: That's such a shame. Pretty soon the neighborhood
will just be a bunch of malls. And maybe there
won't be any schools anymore.

Mia: Probably not. Kids will study from their computers anywhere they want.

Tom: So they won't hang out with their friends after school? That's too bad.
I enjoyed meeting our friends at that burger place after class.

Mia: Seriously? That's a thing of the past! Nowadays, kids only meet online.

▶ **B** Listen to the rest of the conversation. What else has changed in their neighborhood?

3 GRAMMAR FOCUS

Time contrasts

Past	Present	Future
A few years ago, there **were** just houses here.	These days, they**'re building** lots of apartments.	Soon, there **will be** apartment blocks everywhere.
We **used to go** to a burger place after class every day.	Today, people **order** food from their phones.	In the future, restaurants **might not exist**.
In the past, kids **used to hang out** with friends after school.	Nowadays, kids only **meet** online.	In a few years, we **are going to have** virtual friends.

GRAMMAR PLUS *see page 140*

A Complete the sentences in column A with the appropriate information from column B. Then compare with a partner.

A
1. In the early 1990s, ___
2. Before the airplane, ___
3. Before there were supermarkets, ___
4. In many companies these days, ___
5. In most big cities nowadays, ___
6. In many schools today, ___
7. In the next 100 years, ___
8. Sometime in the near future, ___

B
a. students have their own tablets.
b. pollution is becoming a serious problem.
c. there will probably be cities in space.
d. few people had cell phones.
e. people used to shop at small grocery stores.
f. women still receive lower salaries than men.
g. doctors might find a cure for the common cold.
h. ocean liners were the only way to travel across the Atlantic.

B Complete four of the phrases in part A, column A, with your own ideas. Then compare with a partner.

4 PRONUNCIATION Intonation in statements with time phrases

A Listen and practice. Notice the intonation in these statements beginning with a time phrase.

In the past, few women went to college.

Today, there are more women than men in college in the United States.

In the future, women all over the world will go to college.

B **PAIR WORK** Complete these statements with your own information. Then read your statements to a partner. Pay attention to intonation.

As a child, I used to . . .
Five years ago, I . . .
Nowadays, I . . .

These days, . . .
In five years, I'll . . .
In ten years, I might . . .

5 LISTENING On the other side of the world

A Listen to Katie talk to her grandfather about an upcoming trip. Check (✓) the three concerns her grandfather has about the trip.

Concern

1. ☐ language   ☐ transportation
2. ☐ meeting people   ☐ money
3. ☐ communication   ☐ food

Katie's response

_____

_____

_____

B Listen again. Write what Katie says in response to these concerns.

C **PAIR WORK** What other problems might someone experience when they travel to another country? How might these problems change in the future?

6 SPEAKING Not anymore.

GROUP WORK How have things changed? How will things be different in the future? Choose four of these topics. Then discuss the questions below.

communications   education   housing
entertainment   fashion   shopping
environment   food   traveling
health

What was it like in the past?
What is it like today?
What will it be like in the future?

A: In the past, people cooked all their meals at home.
B: Not anymore. Nowadays, we eat takeout food all the time.
C: In the future, . . .

7 WRITING He's changed a lot.

A **PAIR WORK** Interview your partner about his or her past, present, and hopes for the future.

B Write a paragraph describing how your partner has changed. Make some predictions about the future. Don't write your partner's name.

> This person came to our school about two years ago. He used to be a little shy in class, and he didn't have many friends. Now, he's on the basketball team and he is very popular. He's a very talented player and, someday, he'll play on the national team. He'll be famous and very rich. I think he'll . . .

C **CLASS ACTIVITY** Read your paragraph to the class. Can they guess who it is about?

A Listen to some possible consequences of getting a high-paying job. Check (✓) the statements you agree with.

If you get a high-paying job, . . .

- ☐ your friends might ask you for a loan.
- ☐ you'll have a lot of money to spend.
- ☐ more people may want to be your friend.
- ☐ you won't have much time for your family.
- ☐ you'll be able to buy anything you want.
- ☐ you won't be able to take long vacations.
- ☐ you'll have to pay higher taxes.
- ☐ you won't have to worry about the future.

B **PAIR WORK** Look at the statements again. Which are advantages of getting a high-paying job? Which are disadvantages?

"The first one is a disadvantage. I'd like to help my friends, but I wouldn't like to lend them money."

9 GRAMMAR FOCUS

Conditional sentences with *if* clauses

Possible situation (present)	Consequence (future with *will*, *may*, or *might*)
If you **get** a high-paying job,	you**'ll have** more cash to spend.
If you **have** more cash to spend,	you**'ll be able to buy** anything you want.
If you **can buy** anything you want,	you **won't save** your money.
If you **don't save** your money,	you **may have to get** a weekend job.
If you **have to get** a weekend job,	you **might not have** any free time.

GRAMMAR PLUS *see page 140*

A Match the *if* clauses in column A with the appropriate consequences from column B. Then compare with a partner.

A
1. If you eat less fast food, ____
2. If you walk to work every day, ____
3. If you don't get enough sleep, ____
4. If you change jobs, ____
5. If you don't study regularly, ____
6. If you travel abroad, ____

B
a. you may not learn to speak fluently.
b. you might feel a lot healthier.
c. you'll stay in shape without joining a gym.
d. you'll be able to experience a new culture.
e. you won't be able to stay awake in class.
f. you may not like it better than your old one.

B Add your own consequences to the *if* clauses in column A. Then practice with a partner.

"If you eat less fast food, you will probably live longer."

10 WORD POWER Collocations

A **PAIR WORK** Find phrases from the list that usually go with each verb.
(Sometimes more than one answer is possible.)

a club	a gym	in shape	money	tired
✓ a degree	a living	into college	stressed	work experience
a group	energy	jealous	time	your own money

earn ___*a degree*___ _____ _____

get _____ _____ _____

join _____ _____ _____

spend _____ _____ _____

feel _____ _____ _____

B **GROUP WORK** Share your answers with the group.
Can you add one more phrase to each verb?

11 SPEAKING Who knows what will happen?

A **GROUP WORK** Choose three possible events from below. One student completes an event with a
consequence. The next student adds a consequence. Suggest at least five consequences.

fall in love   get a part-time job
join a gym   move to a foreign country
study very hard

If you fall in love, you'll probably want to get married.

If you get married, you'll have to earn your own money.

If you want to earn your own money, you'll need to get a job.

If you get a job, you may spend less time at the gym.

If you spend less time at the gym, you won't keep in shape.

B **CLASS ACTIVITY** Who has the most interesting consequences for each event?

12 INTERCHANGE 9 Cause and effect

Give your opinion about some issues. Go to Interchange 9 on page 123.

A Scan the article. Where is Aguaviva? Who is Luis Bricio?

AGUAVIVA: FIGHTING FOR A FUTURE

Twenty years ago, Aguaviva, a small village in the north of Spain, was dying. Young people wanted more opportunities, so they moved away to the cities. By 1991, there were only 618 people left, and most of them were old. Many of the houses were empty and falling down, and the local school had very few children. Aguaviva's future looked dark.

In 2000, the mayor, Luis Bricio, decided something had to change. He wondered, "How can I bring this place back to life?" He knew the village needed people, but from where? Then he had a brilliant idea. He flew 6,300 miles to Buenos Aires and started telling everyone about Aguaviva. He spoke on the radio and put advertisements in newspapers. The ads said, "If you are married with two children under the age of 12, we'll offer you a home, a job, free health care and education for at least five years." The following year, he did the same thing in Romania.

Many families accepted the offer and Aguaviva began to change. The village school went from having 37 students to more than 80 in three years. The sound of children shouting and playing has made the local people feel so much younger. The economy began to improve, too. There was work for builders repairing the old houses, and a factory making electrical parts for cars opened.

Of course, not everything was easy. The people from Buenos Aires were used to a big city, so living in a small village with little public transportation was difficult at first. The Romanians had to learn a new language. And they all missed their family and friends back home. But everybody had new opportunities, too. Before, many of the parents had worried about finding a job and having enough money to look after their children. After moving to Spain, their future looked brighter. Many of them thought, "We're going to stay here for many years – this place will be our home."

B Read the article. Then answer the questions.

1. Why did young people start leaving Aguaviva?
2. How did Luis Bricio try to attract people to Aguaviva?
3. How did the school change after the year 2000?
4. What kinds of new jobs were there in Aguaviva?
5. What problems did the families from Argentina and Romania have?

C Who would make the following comments? Choose the correct words from the box.

| Luis Bricio | young people from Aguaviva |
| elderly people from Aguaviva | new immigrants |

1. "I'm not going back home because life is better here."
2. "I can't stay here. There are no jobs for people of my age."
3. "I'm going to make this village a better place."
4. "I love having all these kids around me – I don't feel so old."

D Do you think Luis Bricio had a good idea? Would you move to a place like this? What would you miss most about home?

10 I like working with people.

▶ Discuss job skills
▶ Discuss kinds of jobs

1 SNAPSHOT

21ST CENTURY SKILLS

☐ Can you use technology to find the information you need?
☐ Can you evaluate the information you find?
☐ Do you work well with different kinds of people?
☐ Can you communicate with people from different cultures?
☐ Are you good at analyzing and solving problems?
☐ Can you develop new ideas?
☐ Do you enjoy learning new things?
☐ Can you teach others how to do things?

21st century life
citizen skills
creativity successful
digital
effective
knowledge
information
responsibility
network
fluency
flexibility
technology
collaborate
ability thinking
global critical

Which of these skills do you think are most important for work? in life? Why?
Check (✓) the skills that you think you have.
Look at the skills you checked. What jobs do you think you might be good at?

2 CONVERSATION I love playing video games.

▶ **A** Listen and practice.

Mai: What are you doing this summer?
Jeff: Nothing much. I'm broke. I need to find a job!
Mai: So do I. Have you seen anything interesting?
Jeff: No, not yet.
Mai: Why don't you get a job at your uncle's restaurant?
Jeff: No way. They're open evenings and weekends, and I hate working on weekends.
Mai: Well, I don't mind working on weekends. Besides, I really enjoy working with people. Do you think he would give me a job?
Jeff: Why don't you go over this weekend and talk to him?
Mai: Yeah. I'll do that. Oh, I found one for you: video game tester.
Jeff: That sounds like fun. I love playing video games. I'll check that one out.

▶ **B** Listen to the rest of the conversation. What is one problem with the job? What does Jeff decide to do?

3 GRAMMAR FOCUS

▶ **Gerunds; short responses**

Affirmative statements with gerunds	Agree	Disagree	Other verbs or phrases followed by gerunds
I love playing video games.	So do I.	I don't.	*like*
I hate working on weekends.	So do I.	Really? I like it.	*enjoy*
I'm good at solving problems.	So am I.	Oh, I'm not.	*be interested in*
Negative statements with gerunds			
I don't mind working evenings.	Neither do I.	I do.	
I'm not good at selling.	Neither am I.	Well, I am.	
I can't stand commuting.	Neither can I.	Oh, I don't mind it.	

GRAMMAR PLUS see page 141

A PAIR WORK Match the phrases in columns A and B to make statements about yourself. Then take turns reading your sentences and giving short responses.

A
1. I can't stand _____
2. I'm not very good at _____
3. I'm good at _____
4. I don't like _____
5. I hate _____
6. I'm interested in _____
7. I don't mind _____
8. I enjoy _____

B
a. working the night shift.
b. solving other people's problems.
c. working alone.
d. sitting in long meetings.
e. working on weekends.
f. speaking in public.
g. managing my time.
h. learning foreign languages.

A: I can't stand sitting in long meetings.
B: Neither can I.

B GROUP WORK Complete the phrases in column A with your own information. Then take turns reading your statements. Ask questions to get more information.

4 PRONUNCIATION Unreleased and released /t/ and /d/

▶ **A** Listen and practice. Notice that when the sound /t/ or /d/ at the end of a word is followed by a consonant, it's unreleased. When it is followed by a vowel sound, it's released.

Unreleased
She's not good at dealing with stress.
I hate working on Sundays.
You need to manage money well.

Released
He's not a good artist.
They really hate it!
I need a cup of coffee.

B PAIR WORK Write three sentences starting with *I'm not very good at* and *I don't mind*. Then practice the sentences. Pay attention to the unreleased and released sounds /t/ and /d/.

5 SPEAKING Do what you love.

A **PAIR WORK** How does your partner feel about doing these things? Interview your partner. Check (✓) his or her answers.

How do you feel about . . . ?	I enjoy it.	I don't mind it.	I hate it.
dealing with the public	☐	☐	☐
working alone	☐	☐	☐
being part of a team	☐	☐	☐
meeting deadlines	☐	☐	☐
leading a team	☐	☐	☐
working on weekends	☐	☐	☐
learning new skills	☐	☐	☐
doing the same thing every day	☐	☐	☐
traveling	☐	☐	☐
making decisions	☐	☐	☐
helping people	☐	☐	☐
solving problems	☐	☐	☐

B **PAIR WORK** Look back at the information in part A. Suggest a job for your partner.

A: You enjoy dealing with the public, and you hate working alone. You'd be a good salesperson.
B: But I hate working on weekends.
A: Maybe you could . . .

6 LISTENING My ideal career

A Listen to people talk about the kind of work they are looking for. Then check (✓) each person's ideal job.

1. Alex
☐ architect
☐ accountant
☐ teacher

2. Evelyn
☐ banker
☐ doctor
☐ lawyer

3. Edward
☐ marine biologist
☐ songwriter
☐ flight attendant

B Listen again. Write two reasons each person gives for his or her ideal job.

1. Alex _____   _____
2. Evelyn _____   _____
3. Edward _____   _____

7 INTERCHANGE 10 You're hired.

Choose the right person for the job. Go to Interchange 10 on page 124.

8 WORD POWER Personality traits

A Which of these adjectives are positive (**P**)? Which are negative (**N**)?

creative	P	impatient	
critical		level-headed	
disorganized		moody	
efficient		punctual	
forgetful		reliable	
generous		short-tempered	
hardworking		strict	

disorganized

B **PAIR WORK** Tell your partner about people you know with these personality traits.

"My boss is very short-tempered. She often shouts at people . . ."

hardworking

C Listen to four conversations. Then check (✓) the adjective that best describes each person.

1. a boss
- [ ] creative
- [ ] forgetful
- [ ] serious

2. a co-worker
- [ ] unfriendly
- [ ] generous
- [ ] strange

3. a teacher
- [ ] moody
- [ ] patient
- [ ] hardworking

4. a relative
- [ ] short-tempered
- [ ] disorganized
- [ ] reliable

9 PERSPECTIVES Making the right choice

A Listen to these people answer the question, "What kind of work would you like to do?" What job does each person talk about? Do they want that job?

Paula
"Well, I think I'd make a good journalist because I'm good at writing. When I was in high school, I worked as a reporter for the school website. I really enjoyed writing different kinds of articles."

Shawn
"I know what I *don't* want to do! A lot of my friends work in the stock market, but I could never be a stockbroker because I can't make decisions quickly. I don't mind working hard, but I'm terrible under pressure!"

Dalia
"I'm still in school. My parents want me to be a teacher, but I'm not sure yet. I guess I could be a teacher because I'm very creative. I'm also very impatient, so maybe I shouldn't work with kids."

B **PAIR WORK** Look at the interviews again. Who are you most like? least like? Why?

10 GRAMMAR FOCUS

▶ **Clauses with *because***

The word *because* introduces a cause or reason.

I'd make a good journalist **because I'm good at writing**.

I could be a teacher **because I'm very creative**.

I wouldn't want to be a teacher **because I'm very impatient**.

I could never be a stockbroker **because I can't make decisions quickly**.

GRAMMAR PLUS *see page 141*

A Complete the sentences in column A with appropriate information from column B. Then compare with a partner.

A

1. I'd like to be a physical therapist ____
2. I would make a bad librarian ____
3. I couldn't be a diplomat ____
4. I wouldn't mind working as a veterinarian ____
5. I could be a flight attendant ____
6. I could never be a financial advisor ____

B

a. because I'm very disorganized.
b. because I love animals.
c. because I enjoy helping people.
d. because I'm not good at managing money.
e. because I'm short-tempered.
f. because I really enjoy traveling.

B **GROUP WORK** Think about your personal qualities and skills. Then complete these statements. Take turns discussing them with your group.

I could never be a . . . because . . .
I wouldn't mind working as a . . . because . . .

I'd make a good . . . because . . .
The best job for me is . . . because . . .

11 WRITING An online cover letter for a job application

A Imagine you are applying for one of the jobs in this unit. Write a short cover letter for a job application.

> ● ● ●   Reply   Forward
> **To:** Catherine West
> **Subject:** News reporter position – ref. 04532
>
> Dear Ms. West,
> I was excited to see your opening for a news reporter, and I hope to be invited for an interview. I think I could make a great addition to your team because I'm very hardworking, and I really enjoy writing.
>
> As you can see from my résumé, I've had a lot of experience writing for my high school newspaper and for my college website. I also worked . . .

B **PAIR WORK** Exchange papers. If you received this cover letter, would you invite the applicant for a job interview? Why or why not?

A Skim the advertisement. Which three cross-cultural problems does it mention?

GLOBAL WORK SOLUTIONS

At GW Solutions, we recognize the importance of cross-cultural training for U.S. employees working abroad. Lack of cultural understanding results in lost contracts and less business. Here are some examples of what our courses can teach you.

In the U.S.A., we say that time is money. For American workers, punctuality and timetables are always important. At work, people concentrate on the task they are doing. They usually do not spend a lot of time on small talk. However, it's important to realize that not all cultures see time in this way. In many African countries, for example, getting work done isn't the only valuable use of time. Spending time at work to build close relationships with colleagues is equally important. It's important to ask about your colleague's personal life. Understanding these cultural differences is essential for working in a global team. If an American doesn't realize this, he or she might think that an African colleague who spends a lot of time chatting with co-workers is being lazy or avoiding doing his or her work. And an African worker might think their American colleague is the rudest person they've ever met!

In the U.S.A., written agreements are essential. Business deals are always agreed through a contract and once it has been signed, we consider it to be final. The conditions of the agreement don't usually change without the signing of another contract. But you may do business in places where this is not the case. In China, for example, people generally place more trust in a person's word than in a signed contract. Once a good relationship exists, a simple handshake might be enough to reach a business deal.

In the U.S.A., workers generally speak directly, and they openly disagree with colleagues. This kind of "straight talk" is seen as a mark of honesty. But where we see honesty, others may see rudeness. In some parts of Asia, open disagreement with colleagues may not be acceptable because it makes people feel embarrassed. Instead, you should stop and think for a while. Afterward you could say, "I agree in general, but could a different idea work in this situation?" And your body language is important, too. In the West, direct eye contact is good because it's a sign of honesty. In some Asian cultures, it's polite to avoid looking directly at your colleagues in order to show respect.

Did you learn something new? Need to know more? Sign up for one of our training courses and learn how to do business wherever you go.

B Read the advertisement. Then correct the sentences.

1. Ideas about work time are the same in Africa and the U.S.A.
2. Written contracts are more important in China than in the U.S.A.
3. American and Asian workers have similar ways of communicating.

C Complete these sentences with words from the advertisement.

1. In the U.S.A., being _____ is very important at work.
2. African workers like to have strong _____ with their co-workers.
3. In China, people might agree to a business deal with a _____.
4. For Americans, it's normal to _____ openly when they have a different opinion.
5. Some workers _____ making eye contact when talking to others.

D Look at the sentences in part C. Are they true for your country? What advice would you give to a foreigner coming to work in your country?

Units 9–10 Progress check

SELF-ASSESSMENT

How well can you do these things? Check (✓) the boxes.

I can . . .	Very well	OK	A little
Describe people and things in the past, present, and future (Ex. 1)	☐	☐	☐
Discuss possible consequences of actions (Ex. 2)	☐	☐	☐
Understand descriptions of skills and personality traits (Ex. 3, 4)	☐	☐	☐
Discuss job skills (Ex. 4)	☐	☐	☐
Give reasons for my opinions (Ex. 4)	☐	☐	☐

1 SPEAKING Things have changed.

A PAIR WORK Think of one more question for each category. Then interview a partner.

Free time How did you spend your free time as a child? What do you like to do these days? How are you going to spend your free time next year?

Friends Who used to be your friends when you were a kid? How do you meet new people nowadays? How do you think people will meet in the future?

B GROUP WORK Share one interesting thing about your partner.

2 GAME Share the consequences

A Add two situations and two consequences to the lists below.

Situation
- ☐ you spend too much time online
- ☐ you get a well-paid job
- ☐ you move to a foreign country
- ☐ it's sunny tomorrow
- ☐ you don't study hard
- ☐ you fall in love
- ☐ _____
- ☐ _____

Consequences
- ☐ learn about a different culture
- ☐ get good grades
- ☐ buy an expensive car
- ☐ feel jealous sometimes
- ☐ go to the beach
- ☐ have time for your family and friends
- ☐ _____
- ☐ _____

B CLASS ACTIVITY Go around the class and make sentences. Check (✓) each *if* clause after you use it. The student who uses the most clauses correctly wins.

"If you spend too much time online, you won't . . ."

3 LISTENING What do you want to do?

▶ **A** Listen to Michelle and Robbie discuss four jobs. Write down the jobs and check (✓) if they would be good or bad at them.

	Job	Good	Bad	Reason
1. Michelle	_____	☐	☐	_____
	_____	☐	☐	_____
2. Robbie	_____	☐	☐	_____
	_____	☐	☐	_____

▶ **B** Listen again. Write down the reasons they give.

C **PAIR WORK** Look at the jobs from part A. Which ones would you be good at? Why?

4 DISCUSSION Job profile

A Prepare a personal job profile. Write your name, skills, and job preferences. Think about the questions below. Then compare with a partner.

Do you . . . ?
enjoy helping people
have any special skills
have any experience
have a good memory

Are you good at . . . ?
communicating with people
solving problems
making decisions quickly
learning foreign languages

Do you mind . . . ?
wearing a uniform
traveling frequently
working with a team
working long hours

A: Do you enjoy helping people?
B: Sure. I often do volunteer work.
A: So do I. I help at our local . . .

B **GROUP WORK** Make suggestions for possible jobs based on your classmates' job profiles. Give reasons for your opinions. What do you think of their suggestions for you?

A: Victor would be a good psychologist because he's good at communicating with people.
B: No way! I could never be a psychologist. I'm very moody and short-tempered!

WHAT'S NEXT?

Look at your Self-assessment again. Do you need to review anything?

11 It's really worth seeing!

▸ Discuss famous landmarks, monuments, and works of art
▸ Discuss countries around the world

1 SNAPSHOT

AMAZING FACTS ABOUT AMAZING LANDMARKS

Machu Picchu – It is located 2,430 m (7,972 ft) above sea level, and it has resisted several earthquakes. When there is an earthquake, the stones "dance" and fall back into place.

Mount Fuji – The highest mountain in Japan is made up of a few volcanoes. The last recorded eruption started in 1707.

Big Ben – The tower is named Elizabeth Tower. Big Ben is the name of the bell inside it.

The Eiffel Tower – When it was opened in 1889, the tower was red. After a decade, it was painted yellow, and later, it was covered in different shades of brown.

The Neuschwanstein Castle – This beautiful castle in Germany was the inspiration for the Walt Disney Magic Kingdom Sleeping Beauty Castle.

The Statue of Liberty – The 350 pieces were made in France and then shipped to the United States.

Did you know these facts about the landmarks above? What else do you know about them?
Have you ever visited any of them? Which would you like to visit? Why?
Do you know any interesting facts about landmarks in your country?

2 PERSPECTIVES Where dreams come true

A How much do you know about the Walt Disney Company and theme parks?
Find three mistakes in the statements below. Then listen and check your answers.

1. The Walt Disney Company was founded in 1923 in California by Walt Disney and his brother Roy.
2. Their most famous character, Donald Duck, first appeared in a movie in 1928.
3. The first Disney theme park, Disneyland, was opened in 1955 in New York and soon became an international attraction.
4. The official opening was broadcast live by the ABC television network.
5. In 1971, the company opened their second park, Disney World.
6. Some of their most popular parks in Florida include Magic Kingdom, Animal Kingdom, and Epcot Center.
7. In 1983, the company opened their first foreign park, London Disneyland. Later, theme parks were also opened in Paris, Hong Kong, and Shanghai.

B **GROUP WORK** Have you been to a Disney park? Which one?
How did you like it? Which one would you like to go to? Why?

3 GRAMMAR FOCUS

▶ **Passive with *by* (simple past)**

The passive changes the focus of a sentence.

For the simple past, use the past of *be* + past participle.

Active	Passive
The Disney brothers **founded** the company in 1923.	It **was founded by** the Disney brothers in 1923.
Walt Disney **opened** Disneyland in 1955.	Disneyland **was opened by** Walt Disney in 1955.
The ABC network **broadcast** the opening of the park.	The opening **was broadcast by** ABC.

GRAMMAR PLUS *see page 142*

A Complete the sentences with the simple past passive form of the verbs. Then compare with a partner.

1. *Mont Sainte-Victoire* _____ (paint) by the French artist Paul Cézanne.

2. The first Star Wars film _____ (write) and _____ (direct) by George Lucas.

3. The Statue of Liberty _____ (design) by the French sculptor Frédéric Auguste Bartholdi.

4. The 2014 World Cup final _____ (win) by Germany. The final match _____ (see) by almost 1 billion people all over the world.

5. The songs *Revolution* and *Hey Jude* _____ (record) by the Beatles in 1968.

6. In the 2007 film *I'm Not There*, the American musician Bob Dylan _____ (play) by six different people, including Australian actress Cate Blanchett.

7. The 2016 Oscar for Best Actress _____ (give) to Brie Larson for her role in the movie *Room*.

8. The first iPad _____ (release) in 2010.

B **PAIR WORK** Change these sentences into passive sentences with *by*. Then take turns reading them aloud.

1. Eddie Redmayne played Stephen Hawking in the 2014 film *The Theory of Everything*.
_____

2. Gabriel García Márquez wrote the novel *One Hundred Years of Solitude* in 1967.
_____

3. The American architect William Lamb designed the Empire State Building.
_____

4. Woo Paik produced the first digital HDTV in 1991.
_____

5. J. K. Rowling wrote the first Harry Potter book on an old manual typewriter.
_____

6. *Empire* magazine readers chose Indiana Jones as the greatest movie character of all time.
_____

4 INTERCHANGE 11 True or false?

Who created these well-known works? Go to Interchange 11 on page 125.

5 PRONUNCIATION The letter o

▶ A Listen and practice. Notice how the letter o is pronounced in the following words.

/a/	/ou/	/u/	/ʌ/
not	no	do	one
top	don't	food	love
___	___	___	___
___	___	___	___

▶ B How is the letter o pronounced in these words? Write them in the correct column in part A. Then listen and check your answers.

come   done   lock   own   shot   soon   who   wrote

6 LISTENING Man-made wonders of the world

▶ A Listen to three tour guides describe some famous monuments. Take notes to answer the questions below. Then compare with a partner.

1. Taj Mahal
Why was it built?
What do the changing colors of the building represent?

2. Palace of Versailles
What did King Louis XIV want the Hall of Mirrors to show?
What problem did the candles cause? How did the mirrors help?

3. La Sagrada Familia
What did the architect think about man-made structures versus nature?
Why are no straight lines used?

B PAIR WORK Think of another famous monument. Describe it to the rest of the class. They will try to guess the monument.

7 WORD POWER Country fast facts

A Complete the sentences with words from the list.

✓ cattle	dialects	electronics	handicrafts	languages
sheep	souvenirs	✓ soybeans	textiles	wheat

1. The United States **grows** ___soybeans___ and _____.
2. Australia **raises** ___cattle___ and _____.
3. China **manufactures** _____ and _____.
4. In India, people **speak** many different _____ and _____.
5. You can **find** _____ and _____ at different shops in Brazil.

B PAIR WORK Talk about your country. Use the sentences in part A with your own information.

"We raise cattle and chickens. We grow corn and oats. You can find . . . "

8 CONVERSATION What do you want to know?

▶ **A** Listen and practice.

Lisa: Erik, you're from Amsterdam, aren't you?

Erik: Yeah . . . Why?

Lisa: I'm going there for a conference, and I'd like some information.

Erik: Sure. What do you want to know?

Lisa: Do you use the euro in the Netherlands?

Erik: Yes. The euro is used in most of Europe, you know.

Lisa: And do I need to take euros with me?

Erik: Not really. International credit cards are accepted everywhere, and they're much safer.

Lisa: Of course. And what should I buy there?

Erik: Cheese, definitely. We raise dairy cows, and some really excellent cheese is made from their milk.

Lisa: Good. I love cheese. Where is it sold?

Erik: You can find it at cheese shops all around the city. And don't forget to bring me a piece.

NORTH SEA

AMSTERDAM

GERMANY

BELGIUM

▶ **B** Listen to the rest of the conversation. What other suggestion does Erik give Lisa?

9 GRAMMAR FOCUS

▶ **Passive without *by* (simple present)**

For the simple present, use the present of *be* + past participle.

Active	Passive
They **use** the euro in most of Europe.	The euro **is used** in most of Europe.
Most places **accept** credit cards.	Credit cards **are accepted** at most places.
We **raise** dairy cattle in the Netherlands.	Dairy cattle **are raised** in the Netherlands.

GRAMMAR PLUS *see page 142*

A Complete the sentences. Use the passive of these verbs.

grow   manufacture   raise   speak   sell   use

1. French and Flemish _____ in Belgium.
2. Rice _____ in many Asian countries.
3. Cars and electronics _____ in Japan.
4. Sheep's milk _____ for making feta cheese.
5. Handicrafts _____ in the streets in Thailand.
6. A lot of cattle _____ in Australia.

B Complete this passage using the simple present passive form.

Many crops _____ (grow) in Taiwan. Some crops _____ (consume) locally, but others _____ (export). Tea _____ (grow) in cooler parts of the island, and rice _____ (cultivate) in warmer parts. Fishing is also an important industry. A wide variety of seafood _____ (catch) and _____ (ship) all over the world. Many people _____ (employ) in the food-processing industry.

C **PAIR WORK** Use the passive of the verbs in part A to talk about your country and other countries you know.

It's really worth seeing! **75**

10 LISTENING Is all tourism good?

A Listen to a news report about tourism in Costa Rica. Select the six effects of mass tourism that are mentioned. (There are two extra effects.) Indicate if they are positive (**P**) or negative (**N**).

Costa Rica

P	English is spoken.	The ocean is polluted.
	Tourism jobs are available all over the country.	High-rise hotels are built.
	More foreigners are investing there.	Fish and lobster are hunted.
	Acres of jungle are cut down.	The government becomes corrupt.

B Listen again. Write down three criteria the hotel fulfills in order to be an ecotourism business in Costa Rica.

_____ _____ _____

C **GROUP WORK** What is tourism like in your country? Talk about some positive and negative aspects.

11 SPEAKING Give me a clue.

A **PAIR WORK** Choose a country. Then answer these questions.

Where is it located?

What traditional dishes are eaten there?

What languages are spoken?

What currency is used?

What famous tourist attraction is found there?

What souvenirs are found there?

B **CLASS ACTIVITY** Give a short talk about the country you chose. Don't say the country's name. Can the class guess the country?

12 WRITING A city guide

A Choose a city or area in your country and write the introduction for an online city guide. Include the location, size, population, main attractions, shopping and travel tips, etc.

> Bruges is located in the northwest of Belgium, and it has a population of about 120,000 people. It is known for its canals and medieval buildings. In 2000, it was declared a World Heritage City by UNESCO. Bruges is also a good place to buy Belgium chocolate. It is sold . . .

Bruges, Belgium

B **GROUP WORK** Exchange papers. Do you think the introduction gives a good idea of the place? Would it attract tourists or businesses to the place? What other information should be included?

A Scan the advertisements. How many types of toilets can you see at the museum? When were the underwater sculptures designed? How big is the world's smallest book?

A SULABH INTERNATIONAL MUSEUM OF TOILETS, NEW DELHI, INDIA

Ever wondered about the history of toilets? Probably not! But visit the fascinating Sulabh Museum and see just how interesting they can be. Admire nearly 300 different toilets dating back to 2500 B.C.E. Some are beautifully decorated, one is made of solid gold, and there is an electric toilet that works without water. The star of the collection is a copy of a 16th century toilet. It was used by King Louis XIV of France – sometimes while speaking to his government. See drawings, photographs, and poems about toilets, too. One photo shows a toilet that was used by an elephant!

B UNDERWATER MUSEUM, CANCUN, MEXICO

Join one of our unique tours and discover an amazing underwater world 27 feet below the sea. Designed by Jason deCaires Taylor in 2009, it has over 450 sculptures. They are made from natural materials and show art and nature existing side by side. The *Silent Evolution* shows men, women, and children standing together on the seabed. They look so real that you'll want to talk to them. There are also sculptures of a house and a life-size Beetle car. The sculptures are covered in beautiful corals, and their appearances are constantly changing. Watch as an incredible variety of fish swim in and out of them.

C MICROMINIATURE MUSEUM, KIEV, UKRAINE

Small really is beautiful in this museum of art with a difference. The exhibits, created by artist Nikolai Syadristy, are so tiny they can only be seen clearly with a microscope. Read the world's smallest book – it is only 0.6 millimeters in size, but contains twelve pages of poems and drawings. There is a chess set on the head of a pin and the world's smallest electric motor. It is 20 times smaller than a piece of sand. Look closely at the eye of a needle and discover the seven camels inside. Read the words "Long Live Peace" not on paper, but written on a human hair!

B Read the advertisements. Find the words in *italics* below. Then circle the meaning of each word.

1. Something *fascinating* makes you feel very **interested / angry**.
2. The *star* of a collection is the **worst / best** part.
3. A *unique* thing is **different from / the same as** all others.
4. If something is changing *constantly*, it's changing **very little / all the time**.
5. An *exhibit* is an object that is **on show / for sale**.
6. A *needle* is a metal object that is used for **cutting / sewing**.

C Read the comments of three visitors to the museums. Write the letter (A, B, or C) of the museum you think they visited.

_____ **1.** "I just don't know how he made such little things."

_____ **2.** "I can't believe that an animal would use something like that."

_____ **3.** "I felt a little afraid about going down, but it was a great experience in the end."

D Which museum would you most like to visit? Why?

12 It's a long story.

▶ **Tell stories**
▶ **Discuss recent activities**

1 SNAPSHOT

True Stories of Incredible Coincidences

One day, the American novelist Anne Parrish was in a bookstore in Paris and she saw an old, used copy of one of her favorite childhood books. When she opened it, she saw on the first page: "Anne Parrish, 209 N. Weber Street, Colorado Springs." It was Anne's own book.

A 10-year-old girl named Laura Buxton released a bunch of balloons into the air. She attached a note to the balloons that asked the person who found it to write back to her. A couple of weeks later, she received a reply. It was from another 10-year-old girl also named Laura Buxton who lived 150 miles away.

Which of these stories do you think is more amazing? more difficult to believe?
Have you ever had an experience that is hard to believe?
Do you know of anyone who has? What happened?

2 PERSPECTIVES What next?

▶ **A** Listen to what happened to these people. Check (✓) the things that have happened to you.

- ☐ "I was having lunch when I spilled a cup of coffee on my clothes."
- ☐ "I was driving to the airport to pick up a friend, but I got a flat tire."
- ☐ "I was studying for an important test when the lights went out."
- ☐ "While I was walking down the street, I found a wallet with lots of money."
- ☐ "I was traveling in another country when I met an old school friend."
- ☐ "I was getting off a bus when I slipped and fell on the sidewalk."
- ☐ "While I was shopping one day, a celebrity walked into the store."

B Choose one statement that you checked. What happened next?

"I tried to clean it, but I couldn't. So I had to wear a jacket for the rest of the day."

3 GRAMMAR FOCUS

▶ Past continuous vs. simple past

Use the past continuous for an action in progress in the past.
Use the simple past for an action that interrupts it.

I **was having** lunch	when I **spilled** coffee on my clothes.
I **was driving** to the airport,	but I **got** a flat tire.
While I **was shopping** one day,	a celebrity **walked** into the store.

GRAMMAR PLUS *see page 143*

A Complete these sentences. Then compare with a partner.

1. My sister _____ (text) while she _____ (drive), and she almost _____ (crash) her car.

2. While I _____ (cook) dinner last night, a friend _____ (call) and I _____ (burn) the food.

3. My father _____ (ski) when he _____ (break) his leg in several places.

4. We _____ (have) our first child while we _____ (live) in a tiny apartment.

5. While I _____ (drive) in England a few years ago, I _____ (realize) I was on the wrong side of the road!

6. Once I _____ (read) a good book, but someone _____ (tell) me the ending.

7. My parents _____ (meet) each other while they _____ (work) at the same restaurant in Vancouver.

B Complete these statements with information about yourself. Use the simple past or the past continuous.

1. I was taking a selfie when . . .
2. While I was going home one day, . . .
3. I was . . .
4. While I was . . .
5. Last month, . . .
6. Some time ago, . . .

C **PAIR WORK** Take turns reading your sentences from part B. Then ask and answer follow-up questions.

A: I was taking a selfie when a man came and stole my phone.

B: Oh, no! What did you do?

A: I went to the police . . . and they told me to be more careful.

4 LISTENING How did it all begin?

A Listen to this story about a successful inventor. Put the sentences into the correct order from 1 to 8.

___1___ Mark Zuckerberg started writing computer programs.

_____ His friends invested in Facebook.

_____ He didn't accept Microsoft's offer.

_____ He invented FaceMash.

_____ Facebook became available to the public.

_____ Zuckerberg wrote his very own messenger program.

_____ He created a program that recommended music.

_____ Three classmates asked for his help.

B Listen again. How did the invention change his life?

C PAIR WORK Think of other websites and apps that were successful inventions.

5 WORD POWER What happened?

A Some adverbs are often used in storytelling to emphasize that something interesting is about to happen. Which of these adverbs are positive (**P**)? Which are negative (**N**)? Which could be either (**E**)?

coincidentally	_____	strangely	_____
fortunately	_____	suddenly	_____
luckily	_____	surprisingly	_____
miraculously	_____	unexpectedly	_____
sadly	_____	unfortunately	_____

B PAIR WORK Complete these statements with adverbs from part A to make up creative sentences.

We were having a party when, . . .

I was walking down the street when, . . .

It started out as a normal day, but, . . .

A: We were having a party when, suddenly, the lights went out!

B: Once I was dancing at a party when, unfortunately, I fell down!

6 WRITING What's your story?

A Write a short story about something that happened to you recently. Try to include some of the adverbs from Exercise 5.

> I was shopping at a big department store when, suddenly, I saw a little girl crying in a corner all by herself. The girl said she couldn't find her mother. I was taking her to the store manager when I saw an old school friend, running towards me. Coincidentally, she was the girl's mother, and . . .

B GROUP WORK Take turns reading your stories. Answer any questions from the group.

7 CONVERSATION What have you been doing?

▶ **A** Listen and practice.

Steve: Hey, Luiza! I haven't seen you in ages. What have you been doing lately?

Luiza: I haven't been going out much. I've been working two jobs for the last six months.

Steve: How come?

Luiza: I'm saving up money for a trip to Morocco.

Steve: Well, that's exciting!

Luiza: Yeah, it is. What about you?

Steve: Well, I've only been *spending* money. I've been trying to become an actor. I've been taking courses and going to a lot of auditions.

Luiza: Really? How long have you been trying?

Steve: Since I graduated. But I haven't had any luck yet. No one recognizes my talent.

▶ **B** Listen to two other people at the party. What has happened since they last saw each other?

8 GRAMMAR FOCUS

▶ **Present perfect continuous**

Use the present perfect continuous for actions that start in the past and continue into the present.

What **have** you **been doing** lately?   I**'ve been working** two jobs for the last six months.

How long **have** you **been trying**?   I**'ve been trying** since I graduated.

Have you **been saving** money?   No, I **haven't been saving** money. I**'ve been spending** it!

GRAMMAR PLUS *see page 143*

A Complete the conversations with the present perfect continuous.

1. **A:** _____ you _____ (learn) any new skills this year?
   B: Yes, I have. I _____ (take) some art courses.

2. **A:** What _____ you _____ (do) lately?
   B: Well, I _____ (look for) a new job.

3. **A:** How _____ you _____ (feel) recently?
   B: Great! I _____ (run) three times a week. And I _____ (not drink) as much coffee since I stopped working at the coffee shop.

4. **A:** _____ you _____ (get) enough exercise lately?
   B: No, I haven't. I _____ (study) a lot for a big exam.

B **PAIR WORK** Read the conversations in part A together. Then read them again and answer the questions with your own information.

A: Have you been learning any new skills this year?

B: Yes, I've been taking guitar lessons.

9 PRONUNCIATION Contrastive stress in responses

▶ **A** Listen and practice. Notice how the stress changes to emphasize a contrast.

A: Has your brother been studying German?

B: No, I've been studying German.

A: Have you been teaching French?

B: No, I've been studying French.

▶ **B** Mark the stress changes in these conversations. Listen and check.
Then practice the conversations.

A: Have you been studying for ten years?
B: No, I've been studying for two years.

A: Have you been studying at school?
B: No, I've been studying at home.

10 SPEAKING Tell me about it.

GROUP WORK Add three questions to this list. Then take turns asking and answering the questions. Remember to ask for further information.

Have you been . . . lately?

traveling

watching any good TV series

taking any lessons

working out

working long hours

going out a lot

staying up late

_____

_____

_____

useful expressions
Really?
I didn't know that!
Oh, I see.
I had no idea.
Wow! Tell me more.

A: Have you been traveling lately?
B: Yes, I have. I've been going abroad about once a month.
C: Really? Lucky you!
B: Not exactly. I've been traveling for work, not on vacation.

11 INTERCHANGE 12 It's my life.

Play a board game. Go to Interchange 12 on page 126.

A Skim the article. What is special about these musicians? How have they influenced other people?

BREAKING DOWN THE SOUND OF SILENCE

Ten years before he died, the composer Beethoven went deaf. He called this disability his "nightmare." Fortunately for thousands of classical music fans, he didn't stop writing brilliant music. One hundred and eighty years later, being deaf hasn't stopped three Americans – Steve Longo, Ed Chevy, and Bob Hiltermann – from playing music, either. In their case, the music is rock, and their band is called Beethoven's Nightmare.

The three boys grew up in different cities, but they all showed a surprising interest in music. Although they couldn't hear it, they were amazed by the energy of 1960s bands like the Beatles. They could see the effect the music had on the audiences – the happy faces of friends and family as they watched. Something exciting was obviously happening. "I'm going to do that, too," they all said. "Why? You can't hear," asked parents, teachers, and friends alike. Each boy used sign language to answer, "Because I can feel it."

Longo and Chevy started playing the guitar. They put on headphones and turned up the volume. With the help of powerful hearing aids, they could get some of the notes – the rest they felt through vibrations. Drummer Hiltermann came from a musical family. His parents thought that teaching their son to play an instrument was a waste of time. But they changed their minds after he nearly drove them crazy by using knives and forks to drum on the furniture of the house.

The three men first met in college in Washington, D.C. They started a band and played many concerts until they graduated in 1975. In 2001, Hiltermann had the idea to bring his old friends together again. They have been performing ever since. In 2013, a new member, Paul Raci, joined the band as a singer. At concerts, dancers put on a spectacular show and use sign language to explain the words of the songs to the audience. And, of course, the band plays very loudly!

The group has encouraged many deaf people, and people with other disabilities, to follow their dreams. Chevy says, "The only thing deaf people *can't* do is hear."

Dennis McCarthy, "Deaf band 'Beethoven's Nightmare' feels the music," *Los Angeles Daily News* (Oct. 31, 2013). Used with permission.

B Read the article. Choose the correct word(s) in the sentences below.

1. After going deaf, Beethoven **continued / refused** to compose music.
2. The boys knew music was powerful because of something they **read / saw.**
3. Many people didn't **understand / like** the boys' ambition to play music.
4. Hiltermann's parents **wanted / didn't want** him to learn to play at first.
5. The three young men started playing together **before / after** finishing college.

C Answer the questions.

1. Which band inspired the three boys to play music?
2. What did Longo and Chevy use to hear some parts of the music?
3. What did Hiltermann use to make noise in his house?
4. Where did the three men get to know each other?
5. When did Beethoven's Nightmare start playing?

D Do you think it's very difficult for people in your country to achieve their dreams? What new technology and facilities make it easier for them?

SELF-ASSESSMENT

How well can you do these things? Check (✓) the boxes.

I can . . .	Very well	OK	A little
Give information about books, movies, songs, etc. (Ex. 1)	☐	☐	☐
Understand information about countries (Ex. 2)	☐	☐	☐
Describe a situation (Ex. 3)	☐	☐	☐
Ask and answer questions about past events (Ex. 4, 5)	☐	☐	☐
Ask and answer questions about recent activities (Ex. 5)	☐	☐	☐

1 SPEAKING Trivia questions

A List six books, movies, songs, albums, or other popular works. Then write one *who* question for each of the six items.

> *Harry Potter books*
>> *Who wrote the Harry Potter books?*

B **PAIR WORK** Take turns asking your questions. Use the passive with *by* to answer.

A: Who wrote the *Harry Potter* books?
B: I think they were written by J. K. Rowling.

2 LISTENING Did you know?

▶ A Listen to a game show about Spain. Write the correct answers.

1. How many languages are officially recognized? _____
2. What day is considered bad luck? _____
3. What is the most valuable soccer team in the world? _____
4. In how many countries is Spanish the official language? _____
5. What fruit is thrown at the world's biggest food fight? _____
6. What is Spain's famous dance called? _____

▶ B Listen again. Keep score. How much money does each contestant have?

3 GAME What happened?

GROUP WORK Use the passive to write details about these situations. Then compare with the class. Which group wrote the most sentences?

The lights went out.

Our class was canceled.

It snowed a lot yesterday.

Many roads were blocked.

Your roommate cleaned the apartment.

The dishes were done.

4 ROLE PLAY Do you have an alibi?

A famous painting has been stolen from a local museum. It disappeared last Sunday afternoon between 12:00 P.M. and 4:00 P.M.

Student A: Student B suspects you stole the painting. Make up an alibi. Take notes on what you were doing that day. Then answer Student B's questions.

Student B: You are a police detective. You think Student A stole the painting. Add two questions to the notebook. Then ask Student A the questions.

Change roles and try the role play again.

Where were you last Sunday?

Where did you go for lunch?

Did anyone see you?

What were you wearing that day?

What were you doing between noon and 4:00 P.M.?

Was anyone with you?

_____

_____

5 DISCUSSION Is that so?

A GROUP WORK What interesting things can you find out about your classmates? Ask these questions and others of your own.

Have you been doing anything exciting recently?

Where do you live? How long have you been living there?

Have you met anyone interesting lately?

Who is your best friend? How did you meet? How long have you been friends?

Where were you living ten years ago? Did you like it there? What do you remember about it?

useful expressions

Really?

I didn't know that!

Oh, I see.

I had no idea.

Wow! Tell me more.

B CLASS ACTIVITY Tell the class the most interesting thing you learned.

WHAT'S NEXT?

Look at your Self-assessment again. Do you need to review anything?

13 That's entertainment!

▶ Discuss popular entertainment
▶ Discuss movies and famous Hollywood names

1 SNAPSHOT

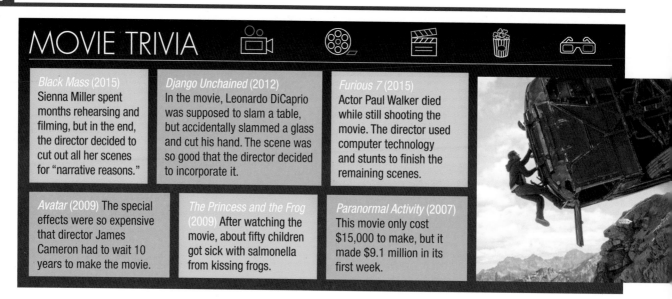

MOVIE TRIVIA

Black Mass (2015)
Sienna Miller spent months rehearsing and filming, but in the end, the director decided to cut out all her scenes for "narrative reasons."

Django Unchained (2012)
In the movie, Leonardo DiCaprio was supposed to slam a table, but accidentally slammed a glass and cut his hand. The scene was so good that the director decided to incorporate it.

Furious 7 (2015)
Actor Paul Walker died while still shooting the movie. The director used computer technology and stunts to finish the remaining scenes.

Avatar (2009) The special effects were so expensive that director James Cameron had to wait 10 years to make the movie.

The Princess and the Frog (2009) After watching the movie, about fifty children got sick with salmonella from kissing frogs.

Paranormal Activity (2007) This movie only cost $15,000 to make, but it made $9.1 million in its first week.

Which of the movie trivia do you find most interesting?

Do you know any other movie trivia?

Which of these movies have you seen? Did you enjoy it? Which would you like to watch?

2 CONVERSATION I think they're boring.

▶ **A** Listen and practice.

Danny: It's so hot out. Do you want to stay in and watch a movie this afternoon?

Gina: Hmm. Maybe. What do you want to see?

Danny: How about an *X-Men* movie? I've heard that the early ones are really interesting.

Gina: For you, maybe. I'm not interested in action movies. Actually, I think they're boring.

Danny: What about that new movie based on one of Stephen King's novels?

Gina: I don't know. I'm always fascinated by his books, but I'm not in the mood for a horror movie.

Danny: Well, what do you want to see?

Gina: How about a *Game of Thrones* marathon? It's my favorite series ever.

Danny: OK, but only if you make us some popcorn.

▶ **B** Listen to the rest of the conversation. What happens next? What do they decide to do?

3 GRAMMAR FOCUS

▶ **Participles as adjectives**

Present participles	Past participles
That *X-Men* movie sounds **interesting**.	I'm not **interested** in action movies.
Stephen King's books are **fascinating**.	I'm **fascinated** by Stephen King's books.
I think action movies are **boring**.	I'm **bored** by action movies.

GRAMMAR PLUS *see page 144*

A Complete these sentences. Then compare with a partner.

1. John Cho is such an _____ actor. I'm always _____ by his incredible talent. (amaze)

2. Most TV shows are really _____. I often get so _____ watching them that I fall asleep. (bore)

3. I was _____ in watching *The Martian* after I read the book. And I was surprised that the movie is really _____. (interest)

4. I'm _____ to watch *The Avengers*. Everybody has told me it's really _____. (excite)

5. I find animated films very _____. I've been _____ by them since I was a little kid. (amuse / fascinate)

6. It's _____ that horror movies are so popular. I can't understand why people go to the movies to feel _____. (surprise / terrify)

John Cho

B PAIR WORK Complete the description below with the correct forms of the words.

amaze	annoy	confuse	disgust	embarrass	shock

I had a terrible time at the movies last weekend. First, my ticket cost $25. I was really _____ by the price. By mistake, I gave the cashier two $5 bills instead of a twenty and a five. I was a little _____. Then there was trash all over the theater. The mess was _____. The people behind me were talking during the movie, which was _____. The story was hard to follow. I always find thrillers so _____. I liked the special effects, though. They were _____!

4 WORD POWER How do you like it?

A PAIR WORK Complete the chart with synonyms from the list.

amusing	dumb	horrible	odd	silly
bizarre	fantastic	hysterical	outstanding	terrible
disgusting	hilarious	incredible	ridiculous	weird

Awful	Wonderful	Stupid	Strange	Funny

B GROUP WORK Share your opinions about a movie, an actor, an actress, a TV show, and a book. Use words from part A.

5 LISTENING What did you think?

A Listen to people talk about books, movies, and TV programs. Match each conversation to the statement that best describes the people's opinions.

1. _____   **a.** This special offers an amazing look into an exotic country.
2. _____   **b.** The new investigation into these creatures was a waste of time.
3. _____   **c.** The bad acting with this boring idea makes it terrible.
4. _____   **d.** She is excited to read more of this clever mystery series.

B Listen again. Write a reason each person gives to support his or her opinion.

1. _____   3. _____
2. _____   4. _____

6 PRONUNCIATION Emphatic stress

A Listen and practice. Notice how stress and a higher pitch are used to express strong opinions.

That was terrible!

He was amazing!

That's fascinating!

B **PAIR WORK** Write four statements using these words. Then take turns reading them. Pay attention to emphatic stress.

fantastic   horrible   ridiculous   weird

7 DISCUSSION I give it two thumbs up!

A **PAIR WORK** Take turns asking and answering these questions and others of your own.

What kinds of movies are you interested in? Why?
What kinds of movies do you find boring?
Who are your favorite actors and actresses? Why?
Are there actors or actresses you don't like?
What's the worst movie you've ever seen?
Are there any outstanding movies playing now?
Do you prefer to watch films dubbed or with subtitles? Why?

A: What kinds of movies are you interested in?
B: I like romantic comedies.
A: Really? Why is that?
B: They're entertaining! What about you?
A: I think romantic comedies are kind of dumb. I prefer . . .

B **GROUP WORK** Compare your information. Whose taste in movies is most like yours?

ACTION
COMEDY
ANIMATION
FANTASY
BIOGRAPHY
SCI-FI
THRILLER
HORROR
DRAMA
WAR
DOCUMENTARY

8 PERSPECTIVES And the Oscar goes to . . .

A Listen to people talk about some of their Hollywood favorites. Can you guess the actress, actor, or movie each person is describing?

1. He's a famous American actor who is also a successful director and producer. He won the Oscar for Best Motion Picture in 2013 with *Argo*, which he directed and co-produced.

2. The first movie in the series came out in 1977. It's a science fiction fantasy that has become a blockbuster franchise. The story takes place "a long time ago in a galaxy far, far away."

3. I really like animated movies, and the third one in this series is my favorite. It's about a boy's toys that have a secret life full of adventures when they are alone.

4. She's an actress that is excellent in both dramas and comedies. I loved her in *Mamma Mia!* and *The Devil Wears Prada*. In 2011, she won her third Oscar for her performance in *The Iron Lady*.

B Do you like the people and movies described in part A? What else do you know about them?

9 GRAMMAR FOCUS

Relative pronouns for people and things

Use *who* or *that* for people.	**Use *which* or *that* for things.**
He's an actor. He's also a director and producer.	It's a science fiction fantasy. It has become a blockbuster franchise.
He's an actor **who/that** is also a director and producer.	It's a science fiction fantasy **which/that** has become a blockbuster franchise.

GRAMMAR PLUS *see page 144*

A Combine the sentences using relative pronouns. Then compare with a partner.

1. Jennifer Hudson is a singer. She's acted in several films.
2. *The Phantom of the Opera* is based on a French novel. It was published in 1911.
3. *Spiderman* and *Transformers* are successful franchises. They were adapted from comic books.
4. Michael Keaton is a famous Hollywood actor. He began his career as a cameraman.
5. Dakota Fanning is an actress. She made her first movie when she was only seven years old.
6. Wii Fit is a video game. It helps people to get more exercise.
7. Stephenie Meyer is an American writer. She wrote the *Twilight* series.
8. Many Hollywood stars live in Beverly Hills. It's a small city near Los Angeles, California.

Jennifer Hudson

B **PAIR WORK** Complete these sentences. Then compare your information around the class.

1. Adele is a singer and songwriter . . .
2. *Fantastic Four* is a movie franchise . . .
3. *The Voice* is a reality show . . .
4. Scarlett Johansson is an actress . . .

10 INTERCHANGE 13 It was hilarious!

How do you like movies and TV shows? Go to Interchange 13 on page 127.

11 SPEAKING Pilot episode

A PAIR WORK A TV studio is looking for ideas for a new TV show. Brainstorm possible ideas and agree on an idea. Make brief notes.

What kind of TV show is it?

What's it about?

Who are the main characters?

Who is this show for?

B CLASS ACTIVITY Tell the class about your TV show.

"Our TV show is a comedy. It's about two very lazy friends who discover a time machine and travel to the time of the dinosaurs. Then . . ."

12 LISTENING At the movies

A Listen to two critics, Nicole and Anthony, talk about a new movie. Check (✓) the features of the movie that they discuss. (There are two extra features.)

	Nicole's opinion	Anthony's opinion
☐ acting		
☐ story		
☐ writing		
☐ music		
☐ love story		
☐ special effects		

B Listen again. Write Nicole and Anthony's opinions of each feature.

13 WRITING A movie review

A PAIR WORK Choose a movie you both have seen and discuss it. Then write a review of it.

What was the movie about?

What did you like about it?

What didn't you like about it?

How was the acting?

How would you rate it?

B CLASS ACTIVITY Read your review to the class. Who else has seen the movie?

Do they agree with your review?

MOVIE TALK   LOGIN / REGISTER

We recently streamed *Birdman*, which won the Academy Award for Best Picture in 2015. It's about an actor who made successful movies in Hollywood in the past, and now tries to reinvent his career on Broadway.

BEST PICTURE
BIRDMAN
OR (THE UNEXPECTED VIRTUE OF IGNORANCE)

It stars Michael Keaton and Emma Stone as a father and daughter. We liked the movie because it is both a drama and a comedy. I didn't like . . .

💬 14   ♡ 12

A Scan the article. Which movies are mentioned? When were they released?

THE REAL ART OF ACTING

Natalie Portman

1 Acting can bring fame, money, and success. But it's not always easy. Good acting is not only about learning lines and dressing up. It's also about convincing the audience that you really are somebody else. [a] To achieve this, good actors sometimes put themselves through unpleasant experiences.

2 Actors often have to lose or gain a lot of weight in order to play a part. In *The Machinist* (2005), Christian Bale plays an extremely thin factory worker who suffers from insomnia. [b] Four months before he began filming, Bale started a crazy diet.

Christian Bale

He only ate an apple and a can of tuna a day and lost 63 pounds. Although he wanted to lose another 20 pounds, the producers persuaded him to stop because they were worried about his health. When filming ended, he had just six months to gain the incredible 100 pounds he needed to play Bruce Wayne in *Batman Begins*. [c]

3 Physical training can also be a challenge. Steven Spielberg wanted to show the real horror of war in *Saving Private Ryan* (1998) and he wanted his actors to feel like real soldiers. So he sent a group of them, including Tom Hanks, to a 10-day military boot camp. [d] They ran miles every day, slept outside in the freezing cold, and were given little food. In the end, all of them were physically and mentally exhausted. Natalie Portman also had to make a great physical effort when she got the role of a ballerina in *Black Swan* (2010). Before filming, she spent a whole year training for eight hours a day, six days

a week in order to learn to dance. Once filming began, things didn't get easier either. Portman dislocated a rib while dancing. Nevertheless, she bravely continued filming during the six weeks it took her to recover.

4 Sometimes "becoming" a character can mean saying goodbye to the real world and everybody in it completely. Actor Heath Ledger locked himself in a hotel room for six weeks when he was preparing to play the role of Joker in *The Dark Knight* (2008). He slept only two hours a day and he spent the rest of the time practicing how to walk, talk, and move like his character. [e] It seems he was successful in the end, as audiences and critics loved his work, and he won an Oscar for the part.

B Read the article. Where do these sentences belong? Write a–e.

1. The actors' lives became very hard. ____

2. Not sleeping is making him sick. ____

3. And he didn't speak to anybody at all. ____

4. The character has to be believable. ____

5. So he ate lots of pizza and ice cream. ____

C Find words in the text to match these definitions.

1. The words that actors say in a movie (paragraph 1) _____

2. People who control how a movie is made (paragraph 2) _____

3. A bone in a person's chest (paragraph 3) _____

4. The people who write reviews of movies or books (paragraph 4) _____

D Which of these unpleasant experiences is the worst? Do you think it's necessary for an actor to do this kind of thing for a part?

14 Now I get it!

▸ Discuss the meaning of gestures and body language
▸ Discuss rules and recognize common signs

1 SNAPSHOT

POPULAR EMOJIS

I am not amused.

I'm laughing so hard, I'm crying!

I'm bored.

Great job!

That's amazing!

I'm so embarrassed.

I love it!

That's awful!

Just kidding!

My heart is breaking.

Do you use these emojis? In what situations do you use them?
What other expressions can you use emojis to convey?
What is the weirdest emoji you've ever seen? the funniest? the hardest to understand?

2 WORD POWER Body language

A What is this woman doing in each picture? Match each description with a picture. Then compare with a partner.

1. She's scratching her head. _____
2. She's biting her nails. _____
3. She's rolling her eyes. _____
4. She's tapping her foot. _____
5. She's pulling her hair out. _____
6. She's wrinkling her nose. _____

a  b 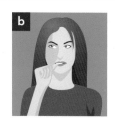 c

d  e  f

B **GROUP WORK** Use the pictures in part A and these adjectives to describe how the woman is feeling.

annoyed	confused	embarrassed	frustrated	irritated
bored	disgusted	exhausted	impatient	nervous

"In the first picture, she's tapping her foot. She looks impatient."

3 CONVERSATION It's pretty confusing.

▶ **A** Listen and practice.

Eva: How was dinner with the new Bulgarian student last night? What's her name – Elena?

Brian: Yeah, Elena. It was nice. We always have a good time, but I still don't understand her very well. You see, when we offer her something to eat or drink, she nods her head up and down. But, at the same time she says no.

Eva: It might mean she wants to accept it, but she thinks it's not polite. In some countries, you have to refuse any offer first. Then the host insists, and you accept it.

Brian: I don't know . . . It's pretty confusing.

Eva: It could mean she doesn't want anything, but she thinks it's rude to say no.

Jack: Actually, in some countries, when people move their heads up and down, it means "no."

Brian: Really? Now I get it!

▶ **B** Now listen to Elena talk to her friend. What does she find unusual about the way people in North America communicate?

4 GRAMMAR FOCUS

▶ **Modals and adverbs**

Modals	**Adverbs**
It **might/may** mean she wants to accept it.	**Maybe/Perhaps** it means she wants to accept it.
It **could** mean she doesn't want anything.	It **probably** means she doesn't want anything.
That **must** mean "no."	That **definitely** means "no."

GRAMMAR PLUS *see page 145*

PAIR WORK What do these gestures mean? Take turns making statements about each gesture. Use the meanings in the box or your own ideas.

possible meanings
I don't know.
Be quiet.
Call me.
That sounds crazy!
I can't hear you.
Come here.

A: What do you think the first gesture means?
B: It probably means . . . , OR It might mean . . .

5 PRONUNCIATION Pitch

▶ **A** Listen and practice. Notice how pitch is used to express certainty or doubt.

		Certain	**Uncertain**
A: Do you think her gesture means "no"?		**B:** Definitely.	**B:** Probably.
A: Do you understand what her gesture means?		**B:** Absolutely.	**B:** Maybe.

B **PAIR WORK** Take turns asking yes/no questions. Respond by using *absolutely*, *definitely*, *maybe*, *probably*, and your own information. Pay attention to pitch.

6 SPEAKING What's the matter with me?

A **GROUP WORK** Imagine you have one of these problems. What could explain it?

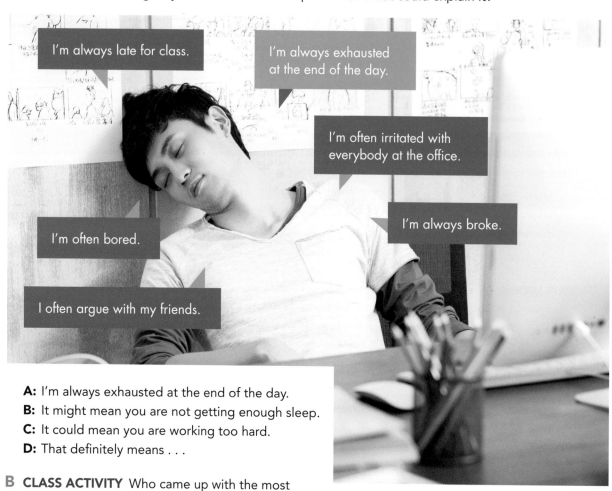

I'm always late for class.

I'm always exhausted at the end of the day.

I'm often irritated with everybody at the office.

I'm always broke.

I'm often bored.

I often argue with my friends.

A: I'm always exhausted at the end of the day.
B: It might mean you are not getting enough sleep.
C: It could mean you are working too hard.
D: That definitely means . . .

B **CLASS ACTIVITY** Who came up with the most interesting explanation in your group? the most unexpected?

7 INTERCHANGE 14 Casual observers

Interpret people's body language. Go to Interchange 14 on page 128.

8 PERSPECTIVES Rules and regulations

A What do you think these signs mean? Listen and match each sign with the correct meaning.

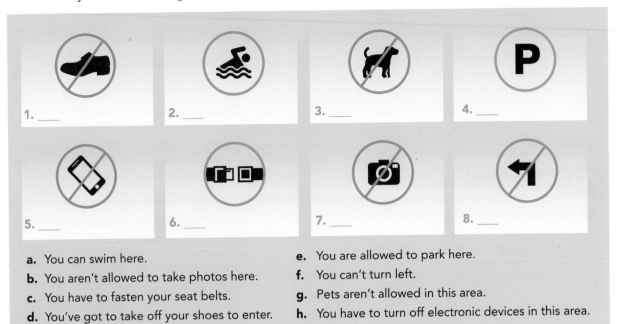

1. ____ 2. ____ 3. ____ 4. ____

5. ____ 6. ____ 7. ____ 8. ____

a. You can swim here.
b. You aren't allowed to take photos here.
c. You have to fasten your seat belts.
d. You've got to take off your shoes to enter.
e. You are allowed to park here.
f. You can't turn left.
g. Pets aren't allowed in this area.
h. You have to turn off electronic devices in this area.

B **PAIR WORK** Where might you see the signs in part A? Give two suggestions for each one.

"You might see this one by a lake . . ."

9 GRAMMAR FOCUS

Permission, obligation, and prohibition

Permission	Obligation	Prohibition
You **can** swim here.	You **have to** fasten your seat belt.	You **can't** turn left.
You**'re allowed to** park here.	You**'ve got to** take off your shoes.	Pets **aren't allowed** in this area.

GRAMMAR PLUS *see page 145*

A **PAIR WORK** Use the language in the grammar box to talk about these signs.

A: This first sign means you've got to use the stairs in case of a fire.

B: Yes, I think you're right. And the second one means you aren't allowed to . . .

B **CLASS ACTIVITY** What are some of the rules in your office or school?

A: In my office, we can't eat at our desks.

B: We can't either, but we're allowed to have water.

C: We're allowed to eat at our desks, but we have to clean up afterward.

10 DISCUSSION Play by the rules.

A PAIR WORK How many rules can you think of for each of these places?

at the gym   at a public swimming pool   on an airplane
in a museum   in a movie theater   at work

"At the gym, you have to wear sneakers or other athletic shoes. You're not allowed to wear regular shoes."

B GROUP WORK Share your ideas. Why do you think these rules exist? Have you ever broken any of them? What happened?

11 LISTENING Road signs

A Listen to four conversations about driving. Number the situations they are discussing in the correct order from 1 to 4.

____ Cars can't be in the bus and taxi lane.

____ Drivers must drive within the speed limit.

____ Drivers have to turn on car headlights on mountain roads.

____ Cars are allowed to park in this area after 6:00 P.M.

B Listen again. How did they find out about the traffic situation? Write what happened.

1. _____
2. _____
3. _____
4. _____

C PAIR WORK How do you move around your city? Give two examples of traffic laws you must obey.

12 WRITING Golden rules

A GROUP WORK Discuss the rules that currently exist at your school. How many can you think of? Are they all good rules?

B GROUP WORK Think of four new rules that you feel would be a good idea. Work together to write brief explanations of why each is necessary.

> 1. You aren't allowed to use your first language. If you need to use it, you need to ask your teacher for permission.
>
> 2. You have to pay a small fine if you hand in your homework late.
>
> 3. You can be late, but you have to come in quietly so you don't disturb the lesson.

C CLASS ACTIVITY Share your lists. Vote on the best new rules.

A Skim the article. Match the pictures 1, 2, and 3 to the paragraphs.

UNDERSTANDING IDIOMS

Idioms can be a problem for language learners. They often seem to make absolutely no sense at all. For example, imagine your English friend Sam tells you his math exam was "a piece of cake." Do you imagine him at school, sitting in front of a sweet dessert with nothing but a pen to eat it with? In fact, he's saying that the exam was really easy. It's important to learn useful English idioms and knowing their origins helps us to remember them. Here are stories of three English idioms.

_____ **A** If you ask a friend to hang out, you might hear, "Sorry, I can't tonight. I'm feeling a little under the weather." It may sound like rain is coming, but really, it means that your friend feels sick. This expression came from sailors, who often got seasick when bad weather tossed the ship from side to side. The sailors went down to the bottom part of the ship, away from the storm and where the ship's rocking was gentler.

_____ **B** If you have a difficult roommate, you might say, "My roommate has loud parties every night, but last night was the last straw. They played music till 5 A.M.! I'm moving out." A "last straw" is a final problem that makes someone take action. This expression is a short form of the phrase "the straw that broke the camel's back." The idea is that even though a single piece of straw is very light, many pieces added together will be too heavy for the camel to carry.

_____ **C** Have you ever asked someone if they know something, and they reply, "That rings a bell"? They're not hearing music! They mean that what you're saying sounds familiar, and they think they've heard it before. This idiom comes from the fact that bells are used to remind people of many things. Traditionally, bells would toll for an important event, like a wedding. School bells tell you that class is starting, and even the alarm chime on your phone reminds you that it's time to get up.

B Read the article and correct the false statements below.

1. You can guess the meaning of an idiom if you understand each word.
_____

2. In the past, people knew about important events when they heard shouting.
_____

3. A camel falls down if it has to carry too much water.
_____

4. Sailors used to feel sicker when they went to the bottom of the ship.
_____

C Complete the sentences with the correct form of one of the idioms.

1. Julie has a bad cold at the moment, and she's _____.
2. I don't remember his face, but his name _____.
3. When the neighbors' noisy kids broke my window with their ball, it _____.

D What idioms are commonly used in your country? Where do you think they come from?

Units 13–14 Progress check

SELF-ASSESSMENT

How well can you do these things? Check (✓) the boxes.

I can . . .	Very well	OK	A little
Ask about and express opinions and emotions (Ex. 1, 4, 5)	☐	☐	☐
Discuss movies (Ex. 2)	☐	☐	☐
Understand descriptions of rules and laws (Ex. 3)	☐	☐	☐
Speculate about things when I'm not sure and recognize emotions (Ex. 4)	☐	☐	☐
Describe rules and laws: permission, obligation, and prohibition (Ex. 5)	☐	☐	☐

1 SURVEY Personal preferences

A Complete the first column of the survey with your opinions.

	Me	My classmate
A fascinating book		
A confusing movie		
A boring TV show		
A shocking news story		
An interesting celebrity		
A singer you are amazed by		
A song you are annoyed by		

B CLASS ACTIVITY Go around the class and find someone who has the same opinions. Write a classmate's name only once.

"I thought *I am Malala* was a fascinating book. What about you?"

2 ROLE PLAY Movie night

Student A: Invite Student B to a movie. Suggest two movie options.
Then answer your partner's questions.
Start like this: *Do you want to see a movie?*

Student B: Student A invites you to a movie.
Find out more about the movie.
Then accept or refuse the invitation.

Change roles and try the role play again.

3 LISTENING Unusual laws around the world

A Listen to two people discuss an article about laws in different places. Match the topic to the place. (There are two extra topics.)

> a. smiling   b. chewing gum   c. stealing
> d. hospitals   e. pigeons   f. carrying money

1. Singapore ____   **2.** Kenya ____   **3.** San Francisco ____   **4.** Milan ____

B Listen again. Complete the sentences to describe each law.

1. In Singapore, you _____.

2. In Kenya, you _____.

3. In San Francisco, you _____.

4. In Milan, you _____.

C **PAIR WORK** Which law seems the strangest to you? the most logical? Why?

4 GAME Miming

A Think of two emotions or ideas you can communicate with gestures. Write them on separate cards.

B **GROUP WORK** Shuffle your cards together. Then take turns picking cards and acting out the meanings with gestures. The student who guesses correctly goes next.

A: That probably means you're disgusted.
B: No.
C: It could mean you're surprised.
B: You're getting closer . . .

I'm confused. I don't understand what you really want.

5 DISCUSSION What's the law?

GROUP WORK Read these laws from the United States. What do you think about them? Are they the same or different in your country?

- You aren't allowed to keep certain wild animals as pets.
- You're allowed to vote when you turn 18.
- In some states, you can get married when you're 16.
- You have to wear a seat belt in the back seat of a car in most states.
- Young men don't have to serve in the military.
- In some states, you can't drive faster than 65 miles per hour (about 100 kph).
- In most states, children have to attend school until they are 16 or 18.

A: In the U.S.A., you aren't allowed to keep certain wild animals as pets.
B: It's the same for us. You've got to have a special permit to keep a wild animal.
C: I've heard that in some countries, you can keep lions and tigers as pets.

WHAT'S NEXT?

Look at your Self-assessment again. Do you need to review anything?

I wouldn't have done that.

▶ **Discuss imaginary situations**
▶ **Discuss difficult situations**

1 SNAPSHOT

NEWS 4 YOU   NEW TODAY   MOST POPULAR   TRENDING   LOGIN | SIGN UP

FLORIDA MOM "CAUGHT" BEING HONEST
Nancy Bloom was caught on the security camera entering a convenience store while the owner was out to lunch. The door was unlocked, so Nancy walked in with her son, picked up some ice cream, and left the money on the counter.

MOST SHARED THIS WEEK

HONESTY IS ITS OWN REWARD
After driving for 20 miles to return a wallet lost in a park, Kate Moore gets only a half-hearted, "Oh. Thanks."

HOMELESS MAN FINDS $40,000 AND TURNS IT IN
When Tom Heart found a backpack full of cash, he didn't think twice. He took it straight to the police. After reading Tom's story, a stranger started a fundraising campaign for Tom that has already raised over $60,000.

Have you heard any stories like these recently?
Have you ever found anything valuable? What did you do?
Do you think that people who return lost things should get a reward?

2 CONVERSATION What would you do?

▶ **A** Listen and practice.

Joon: Look at this. A homeless guy found a backpack with $40,000 inside!

Mia: And what did he do?

Joon: He took it to the police. He gave it all back, every single penny.

Mia: You're kidding! If I found $40,000, I wouldn't return it. I'd keep it.

Joon: Really? What would you do with it?

Mia: Well, I'd spend it. I could buy a new car or take a nice long vacation.

Joon: The real owner might find out about it, though, and then you could go to jail.

Mia: Hmm. You've got a point there.

▶ **B** Listen to the rest of the conversation. What would Joon do if he found $40,000?

3 GRAMMAR FOCUS

▶ Unreal conditional sentences with *if* clauses

Imaginary situation **(simple past)**	**Possible consequence** (*would*, *could*, or *might* + verb)
If I **found** $40,000,	**I would keep** it.
	I wouldn't return it.
	I could buy a new car.
	I might go to the police.
What **would** you **do if** you **found** $40,000?	

GRAMMAR PLUS *see page 146*

A Complete these conversations. Then compare with a partner.

1. **A:** What _____ you _____ (do) if you lost your sister's favorite sweater?
   B: Of course I _____ (buy) her a new one.

2. **A:** If you _____ (have) three months to travel,
   where _____ you _____ (go)?
   B: Oh, that's easy! I _____ (fly) to Europe. I've always wanted to go there.

3. **A:** If your doctor _____ (tell) you to get more exercise, which activity
   _____ you _____ (choose)?
   B: I'm not sure, but I think I _____ (go) jogging two or three times a week.

4. **A:** _____ you _____ (break) into your house if you _____ (lock)
   yourself out?
   B: No way! If I _____ (not have) another key, I _____ (ask) a neighbor for help.

5. **A:** If your friend _____ (want) to marry someone you didn't like,
   _____ you _____ (say) something?
   B: No, I _____ (not say) anything. I _____ (mind) my own business.

6. **A:** What _____ you _____ (do) if you _____ (see) your favorite
   movie star on the street?
   B: I _____ (not be) shy! I _____ (ask) to take a photo with them.

B **PAIR WORK** Take turns asking the questions in part A. Answer with your own information.

4 LISTENING Tough situations

▶ **A** Listen to three people talk about predicaments. Check which predicament they are talking about.

1. ☐ Chris has relationship problems.   ☐ Chris is addicted to the Internet.
2. ☐ Kari spent all her money in Europe.   ☐ Kari lost all her money in Europe.
3. ☐ Zoey saw her classmates cheating.   ☐ Zoey doesn't understand her math class.

▶ **B** Listen again. Write the two suggestions given for each predicament.

1. a. _____   b. _____
2. a. _____   b. _____
3. a. _____   b. _____

C **GROUP WORK** Which suggestions do you agree with? Why?

5 INTERCHANGE 15 Tough choices

What would you do in some difficult situations? Go to Interchange 15 on page 130.

6 WORD POWER Opposites

A Find nine pairs of opposites in this list. Complete the chart. Then compare with a partner.

accept	borrow	dislike	find	lose	remember
admit	deny	divorce	forget	marry	save
agree	disagree	enjoy	lend	refuse	spend

accept	≠	refuse		≠			≠
	≠			≠			≠
	≠			≠			≠

B PAIR WORK Choose four pairs of opposites. Write sentences using each pair.

I can't remember my dreams. As soon as I wake up, I forget them.

7 PERSPECTIVES That was a big mistake.

A Listen to people talk about recent predicaments. Then check (✓) the best suggestion for each one.

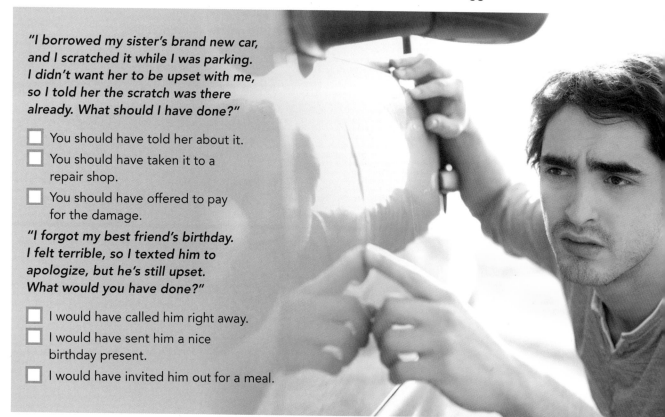

"I borrowed my sister's brand new car, and I scratched it while I was parking. I didn't want her to be upset with me, so I told her the scratch was there already. What should I have done?"

☐ You should have told her about it.

☐ You should have taken it to a repair shop.

☐ You should have offered to pay for the damage.

"I forgot my best friend's birthday. I felt terrible, so I texted him to apologize, but he's still upset. What would you have done?"

☐ I would have called him right away.

☐ I would have sent him a nice birthday present.

☐ I would have invited him out for a meal.

B PAIR WORK Compare with a partner. Do you agree with each other?

▶ **Past modals**

Use *would have* or *should have* + past participle to give opinions or
suggestions about actions in the past.

What **should** I **have done**?

You **should have told** her about it.

You **shouldn't have lied** to your sister.

What **would** you **have done**?

I **would have called** him.

I **wouldn't have texted** him.

GRAMMAR PLUS *see page 146*

A Complete these conversations. Then practice with a partner.

1. **A:** I was in a meeting at work when my girlfriend texted me saying she needed to see me right away. What should I have _____ (do)?
   B: You should have _____ (send) her a message and _____ (tell) her you'd call back later.

2. **A:** The cashier gave me too much change. What should I have _____ (do)?
   B: You should have _____ (say) something. You shouldn't have _____ (take) the money.

3. **A:** I ignored an email from someone I don't like. What would you have _____ (do)?
   B: I would have _____ (reply) to the person. It just takes a minute!

4. **A:** We left all our trash at the campsite. What would you have _____ (do)?
   B: I would have _____ (take) it with me and _____ (throw) it away later.

B Read the situations below. What would have been the best thing to do? Choose suggestions. Then compare with a partner.

Situations

1. The teacher borrowed my favorite book and spilled coffee all over it. _____
2. I saw a classmate cheating on an exam, so I wrote her an email about it. _____
3. A friend of mine always has messy hair, so I gave him a comb for his birthday. _____
4. I hit someone's car when I was leaving a parking lot. Luckily, no one saw me. _____
5. My aunt gave me a wool sweater. I can't wear wool, so I gave it back. _____

Suggestions

a. You should have spoken to him about it.
b. I would have spoken to the teacher about it.
c. I would have waited for the owner to return.
d. I wouldn't have said anything.
e. You should have warned her not to do it again.
f. You should have left a note for the owner.
g. I would have told her that I prefer something else.
h. You should have exchanged it for something else.

C GROUP WORK Make another suggestion for each situation in part B.

▶ **A** Listen and practice. Notice how **have** is reduced in these sentences.

/əv/
What would you have done?

/əv/
I would have told the truth.

B PAIR WORK Practice the conversations in Exercise 8, part A, again. Use the reduced form of **have**.

10 LISTENING Problem solved!

▶ **A** Listen to an advice podcast. Complete the chart.

	Problem	What the person did
Ronnie:		
Becca:		

▶ **B** Listen again. According to Dr. Jones, what should each person have done?

Ronnie: _____

Becca: _____

C **PAIR WORK** What would you have done in each situation?

11 SPEAKING An awful trip

A **PAIR WORK** Imagine a friend has been on a really awful trip and everything went wrong. What should your friend have done? What shouldn't he or she have done?

Your friend spent hours in the sun and got a sunburn.

Your friend drank tap water and got sick.

Your friend stayed at a very bad hotel.

Your friend's wallet was stolen.

Your friend overslept and missed the flight back.

A: She shouldn't have spent so many hours in the sun.
B: She should have used sunscreen.

B **GROUP WORK** Have you ever had any bad experiences on a trip? What happened?

12 WRITING Advice needed

Write a post to a community blog about a real or imaginary problem.
Put your drafts on the wall and choose one to write a reply to.

WHAT WENT WRONG?
submitted by dmartin 10 hours ago

I lent my girlfriend $10,000 to help her pay for her college tuition. That was about a year ago, and at the time, she said she would pay me back as soon as she found a job. She never even looked for a job. Last week, I asked her for my money back, and she accused me of being selfish, unsympathetic, and insensitive. She broke up with me, and now she won't even talk to me anymore. What did I do wrong? What should I have done? What should I do now? Does anyone have any suggestions?

248 comments

A Skim the three posts. What do Jack, Maya, and Andrés ask for advice about?

●●● < >

HOME   NEW   ABOUT   COMMUNITY   👤 SIGN IN

TOPTIPS.COM

1 JACK – LONDON   ♡12

I am overweight, and I'd really like to slim down. I've tried all kinds of diets, but none of them seem to work. And there's so much advice on the Internet – I don't know what to believe any more. What would you recommend?

I had the same problem until I tried a high protein/no carbohydrate diet. It was very strict – in the first couple of weeks you have to eat less than 40 grams of carbohydrates a day, so no bread, pasta, or potatoes! But I lost nine pounds in just 13 days, so for me it was worth it. I had a lot of meat and eggs and some butter, too, which was great! I'd give it a shot if I were you. (Sarah, Edinburgh)

2 MAYA – SAN FRANCISCO   ♡22

I'm traveling to Rio de Janeiro next month, and I'd like to see as much of the city as possible. The problem is that I'm only going to be there for a couple of days, and I'm not sure how to fit everything in. Should I book an organized tour?

I was in Rio a couple of months ago. I travel a lot and like to be independent, so I chose to find my own way around the city. What a mistake! Rio's so big that I kept getting lost! And in the end, I didn't get to see the beach of Ipanema or the cathedral. It would have been nice to have somebody to talk to also. I really should have gone on a guided tour. (Dag, Oslo)

3 ANDRÉS – BOGOTÁ   ♡11

I've just finished my degree, and I'm on the fence about what to do next. Here in Bogotá, there aren't many job possibilities right now. Should I go back to college to get a Master's? Or go stay with my cousin in New York and try to get a job there? (My English is not very good, by the way – a friend wrote this!)

Stay where you are! I moved to the United States from Poland and got a job as a server, but it's long hours and not much money. I haven't really made many friends, and I miss home. I should have stayed there and continued with my studies. (Marta, Krakow)

B Read the posts. Who would say these sentences? Write names from the posts.

1. Should I go abroad or stay where I am? _____
2. It worked for me, so why don't you try it? _____
3. I would have been happier if I hadn't moved. _____
4. How can I choose the right eating plan? _____
5. If I went there again, I'd definitely join a group. _____
6. I don't have much time, so I need to be organized. _____

C Find words or expressions in the posts to match these definitions.

1. Be an important or useful thing to do (post 1) _____
2. Find enough time for something (post 2) _____
3. To be unable to make a decision (post 3) _____

D Do you agree with the advice given above? What advice would you give?

16

Making excuses

▸ **Give reasons and explanations**
▸ **Discuss statements other people made**

1 SNAPSHOT

Good Excuses, Poor Excuses

Not doing homework
• I was sure the assignment was due tomorrow.
• I emailed it to you, but it bounced back.

Arriving late to class
• My father didn't wake me up.
• My bike tire was flat because a dog bit it.

Missing work
• My cat was sick, and I had to take care of her.
• It was my birthday, and I always donate blood on that day.

Arriving late to work
• I worked on the new project until four in the morning, and then I overslept.
• My wife thinks it's funny to hide my car keys in the morning.

Arriving late for a date
• I was taking a telephone survey and lost track of the time.
• A horse running on the highway was holding up traffic.

Which are good excuses? Which are poor ones?
What excuse do you usually use for these situations?
What excuses can you make for missing a date or party?

2 PERSPECTIVES At your request

▶ **A** Who do you think made these requests? Listen and match.

1. She said to arrive on time for the meeting. ____
2. She asked me to pick up some food on the way home. ____
3. He said not to miss practice again. ____
4. She told me to hand in my homework before Friday. ____
5. She said to drink at least six glasses of water a day. ____
6. He asked me not to tell Mom about his new girlfriend. ____
7. He told me not to leave my bike in the apartment hallway. ____

a. my teacher
b. my boss
c. my brother
d. my doctor
e. my neighbor
f. my roommate
g. my coach

B PAIR WORK Can you think of another request each person might make?

A: Our teacher sometimes says, "Open your books."
B: A teacher could also say, "Repeat after me."

▶ **Reported speech: requests**

Original request	Reported request
Arrive on time for the meeting.	She **said to arrive** on time for the meeting.
	She **told me to arrive** on time for the meeting.
Don't leave your bike in the apartment hallway.	He **said not to leave** my bike in the hallway.
	He **told me not to leave** my bike in the hallway.
Can you pick up some food on the way home?	She **asked me to pick up** some food.

GRAMMAR PLUS *see page 147*

A Victor is organizing a surprise birthday party for his teacher. Look at what he told his classmates. Write each request using *say*, *tell*, or *ask*. Then compare with a partner.

1. Meet at my apartment at 7:30.   *He told them to meet at his apartment at 7:30.*
2. Don't arrive late.   _____
3. Can you bring some ice cream?   _____
4. Can you help me make the sandwiches?   _____
5. Can you bring a small gift for her?   _____
6. Don't spend more than $10 on the gift.   _____
7. Keep the party a secret.   _____
8. Don't say anything to the other teachers.   _____

B **GROUP WORK** Imagine you're planning a class party. Write four requests. Then take turns reading your requests and changing them into reported requests.

Edu: Bring something to eat to the party!
Eva: Edu told us to bring something to eat.

Aki: Can you help me clean up after the party?
Jim: Aki asked us to help her clean up.

4 SPEAKING That's asking too much!

A Think of requests that people have made recently. Write two things people asked you to do and two things people asked you *not* to do.

Person	Request
My boss	shave off my beard

B **GROUP WORK** Talk about the requests that each of you listed in part A. Did you do what people requested? Did you give an excuse? What was it?

5 WORD POWER Verb-noun collocations

A Find three more nouns that are usually paired with each verb. The same noun can be paired with more than one verb. Then compare with a partner.

an apology	an invitation	a request
a complaint	a joke	a solution
an excuse	a lie	a story
an explanation	an offer	a suggestion
an idea	a reason	the truth

make	_a request_	_____	_____	_____
give	_an excuse_	_____	_____	_____
tell	_a joke_	_____	_____	_____
accept	_an apology_	_____	_____	_____
refuse	_an invitation_	_____	_____	_____

B **PAIR WORK** How do you deal with the things in part A? Tell a partner.

A: What do you do when a close friend makes a difficult request?

B: I give a good explanation, and I offer to help in another way. What about you?

6 CONVERSATION Are you doing anything on Sunday?

A Listen and practice.

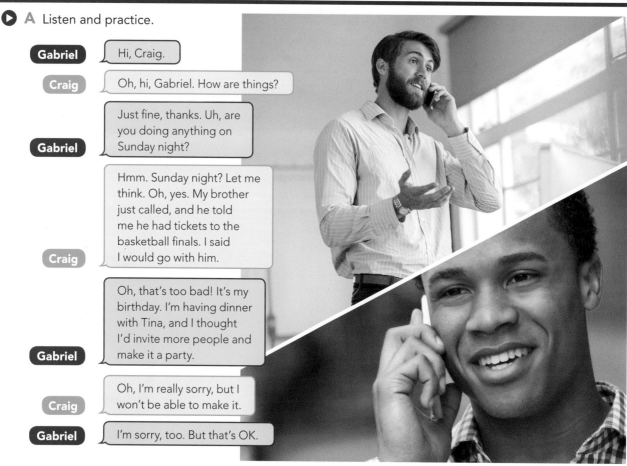

Gabriel Hi, Craig.

Craig Oh, hi, Gabriel. How are things?

Gabriel Just fine, thanks. Uh, are you doing anything on Sunday night?

Craig Hmm. Sunday night? Let me think. Oh, yes. My brother just called, and he told me he had tickets to the basketball finals. I said I would go with him.

Gabriel Oh, that's too bad! It's my birthday. I'm having dinner with Tina, and I thought I'd invite more people and make it a party.

Craig Oh, I'm really sorry, but I won't be able to make it.

Gabriel I'm sorry, too. But that's OK.

B **PAIR WORK** Act out the conversation in part A. Make up your own excuse for not accepting Gabriel's invitation.

▶ **A** Listen to Gabriel invite his friends to his birthday party on Saturday. What excuses do they give for not going? Write them below.

1. Grant: _____
2. Sayo: _____
3. Diego: _____
4. Carrie: _____

▶ **B** Listen. What happens on the night of Gabriel's birthday?

C **PAIR WORK** What was the last party you went to? Describe it to your partner.

8 GRAMMAR FOCUS

▶ **Reported speech: statements**

Direct statements	Reported statements
I'm not feeling well.	She **said** (that) she **wasn't feeling** well.
I **have** houseguests for the weekend.	she **had** houseguests for the weekend.
I **made** a tennis date with Kim.	she **had made** a tennis date with Kim.
I **have planned** an exciting trip.	she **had planned** an exciting trip.
We **can't come** tomorrow.	They **told me** (that) they **couldn't come** tomorrow.
We **will be** out of town.	they **would be** out of town.
We **may go** out with friends.	they **might go** out with friends.

GRAMMAR PLUS see page 147

A Isabella is having a party at her house on Saturday. Look at these excuses. Change them into reported speech. Then compare with a partner.

1. Mason: "I already have plans for Saturday."
2. Olivia: "My in-laws are coming over for dinner that night."
3. Ben and Ava: "We've been invited to a graduation party on Saturday."
4. Felipe: "I promised to help my sister with her homework."
5. Tae-yun: "I can't come because I broke my leg."
6. Osvaldo: "I'll be moving this weekend."
7. Lisa and Henry: "We have to pick someone up at the airport that evening."
8. Omar: "I may have to work the night shift on Saturday."

> Mason said he already had plans for Saturday. OR
>
> Mason told her he already had plans for Saturday.

B **GROUP WORK** Imagine you don't want to go to Isabella's party. Take turns making excuses and changing them into reported speech.

A: I'm sorry, I can't go. I'm going camping this weekend.

B: Lucky guy! He said he was going camping this weekend.

9 PRONUNCIATION Reduction of *had* and *would*

▶ **A** Listen and practice. Notice how *had* and *would* are reduced in the following sentences.

She said she**'d made** the bed. (She said she **had made** the bed.)
She said she**'d make** the bed. (She said she **would make** the bed.)

▶ **B** Listen to four sentences. Check (✓) the reduced form that you hear.

1. ☐ had		**2.** ☐ had		**3.** ☐ had		**4.** ☐ had	
☐ would		☐ would		☐ would		☐ would	

10 WRITING About my classmates

A Interview your classmates and take notes. Use your notes to write a report describing what people told you. Use reported speech.

	Name	Response
What did you do last night?		
What movie have you seen recently?		
Where are you going after class?		
What are your plans for the weekend?		
What will you do on your next birthday?		

B GROUP WORK Read your report, but don't give names. Others guess the person.

"Someone said that he'd go to Paris on his next vacation."

11 SPEAKING You can make it.

A GROUP WORK What are some things you would like to do in the future? Think of three intentions.

A: I'm going to take an English course abroad.
B: That sounds fun. Have you decided where?

B CLASS ACTIVITY Report the best intentions you heard. Then give suggestions.

B: Noriko said she was going to take an English course abroad, but she hadn't decided where.
C: She could go to Australia. My brother attended a very good school there. He told me he studied incredibly hard!

12 INTERCHANGE 16 Just a bunch of excuses

Make some plans. Student A, go to Interchange 16A on page 129; Student B, go to Interchange 16B on page 131.

A Scan the article. What are three common reasons for missing work?

A GOOD EXCUSE FOR A
DAY OFF WORK

1 On average, U.S. employees take 4.9 sick days per year. Usually this does not cause any particular problems. But when employees take sick leave without a good reason, it can quickly become an issue. In fact, in one survey, 18 percent of employers said that they had fired an employee for taking days off without a good reason. The key is to understand what reasons are acceptable and what reasons are not. Generally, most excuses for sick days fall into one of three categories.

2 The most common reasons for not going to work are health-related. It would probably be OK to tell your boss that you ate something bad last night and that you have a stomachache. Of course you might not want to share the details of a health issue with your boss – after all, you do have the right to privacy. If you don't want to be too specific, you can just tell your boss that you have a small medical issue and need to take the day off.

3 Household accidents are the second category of reasons for not going in to work. You might call your boss to say you slipped in the shower and hurt your knee. This is a common accident and one that your boss will sympathize with. However, if you are going to be out of work for several days due to an injury, it's important to make arrangements with your employer. See if you can work from home, or at least make sure there is someone to cover your work.

4 The third type of sick day use isn't really about illness, but it's about something else you can't control: transportation problems. The car might not start, there may be a terrible traffic jam, or there could be delays on the subway. Some employers may be sympathetic to absences due to transportation problems, but others may not. It's important to know your boss and to understand whether he or she will accept an excuse like this.

5 Regardless of the reason for the sick day, there are a few things you can do to make missing work more acceptable to your employer. Try to keep sick days to a minimum. When you do need to take a sick day, give your employer as much advance notice as possible. Finally, never take a sick day if there isn't anything wrong with you – the only good excuses are the ones that are true.

B Read the article. Then correct four mistakes in the summary of the article.

U.S. workers take just under a month in sick days a year. The least frequently used excuses are for health reasons. When employees take a sick day, it's important to explain the reason to their colleagues. It's OK to take a sick day, even if you feel fine, as long as you give an excuse.

C Find words in the text to match these definitions.

1. told someone to leave his or her job (paragraph 1) _____

2. an explanation given for something (paragraph 1) _____

3. someone's right to keep information about his or her personal life secret (paragraph 2) _____

4. understand or care about someone's problems (paragraph 3) _____

5. a warning that something is about to happen (paragraph 5) _____

D What other excuses do people make for not going to work or class? What's the silliest excuse you have ever heard?

Units 15–16 Progress check

SELF-ASSESSMENT

How well can you do these things? Check (✓) the boxes.

I can . . .	Very well	OK	A little
Discuss imaginary events (Ex. 1)	☐	☐	☐
Ask for and give advice and suggestions about past events (Ex. 2)	☐	☐	☐
Understand and report requests (Ex. 3)	☐	☐	☐
Discuss statements other people made (Ex. 4)	☐	☐	☐

1 DISCUSSION Interesting situations

A What would you do in these situations? Complete the statements.

If I forgot to do my homework, _____.
If I found a valuable piece of jewelry in the park, _____.
If a friend gave me a present I didn't like, _____.
If I wasn't invited to a party I wanted to attend, _____.
If someone took my clothes while I was swimming, _____.

B **GROUP WORK** Compare your responses. For each situation, choose one to tell the class.

A: What would you do if you forgot to do your homework?
B: I'd probably tell the teacher the truth. I'd ask her to let me hand it in next class.

2 SPEAKING Predicaments

A Make up two situations like the one below. Think about experiences you have had or heard about at work, home, or school.

"An old friend from high school visited me recently. We had a great time at first, but he became annoying. He made a big mess, and he left his things all over the place. After two weeks, I told him he had to leave because my sister was coming for the weekend."

B **PAIR WORK** Take turns sharing your situations. Ask for advice and suggestions.

A: What would you have done?
B: Well, I would have told him to pick up his clothes, and I would have asked him to clean up his mess.

3 LISTENING A small request

A Listen to the conversations. Check (✓) the person who is making the request.

1. ☐ child 2. ☐ neighbor 3. ☐ child 4. ☐ teacher 5. ☐ boss 6. ☐ neighbor
   ☐ parent   ☐ teacher   ☐ doctor   ☐ classmate   ☐ neighbor   ☐ teacher

B Listen again. Complete the requests.

1. Please _____.
2. Can _____?
3. Don't _____.
4. Can _____?
5. Please _____.
6. Can _____?

C **PAIR WORK** Work with a partner. Imagine these requests were for you. Take turns reporting the requests to your partner.

"My dad told me to pick up my things."

4 GAME Who is lying?

A Think of situations when you expressed anger, gave an excuse, or made a complaint. Write a brief statement about each situation.

I once complained about the bathroom in a hotel.

B **CLASS ACTIVITY** Play a game. Choose three students to be contestants.

Step 1: The contestants compare their statements and choose one. This statement should be true about only one student. The other two students should pretend they had the experience.

Step 2: The contestants stand in front of the class. Each contestant reads the same statement. The rest of the class must ask questions to find out who isn't telling the truth.

Contestant A, what hotel were you in?

Contestant B, what was wrong with the bathroom?

Contestant C, what did the manager do?

Step 3: Who isn't telling the truth? What did he or she say to make you think that?
"I don't think Contestant B is telling the truth. He said the bathroom was too small!"

WHAT'S NEXT?

Look at your Self-assessment again. Do you need to review anything?

Interchange activities

We have a lot in common.

A **CLASS ACTIVITY** Go around the class and find out the information below. Then ask follow-up questions and take notes. Write a classmate's name only once.

Find someone who . . .	Name	Notes
1. wanted to be a movie star **"Did you ever want to be a movie star?"**		
2. always listened to his or her teachers **"Did you always listen to your teachers?"**		
3. used to look very different **"Did you use to look very different?"**		
4. had a pet when he or she was little **"Did you have a pet when you were little?"**		
5. changed schools when he or she was a child "_____?"		
6. used to argue with his or her brothers and sisters "_____?"		
7. got in trouble a lot as a child "_____?"		
8. used to have a favorite toy "_____?"		

B **GROUP WORK** Tell the group the most interesting thing you learned about your classmates.

INTERCHANGE 2 Top travel destinations

A **PAIR WORK** Look at the photos and slogans below. What do you think the theme of each tourism campaign is?

Possible themes

art	culture	entertainment
food	history	music
nature	shopping	sports

Cartagena
"The Colorful Caribbean"

New Orleans
"The Birthplace of Jazz"

Cairo
"The Earth's Mother"

Bangkok
"Thailand Old and New"

B **GROUP WORK** Imagine you are planning a campaign to attract more tourists to one of the cities above or to a city of your choice.
Use the ideas below or your own ideas to discuss the campaign.

a good time to visit
famous historical attractions
special events or festivals
nice areas to stay
interesting places to see
memorable things to do

A: Do you know when a good time to visit Cartagena is?
B: I think between December and April is a good time because . . .

C **GROUP WORK** What will be the theme of your campaign? What slogan will you use?

A Complete this questionnaire with information about yourself.

My Wish List

1. What possession do you wish you had?
   I wish I had _____

2. What sport do you wish you could play?
   _____

3. Where do you wish you could live?
   _____

4. What skill do you wish you had?
   _____

5. What kind of home do you wish you could have?
   _____

6. What kind of vacation do you wish you could take?
   _____

7. What languages do you wish you could speak?
   _____

8. Which musical instruments do you wish you could play?
   _____

9. What famous person do you wish you could meet?
   _____

10. What kind of pet do you wish you could have?
    _____

B **PAIR WORK** Compare your questionnaires. Take turns asking and answering questions about your wishes.

A: What possession do you wish you had?
B: I wish I had a sailboat.
A: Really? Why?
B: Well, I could sail around the world!

C **CLASS ACTIVITY** Imagine you are at a class reunion. It is ten years since you completed the questionnaire in part A. Tell the class about some wishes that have come true for your partner.

"Victor is now a famous explorer and sailor. He has sailed across the Atlantic and to the South Pole. Right now, he's writing a book about his adventures on his boat."

INTERCHANGE 4 Oh, really?

A How much do you really know about your classmates? Look at the survey and add two more situations to items 1 and 2.

	Name	Notes

1. Find someone who has . . .
  a. cooked for more than twenty people
  b. found something valuable
  c. lost his or her phone
  d. been on TV
  e. cried during a movie
  f. _____
  g. _____		

2. Find someone who has never . . .
  a. been camping
  b. gone horseback riding
  c. fallen asleep at the movies
  d. played a video game
  e. baked cookies
  f. _____
  g. _____		

B **CLASS ACTIVITY** Go around the class and ask the questions. Write the names of classmates who answer "yes" for item 1 and "no" for item 2. Then ask follow-up questions and take notes.

A: Have you ever cooked for more than 20 people?

B: Yes, I have. Last year I cooked for the whole family on Mother's Day.

A: How was it?

B: Well, my mother had to help me.

A: Have you ever been camping?

C: No, I haven't.

A: Why not?

C: Because I don't like mosquitoes.

C **GROUP WORK** Compare the information in your surveys.

STUDENT A

A PAIR WORK You and your partner are going to take a trip. You have a brochure for a surfing trip to Hawaii, and your partner has a brochure for a hiking trip to the Grand Canyon.

First, find out about the hiking trip. Ask your partner questions about these things.

The length of the trip	The cost of the trip	What the price includes
The accommodations	Additional activities	Nighttime activities

B PAIR WORK Now use the information in this brochure to answer your partner's questions about the surfing trip.

SURFING VACATION IN HAWAII

Seven-day surf camp on the magical island of Oahu for surfers of all ability levels

Visit the best attractions on the island:
Kailua Beach Park
The Waikiki Aquarium
Pearl Harbor

Accommodations:
Beachfront studios and apartments

Price includes:
Daily surf lessons
All necessary equipment
Breakfast and lunch

Additional activities:
Catamaran sailing lessons
Snorkeling at Hanauma Bay Beach

Nighttime activities:
Authentic Hawaiian luau
Hula shows

Vacation cost:
$2,100

C PAIR WORK Decide which trip you are going to take. Then explain your choice to the class.

INTERCHANGE 6 I'm terribly sorry.

A PAIR WORK Look at these situations. Act out conversations. Apologize and then give an excuse, admit a mistake, or make an offer or a promise.

> **useful expressions**
>
> I'm sorry. / I didn't realize. / I forgot.   You're right. / I was wrong.
> I'll . . . right away.   I'll make sure to . . . / I promise I'll . . .

Student A: You are trying to watch the movie.
Student B: You are talking on your phone.
A: Excuse me. I'm trying to watch the movie. Could you please turn off your phone?
B: I'm so sorry . . .

Student A: You are the server.
Student B: You are one of the customers.
A: Oh, I'm terribly sorry . . .
B: _____

Student A: You have just arrived for the meeting.
Student B: You are making a presentation.
A: I'm sorry I'm late . . .
B: _____

Student A: You are the host.
Student B: You broke the vase.
A: Oh, no! My vase.
B: _____

B GROUP WORK Have you ever experienced situations like these? What happened? What did you do? Share your stories.

Student B

A PAIR WORK You and your partner are going to take a trip. You have a brochure for a hiking trip to the Grand Canyon, and your partner has a brochure for a surfing trip to Hawaii.

First, use the information in the brochure to answer your partner's questions about the hiking trip.

HIKING TRIP IN THE GRAND CANYON

Ten-day tour of spectacular sights with knowledgeable, friendly tour guides

Places to visit:
The red rock canyons
Zion National Park
The Navajo Nation
Kaibab National Forest

Accommodations:
Single or double rooms at historic lodges inside the national park

Price includes:
Breakfast and dinner every day
Two picnic lunches
Transportation to all attractions

Additional activities:
Rafting the Colorado River
Helicopter tour
Lake Powell boat cruise

Nighttime activities:
Dinner cruise
Stargazing
Campfire sing-alongs

Vacation cost:
$1,980

B PAIR WORK Now find out about the surfing trip. Ask your partner questions about these things.

The length of the trip   The cost of the trip   What the price includes
The accommodations   Additional activities   Nighttime activities

C PAIR WORK Decide which trip you are going to take. Then explain your choice to the class.

A GROUP WORK Look at the problems people have. What advice would you give each person? Discuss possible suggestions and then choose the best one.

"I'm moving to a new apartment with two roommates. How can I be sure we get along well and avoid problems?"

"A co-worker has asked to borrow my brand-new mountain bike for the weekend. I don't want to lend it. What can I say?"

"My family and I are going away on vacation for two weeks. How can we make sure our home is safe from burglars while we're gone?"

"I have an important job interview next week. How can I make sure to be successful and get the job?"

"I'm going to meet my future in-laws tomorrow for the first time. How can I make a good impression?"

"I'm really into social networking, but in the past week, five people I hardly know have asked to be my friends. What should I do?"

B PAIR WORK Choose one of the situations above. Ask your partner for advice. Then give him or her advice about his or her problem.

A: I'm moving to a new apartment with two roommates. How can I be sure we get along well?

B: Make sure you decide how you are going to split the household chores. And remember to . . .

A CLASS ACTIVITY How do your classmates celebrate special occasions?
Go around the class and ask the questions below. If someone answers "yes,"
write down his or her name. Ask for more information and take notes.

Question	Name	Notes
1. Have you ever given someone a surprise party?		
2. What's the best gift you have ever received?		
3. Do you ever wear traditional clothes?		
4. Have you bought flowers for someone special recently?		
5. Do you like to watch parades?		
6 Does your family have big get-togethers?		
7. Has someone given you money recently as a gift?		
8. Will you celebrate your next birthday with a party?		
9. Do you ever give friends birthday presents?		
10. What's your favorite time of the year?		
11. Do you ever celebrate a holiday with fireworks?		

A: Have you ever given someone a surprise party?

B: Yes. Once we gave my co-worker a surprise party on his birthday.

A: How was it?

B: It was great. He never suspected that we were planning it, so he was really surprised.
And he was very happy that we got his favorite cake!

B PAIR WORK Compare your information with a partner.

A Read the questions on the cards. Check (✓) the box for your opinion.

1. **If teens work part-time, they won't do well in school.**
   - ☐ I agree.
   - ☐ I don't agree.
   - ☐ It depends.

2. **If kids play violent video games, they will become violent themselves.**
   - ☐ I agree.
   - ☐ I don't agree.
   - ☐ It depends.

3. **If people decrease their screen time, they'll talk more with their families.**
   - ☐ I agree.
   - ☐ I don't agree.
   - ☐ It depends.

4. **If a woman gets married very early, she won't invest time in her career.**
   - ☐ I agree.
   - ☐ I don't agree.
   - ☐ It depends.

5. **If a woman works outside the home, her children won't be happy.**
   - ☐ I agree.
   - ☐ I don't agree.
   - ☐ It depends.

6. **If a child has brothers and sisters, he or she won't ever feel lonely.**
   - ☐ I agree.
   - ☐ I don't agree.
   - ☐ It depends.

7. **If you have too many online friends, you'll have fewer "real" friends.**
   - ☐ I agree.
   - ☐ I don't agree.
   - ☐ It depends.

8. **If there is a heavy fine for littering, our streets will be much cleaner.**
   - ☐ I agree.
   - ☐ I don't agree.
   - ☐ It depends.

9. **If people work only two days a week, their lives will improve.**
   - ☐ I agree.
   - ☐ I don't agree.
   - ☐ It depends.

10. **If teens have a lot of freedom, they will get in trouble more often.**
   - ☐ I agree.
   - ☐ I don't agree.
   - ☐ It depends.

B **GROUP WORK** Compare your opinions. Be prepared to give reasons for your opinions.

A: I think if teens work part-time, they won't do well in school.

B: I don't really agree.

C: Why not?

B: If they work part-time, they'll become more responsible. That's a positive consequence.

A PAIR WORK Look at the following job description. Write an ad for your ideal job.

JOB FINDER   About   Careers   Education   Job search

Activities Director

Requirements:

Experience working with tourists
A "people person"
Outgoing and creative personality

Responsibilities:

Organize all leisure activities on a popular cruise ship, including planning daily tours, special onboard activities, and nightly entertainment

B PAIR WORK Take turns interviewing your classmates for the job you have created. Get as much information as you can to find the right person for the job.

useful questions

What kind of degree do you have?

What work experience do you have?

What hours can you work?

Do you mind . . . ?

Are you interested in . . . ?

Why should I hire you for the job?

C GROUP WORK Who would you hire for the job you posted? Why?

D CLASS ACTIVITY Compare the ideal jobs you created in part A. How are they similar? How are they different?

A List one movie, one TV show, one song, and one book.

B **GROUP WORK** Take turns making statements about each item.
Does everyone agree with each statement?

A: *Titanic* was filmed on a small lake in Mexico.

B: Are you sure? Wasn't it filmed on the ocean?

C: I'm pretty sure it was filmed in a plastic pool. I read it on the Internet.

C Now think of other famous creations and creators. Complete the chart.
Make some of the items true and some false.

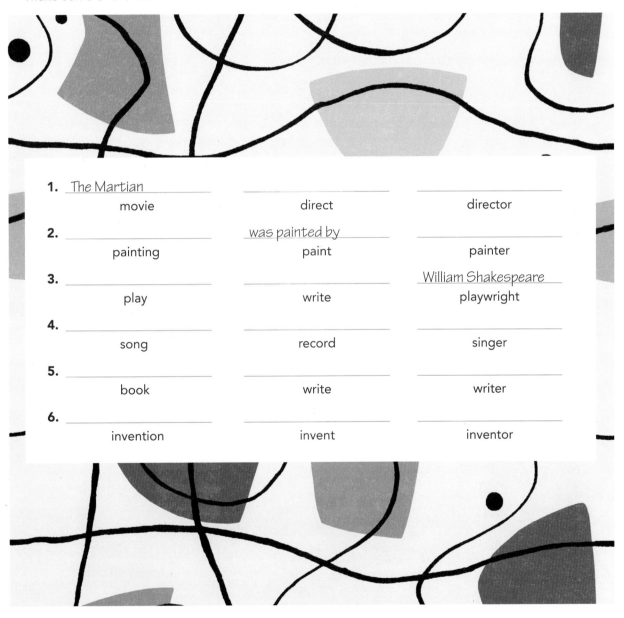

1. <u>The Martian</u>
   movie   direct   director

2. _____ <u>was painted by</u> _____
   painting   paint   painter

3. _____ _____ <u>William Shakespeare</u>
   play   write   playwright

4. _____ _____ _____
   song   record   singer

5. _____ _____ _____
   book   write   writer

6. _____ _____ _____
   invention   invent   inventor

D **GROUP WORK** Make a statement about each item to your group members.
Ask them to decide which statements are true and which are false.

A: The movie *The Martian* was directed by Steven Spielberg.

B: I think that's true.

C: No, that's false. It was directed by Ridley Scott. I'm sure of it.

A GROUP WORK Play the board game. Follow these instructions.

1. Use small pieces of paper with your initials on them as markers.

2. Take turns tossing a coin:

 Move two spaces.

Heads

 Move one space.

Tails

3. Complete the sentence in the space you land on. Others ask two follow-up questions to get more information.

A: When I was little, I lived on the coast.
B: Oh, really? Did you go to the beach every day?
A: No, we only went to the beach on weekends.
C: Did you enjoy living there?

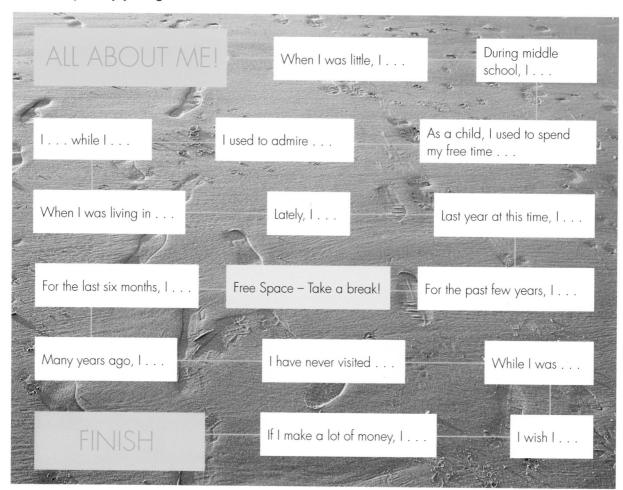

ALL ABOUT ME!

When I was little, I . . .

During middle school, I . . .

I . . . while I . . .

I used to admire . . .

As a child, I used to spend my free time . . .

When I was living in . . .

Lately, I . . .

Last year at this time, I . . .

For the last six months, I . . .

Free Space – Take a break!

For the past few years, I . . .

Many years ago, I . . .

I have never visited . . .

While I was . . .

FINISH

If I make a lot of money, I . . .

I wish I . . .

B CLASS ACTIVITY Tell the class an interesting fact that you learned about someone in your group.

"For the last six months, Marcia has been taking dance classes."

A Complete the questionnaire.

What is the name of a TV show or movie . . . ?

1. that made you laugh a lot
   _____

2. that made you feel sad
   _____

3. that you have seen more than once
   _____

4. which had great music
   _____

5. that was about a silly story
   _____

What is the name of a TV or movie star . . . ?

6. who is very talented
   _____

7. who is famous but not very talented
   _____

8. who does things to help society
   _____

9. who is an excellent comedian
   _____

10. that reminds you of someone you know
    _____

B **PAIR WORK** Compare your questionnaires. Ask follow-up questions of your own.

A: What's the name of a TV show or movie that made you laugh a lot?
B: *Grown Ups 2.*
A: Really? Why?
B: I thought the movie was hilarious.
A: Who was in it?
B: Adam Sandler. I always enjoy his movies.
A: Well, I liked his earlier movies better.

INTERCHANGE 14 Casual observers

A **PAIR WORK** Look at this scene of an airport. What do you think is happening in each of the situations? Look at people's body language for clues.

A: Why do you think the couple in situation 1 looks upset?

B: Well, they might be having a fight. They look . . .

A: Who do you think the woman in situation 6 is?

B: She must be famous. She might . . .

B **GROUP WORK** Compare your interpretations. Do you agree or disagree?

Student A

A **PAIR WORK** You and your partner want to get together. Ask and answer questions to find a day when you are both free. You also want to keep time open for other friends, so give excuses for those days. Write your partner's excuses on the calendar.

A: Do you want to meet on the 2nd?

B: I'm sorry. I'm going to an engagement party. Are you free on the 1st?

A: Well, I . . .

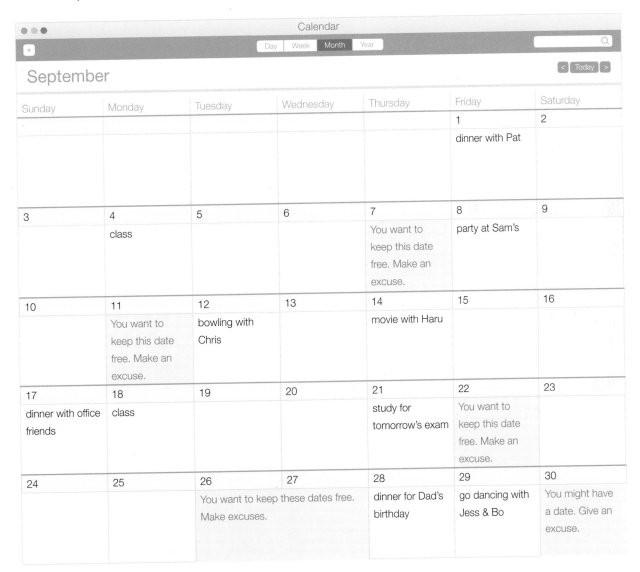

| Calendar |
| Day | Week | **Month** | Year |

September

Sunday	Monday	Tuesday	Wednesday	Thursday	Friday	Saturday
					1 dinner with Pat	2
3	4 class	5	6	7 You want to keep this date free. Make an excuse.	8 party at Sam's	9
10	11 You want to keep this date free. Make an excuse.	12 bowling with Chris	13	14 movie with Haru	15	16
17 dinner with office friends	18 class	19	20	21 study for tomorrow's exam	22 You want to keep this date free. Make an excuse.	23
24	25	26 You want to keep these dates free. Make excuses.	27	28 dinner for Dad's birthday	29 go dancing with Jess & Bo	30 You might have a date. Give an excuse.

B **PAIR WORK** Now work with another student. Discuss the excuses your partner gave you in Part A. Decide which excuses were probably true and which ones were probably not true.

A: Pablo said that on the 7th he had to take care of his neighbors' cats. That was probably not true.

B: I agree. I think . . .

A What would you do in each of these situations? Circle **a**, **b**, or **c**.
   If you think you would do something else, write your suggestion next to **d**.

1 If I saw someone shoplifting in a store,
   I would . . .
   a. pretend I didn't notice.
   b. talk to the store manager.
   c. talk to the shoplifter.
   d. _____ .

2 If I saw an elderly woman trying to cross
   a street, I would . . .
   a. keep walking.
   b. offer to help.
   c. try to stop traffic for her.
   d. _____ .

3 If I saw someone standing on a highway
   next to a car with smoke coming from
   the engine, I would . . .
   a. continue driving.
   b. stop and help.
   c. use my cell phone to call the police.
   d. _____ .

4 If I saw my friend's boyfriend or girlfriend
   with someone other than my friend,
   I would . . .
   a. say nothing.
   b. talk to my friend.
   c. talk to my friend's boyfriend
       or girlfriend.
   d. _____ .

5 If I were eating dinner in a restaurant and
   I found a hair in my food, I would . . .
   a. remove it and continue eating.
   b. mention it to the server.
   c. demand to speak to the manager.
   d. _____ .

B **GROUP WORK** Compare your choices for each situation in part A.

   A: What would you do if you saw someone shoplifting in a store?
   B: I'm not sure. Maybe I would pretend I didn't notice.
   C: Really? I wouldn't. I would . . .

C **CLASS ACTIVITY** Take a class survey. Find out which choice was most popular
   for each situation. Talk about any other suggestions people added for **d**.

Student B

A **PAIR WORK** You and your partner want to get together. Ask and answer questions to find a day when you are both free. You also want to keep time open for other friends, so give excuses for those days. Write your partner's excuses on the calendar.

A: Do you want to meet on the 2nd?

B: I'm sorry. I'm going to an engagement party. Are you free on the 1st?

A: Well, I . . .

Calendar

Day | Week | **Month** | Year

< Today >

September

Sunday	Monday	Tuesday	Wednesday	Thursday	Friday	Saturday
					1	2 Kelly's engagement party
3 You want to keep this date free. Make an excuse.	4 movie with Alex	5	6 You want to keep these dates free. Make excuses.	7	8	9
10 visit Mom and Dad	11 office party	12	13 photography workshop at school	14	15 You want to keep these dates free. Make excuses.	16
17 visit Grandma	18	19 jogging with Andie	20	21	22 party at Cameron's	23 dinner with Farah
24 family get-together	25 You need a break. Make an excuse.	26 study group meeting	27	28 work late: big report due Friday	29	30

B **PAIR WORK** Now work with another student. Discuss the excuses your partner gave you in Part A. Decide which excuses were probably true and which ones were probably not true.

A: Maria said that on the 9th she had to help her brother paint his kitchen. That might be true.

B: I agree. I think . . .

Grammar plus

UNIT 1

1 Past tense   page 3

- Use a form of *be* with *born*: I **was born** here. (NOT: I born here.) Don't use a form of *be* with the verb *die*: He **died** last year. (NOT: He was died last year.)

Complete the conversation.

1. **A:** Do you live around here?
   B: No, I don't. I'm from Costa Rica.
   A: Really? *Were you born* _____ in Costa Rica?
   B: No. Actually, I was born in San Miguelito, Panama.
2. **A:** That's interesting. So where _____?
   B: I grew up in Costa Rica. My family moved there when I was little.
3. **A:** _____ in the capital?
   B: No, my family didn't live in a city. We lived in a small town called Puerto Viejo.
4. **A:** _____ away from Puerto Viejo?
   B: Oh, about eight years ago. I left Puerto Viejo to go to college.
5. **A:** Where _____ to college?
   B: I went to college in San Jose, and I live there now.
6. **A:** And _____ to Miami?
   B: I got here a few days ago. I'm visiting my cousin.

2 *Used to*   page 5

- Use the base form of *used to* in questions and negative statements: Did you **use to** play sports? (NOT: Did you used to play sports?) I didn't **use to** like bananas. (NOT: I didn't used to like bananas.)
- Don't use *never* in negative statements: I **never used to** wear sunglasses. (NOT: I never didn't use to wear sunglasses.)

Complete the conversations with the correct form of *used to*.

1. **A:** Hey, Dad. What kinds of clothes *did you use to* _____ wear – you know, when you were a kid?
   B: Oh, we _____ wear jeans and T-shirts – like you kids do now.
   A: Really? _____ Mom _____ dress like that, too?
   B: No, not really. She never _____ like wearing pants. She always _____ wear skirts and dresses.
2. **A:** _____ you _____ play a sport when you were a kid?
   B: Well, I _____ be a swimmer. My sister and I _____ swim on a team.
   A: Wow, that's cool! Were you good?
   B: Yeah. I _____ win gold medals all the time. And my sister _____ be the fastest swimmer on the team.

1 Expressions of quantity page 9

■ Count nouns have a plural form that usually ends in -s. Noncount nouns don't have a plural form because you can't separate and count them: Are there any **parking garages** around here? BUT Is there any **parking** around here? (NOT: Are there any ~~parkings~~ around here?)

Complete the conversations with the correct words in parentheses.

1. **A:** There's _____ (too many / too much) traffic in this city. There should be _____ (fewer / less) cars downtown.
   B: The problem is there _____ (aren't / isn't) enough public transportation.
   A: You're right. We should have more _____ (bus / buses). There _____ (aren't / isn't) enough of them during rush hour.

2. **A:** How do you like your new neighborhood?
   B: It's terrible, actually. There's _____ (too many / too much) noise and _____ (too few / too little) parking.
   A: That's too bad. There _____ (aren't / isn't) enough parking spaces in my neighborhood either.

3. **A:** Did you hear about the changes to the city center? Starting next month, there will be more bicycle _____ (lane / lanes) and _____ (fewer / less) street parking.
   B: That's good. There _____ (are too many / is too much) pollution downtown. I'm sure there will be _____ (fewer / less) accidents, too.
   A: That's true.

2 Indirect questions from Wh-questions page 11

■ Indirect questions are often polite requests for information. *Can you tell me how much this magazine costs?* sounds more polite than *How much does this magazine cost?*

Complete the conversation with indirect questions.

1. **A:** Excuse me. Can you _tell me where the post office is_____?
   B: Yes, of course. The post office is on the next corner.

2. **A:** And could you _____?
   B: You can find a really good restaurant on Central Avenue.

3. **A:** OK. Do you _____?
   B: Yes. The restaurant is called Giorgio's.

4. **A:** Thanks. Can you _____?
   B: Yes. They serve Italian food.

5. **A:** Oh, good! Do you _____?
   B: It opens at 5:00. Tell them Joe sent you!
   A: OK, Joe. Thanks for everything! Bye now.

1 Evaluations and comparisons page 17

> ■ In evaluations, *enough* goes after adjectives and before nouns.
>
> ■ adjective + *enough*: This house isn't **bright enough**. (NOT: This house isn't ~~enough bright~~.
>
> ■ noun + *enough*: This house doesn't have **enough light**. (NOT: This house doesn't have ~~light enough~~.)

A Read each situation. Then write two sentences describing the problem, one sentence with *not . . . enough* and one with *too*.

1. Our family needs a big house. This house is very small.
   a. _This house isn't big enough for us._
   b. _This house is too small for us._
2. We want to live on a quiet street. This street is very noisy.
   a. _____
   b. _____
3. We need three bedrooms. This house has only two.
   a. _____
   b. _____
4. We want a spacious living room. This one is cramped.
   a. _____
   b. _____

B Rewrite the comparisons using *as . . . as*. Use *just* when possible.

1. My new apartment is smaller than my old one.
   My new apartment isn't as large as my old one.
2. This neighborhood is safer than my old one.

   _____
3. This apartment has a lot of privacy. My old one did, too.

   _____
4. My rent is reasonable now. It was very high before.

   _____

2 Wish page 20

> ■ Use *could* (the past of *can*) and *would* (the past of *will*) with *wish*: **I can't** move right now, but I wish I **could**. My landlord **won't** paint my apartment, but I wish he **would**.

Match the problems with the wishes.

1. My house isn't very nice.   _c_   a. I wish I could find a good roommate.
2. It costs a lot to live here.   ____   b. I wish he'd return my calls.
3. My landlord won't call me back.   ____   c. I wish it were more attractive.
4. I have noisy neighbors.   ____   d. I wish I could afford a car.
5. I don't like living alone.   ____   e. I wish their music weren't so loud.
6. The buses don't run very often.   ____   f. I wish it weren't so expensive.

1 Simple past vs. present perfect page 23

> ■ Use the simple past – not the present perfect – when you say when an event ended:
> I had sushi last night. (NOT: I've had sushi last night.)

Complete the conversations. Choose the best forms.

1. A: What _____ (did you have / have you had) for dinner last night?

   B: I _____ (tried / have tried) Indian food for the first time. _____ (Did you ever have / Have you ever had) it?

   A: A friend and I _____ (ate / have eaten) at an Indian restaurant just last week. It _____ (was / has been) delicious!

2. A: _____ (Did you ever take / Have you ever taken) a cooking class?

   B: No, I _____ (didn't / haven't). How about you?

   A: I _____ (took / have taken) a few classes. My last class _____ (was / has been) in December. We _____ (learned / have learned) how to make some wonderful Spanish dishes.

3. A: I _____ (watched / have watched) a great cooking show on TV yesterday.

   B: Really? I _____ (never saw / have never seen) a cooking show. _____ (Was it / Has it been) boring?

   A: No, it _____ (wasn't / hasn't). It _____ (was / has been) very interesting!

2 Sequence adverbs page 25

> ■ *Then, next,* and *after that* mean the same. *First* comes first, and *finally* comes last; you can use the other adverbs in any order: **First,** put some water in a pan. **Then/Next/After that,** put the eggs in the water. **Finally,** boil the eggs for 7 minutes.

Unscramble the steps in this recipe for hamburgers. Then write the steps in order.

salt and pepper   add   in the bowl   to the meat   then

_____ : _____

2 pounds of chopped beef   put in a bowl   first,

  Step 1   : First, put 2 pounds of chopped beef in a bowl.

put   the burgers   in a pan   finally,   and cook for 10 minutes

_____ : _____

next,   the meat   and the salt and pepper   mix   together

_____ : _____

into four burgers   after that,   with your hands   form the meat

_____ : _____

UNIT 5

1 Future with *be going to* and *will* page 31

> ■ Use the base form of the verb – not the infinitive (*to* + base form) – with *will*:
> I think **I'll go** to Hawaii next winter. (NOT: I think I'll ~~to~~ go to Hawaii next winter.)
>
> ■ Use *be going to* – not *will* – when you know something is going to happen:
> Look at those black clouds. It**'s going to** rain. (NOT: It ~~will~~ rain.)

Complete the conversation with the correct form of *be going to* or *will* and the verbs in parentheses.

A: It's Friday – at last! What _are you going to do_ (do) this weekend?

B: I'm not sure. I'm really tired, so I probably _____ (not do) anything exciting. Maybe I _____ (see) a movie on Saturday. How about you? How _____ (spend) your weekend?

A: My wife and I _____ (do) some work on our house. We _____ (paint) the living room on Saturday. On Sunday, we _____ (clean) all the rugs.

B: _____ (do) anything fun?

A: Oh, I think we _____ (have) a lot of fun. We like working around the house. And Sunday's my birthday, so we _____ (have) dinner at my favorite Italian restaurant.

B: Now that sounds like fun!

2 Modals for necessity and suggestion page 33

> ■ Some modals for necessity and suggestion are stronger than others.
> Weak (for advice or an opinion): *should, ought to*
> Stronger (for a warning): *had better*
> Strongest (for an obligation): *must, need to, have to*

Choose the correct word or words to complete the advice to travelers.

1. You _____ (must / should) show identification at the airport. They won't allow you on a plane without an official ID.

2. Your ID _____ (needs to / ought to) have a picture of you on it. It's required.

3. The picture of you _____ (has to / ought to) be recent. They won't accept an old photo.

4. Travelers _____ (must / should) get to the airport at least two hours before their flight. It's not a good idea to get there later than that.

5. All travelers _____ (have to / had better) go through airport security. It's necessary for passenger safety.

6. Many airlines don't serve food, so passengers on long flights probably _____ (must / ought to) buy something to eat at the airport.

1 Two-part verbs; *will* for responding to requests `page 37`

- Two-part verbs are verb + particle.
- If the object of a two-part verb is a noun, the noun can come before or after the particle: **Take out** the trash./**Take** the trash **out**.
- If the object is a pronoun, the pronoun must come before the particle: **Take** it **out**. (NOT: Take ~~out it~~.)

Write conversations. First, rewrite the request given by changing the position of the particle. Then write a response to the request using *it* or *them*.

1. Put away your clothes, please.
    A: _Put your clothes away, please._
    B: _OK. I'll put them away._

2. Turn the lights on, please.
    A: _____
    B: _____

3. Please turn your music down.
    A: _____
    B: _____

4. Clean up the kitchen, please.
    A: _____
    B: _____

5. Turn off your phone, please.
    A: _____
    B: _____

2 Requests with modals and *Would you mind . . . ?* `page 39`

- Use the base form of the verb – not the infinitive (*to* + base form) – with the modals *can, could,* and *would:* **Could** you **get** me a sandwich? (NOT: Could you ~~to~~ get me a sandwich?)
- Requests with modals and *Would you mind . . . ?* are polite – even without *please*. *Can you get me a sandwich?* sounds much more polite than *Get me a sandwich*.

Change these sentences to polite requests. Use the words in parentheses.

1. Bring in the mail. (could)
    Could you bring in the mail?

2. Put your shoes by the door. (would you mind)
    _____

3. Don't leave dishes in the sink. (would you mind)
    _____

4. Change the TV channel. (can)
    _____

5. Don't play ball inside. (would you mind)
    _____

6. Clean up your mess. (would you mind)
    _____

7. Put away the clean towels. (can)
    _____

8. Pick up your things. (could)
    _____

1 Infinitives and gerunds for uses and purposes page 45

- Sentences with infinitives and gerunds mean the same: *I use my cell phone to send text messages* means the same as *I use my cell phone for sending text messages.*
- Use a gerund – not an infinitive – after *for*: Satellites are used **for studying** weather. (NOT: Satellites are used for ~~to study~~ weather.)

Read each sentence about a technology item. Write two sentences about the item's use and purpose. Use the information in parentheses.

1. My sister's car has a built-in GPS system. (She use / get directions)
   a. *She uses the GPS system to get directions.*
   b. *She uses the GPS system for getting directions.*
2. I love my new smartphone. (I use / take pictures)
   a. _____
   b. _____
3. That's a flash drive. (You use / back up files)
   a. _____
   b. _____
4. My little brother wants his own laptop. (He would only use / watch movies and play games)
   a. _____
   b. _____
5. I'm often on my computer all day long. (I use / shop online and do research)
   a. _____
   b. _____

2 Imperatives and infinitives for giving suggestions page 47

- With imperatives and infinitives, *not* goes before – not after – *to*: Try **not to** talk too long. (NOT: Try ~~to not~~ talk too long.)

Rewrite the sentences as suggestions. Use the words in parentheses.

1. When you go to the movies, turn off your phone. (don't forget)
   When you go to the movies, don't forget to turn off your phone.
2. Don't talk on the phone when you're in an elevator. (try)
   _____
3. Don't eat or drink anything when you're at the computer. (be sure)
   _____
4. Clean your computer screen and keyboard once a week. (remember)
   _____
5. Don't use your tablet outside when it's raining. (make sure)
   _____
6. When the bell rings to start class, put your music player away! (be sure)
   _____

1 Relative clauses of time page 51

■ Relative clauses with *when* describe the word *time* or a noun that refers to a period of time, such as *day, night, month,* and *year.*

Combine the two sentences using *when.*

1. Thanksgiving is a holiday. Entire families get together.
   Thanksgiving is a holiday when entire families get together.

2. It's a wonderful time. People give thanks for the good things in their lives.
   _____

3. It's a day. Everyone eats much more than usual.
   _____

4. I remember one particular year. The whole family came to our house.
   _____

5. That year was very cold. It snowed all Thanksgiving day.
   _____

6. I remember another thing about that Thanksgiving. My brother and I baked eight pies.
   _____

2 Adverbial clauses of time page 54

■ An adverbial clause of time can come before or after the main clause. When it comes before the main clause, use a comma. When it comes after the main clause, don't use a comma: When Ginny and Tom met, they both lived in San Juan. BUT: Ginny and Tom met when they both lived in San Juan.

■ The words *couple* and *family* are collective nouns. They are usually used with singular verbs: When a couple **gets** married, they often receive gifts. (NOT: When a couple ~~get~~ married, they often receive gifts.)

Combine the two sentences using the adverb in parentheses. Write one sentence with the adverbial clause before the main clause and another with the adverbial clause after the main clause.

1. Students complete their courses. A school holds a graduation ceremony. (after)
   a. After students complete their courses, a school holds a graduation ceremony.
   b. A school holds a graduation ceremony after students complete their courses.

2. Students gather to put on robes and special hats. The ceremony starts. (before)
   a. _____
   b. _____

3. Music plays. The students walk in a line to their seats. (when)
   a. _____
   b. _____

4. School officials and teachers make speeches. Students get their diplomas. (after)
   a. _____
   b. _____

5. The ceremony is finished. Students throw their hats into the air and cheer. (when)
   a. _____
   b. _____

UNIT 9

1 Time contrasts page 59

> ■ Use the modal *might* to say something is possible in the present or future: In a few years, movie theaters **might** not exist. = In a few years, maybe movie theaters won't exist.

Complete the conversation with the correct form of the verbs in parentheses. Use the past, present, or future tense.

A: I saw a fascinating program last night. It talked about the past, the present, and the future.

B: What kinds of things did it describe?

A: Well, for example, the normal work week in the 19th century _____ (be) over 60 hours. Nowadays, many people _____ (work) around 40 hours a week.

B: Well, that sounds like progress.

A: You're right. But on the show, they said that most people _____ (work) fewer hours in the future. They also talked about the way we shop. These days, many of us _____ (shop) online. In the old days, there _____ (be) no supermarkets, so people _____ (have to) go to a lot of different stores. In the future, people _____ (do) all their shopping from their phones.

B: I don't believe that.

A: Me neither. What about cars? Do you think people _____ (still drive) cars a hundred years from now?

B: What did they say on the show?

A: They said that before the car, people _____ (walk) everywhere. Nowadays, we _____ (drive) everywhere. And that _____ (not change).

2 Conditional sentences with *if* clauses page 61

> ■ The *if* clause can come before or after the main clause: **If** I change my eating habits, I'll feel healthier./I'll feel healthier **if** I change my eating habits. Always use a comma when the *if* clause comes before the main clause.
>
> ■ For the future of *can*, use *will be able to*: If you save some money, you**'ll be able to buy** a car. (NOT: . . . you'll can buy a car.)
>
> ■ For the future of *must*, use *will have to*: If you get a dog, you**'ll have to take care** of it. (NOT: . . . you'll must take care of it.)

Complete the sentences with the correct form of the verbs in parentheses.

1. If you _____*exercise*_____ (exercise) more often, you'_ll feel_____ (feel) more energetic.

2. If you _____ (join) a gym, exercise _____ (become) part of your routine.

3. You _____ (not have to) worry about staying in shape if you _____ (work out) three or four times a week.

4. If you _____ (ride) a bike or _____ (run) a few times a week, you _____ (lose) weight and _____ (gain) muscle.

5. You _____ (sleep) better at night if you _____ (exercise) regularly.

6. If you _____ (start) exercising, you _____ (might/not have) as many colds and other health problems.

1 Gerunds; short responses page 65

> ■ Short responses with *so* and *neither* are ways of agreeing. The subject (noun or pronoun) comes after the verb: I love traveling. So **do I**. (NOT: So ~~I do~~.) I can't stand talking on the phone. Neither **can I**. (NOT: Neither ~~I can~~.)

Rewrite A's line using the words given. Then write an agreement for B.

1. I hate working alone. (can't stand)
   A: <u>I can't stand working alone.</u>
   B: <u>Neither can I.</u>

2. I don't like reading about politics or politicians. (interested in)
   A: _____
   B: _____

3. I can solve problems. (good at)
   A: _____
   B: _____

4. I have no problem with working on weekends. (don't mind)
   A: _____
   B: _____

5. I love learning new things. (enjoy)
   A: _____
   B: _____

6. I can't develop new ideas. (not good at)
   A: _____
   B: _____

2 Clauses with *because* page 68

> ■ Clauses with *because* answer the question "Why?" or "Why not?": Why would you make a good flight attendant? I'd make a good flight attendant **because** I love traveling, and I'm good with people.

Complete the sentences with *because* and the phrases in the box.

> I don't write very well
> I love arguing with people
> I'm afraid of flying
> ✓ I'm much too short
> I'm not patient enough to work with kids
> I'm really bad with numbers

1. I could never be a fashion model <u>because I'm much too short</u> .
2. I wouldn't make a good high school teacher _____ .
3. I wouldn't want to be a flight attendant _____ .
4. I could never be an accountant _____ .
5. I would make a bad journalist _____ .
6. I'd be an excellent lawyer _____ .

1 Passive with *by* (simple past) <u>page 73</u>

- The past participle of regular verbs is the same form as the simple past: Leonardo da Vinci **painted** *Mona Lisa* in 1503. *Mona Lisa* was **painted** by Leonardo da Vinci in 1503.

- The past participle of some – but not all – irregular verbs is the same form as the simple past: The Egyptians **built** the Pyramids. The Pyramids were **built** by the Egyptians. BUT Jane Austen **wrote** *Pride and Prejudice*. *Pride and Prejudice* was **written** by Jane Austen.

Change the sentences from active to passive with *by*.

1. The Chinese invented paper around 100 C.E.
   Paper was invented by the Chinese around 100 C.E.

2. Marie Curie discovered radium in 1898.
   _____

3. Dr. Felix Hoffmann made the first aspirin in 1899.
   _____

4. Tim Berners-Lee developed the World Wide Web in 1989.
   _____

5. William Herschel identified the planet Uranus in 1781.
   _____

6. Georges Bizet wrote the opera *Carmen* in the 1870s.
   _____

2 Passive without *by* (simple present) <u>page 75</u>

- When it is obvious or not important who is doing the action, don't use a *by* phrase: Both the Olympics and the World Cup are held every four years. (NOT: . . . are held ~~by people~~ . . .)

Complete the information with *is* or *are* and the past participle of the verbs in the box.

base	know
export	✓ speak
import	use

1. Portuguese – not Spanish – <u>is spoken</u> in Brazil.

2. Diamonds and gold from South Africa _____ by countries all over the world.

3. The U.S. dollar _____ in Puerto Rico.

4. Colombia _____ for its delicious coffee.

5. Many electronic products _____ by Japan and South Korea. It's an important industry for these two countries.

6. The economy in many island countries, such as Jamaica, _____ on tourism.

UNIT 12

1 Past continuous vs. simple past page 79

■ When the past continuous is used with the simple past, both actions happened at the same time, but the past continuous action started earlier. The simple past action interrupted the past continuous action.

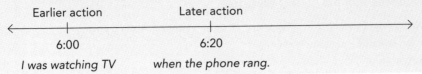

Earlier action   Later action

6:00   6:20

I was watching TV   *when the phone rang.*

Complete the conversations with the correct form of the verbs in parentheses. Use the past continuous or the simple past.

1. A: What happened to you?
   B: I _____fell_____ (fall) while I _____was jogging_____ (jog) in the park.

2. A: _____ you _____ (see) the storm yesterday?
   B: Yes! It _____ (start) while I _____ (drive) to work.

3. A: We finally _____ (move) to a larger apartment.
   B: That's good. I know you _____ (live) in a tiny place when your daughter _____ (be) born.

4. A: My sister _____ (have) a bad accident. She _____ (hurt) her back when she _____ (lift) weights at the gym.
   B: That _____ (happen) to me last year, but I _____ (not lift) weights. I _____ (take) a boxing class, and I _____ (trip).

2 Present perfect continuous page 81

■ The same time expressions used with the present perfect can also be used with the present perfect continuous. Don't confuse *for* and *since*: I've been working here **for** 5 years./I've been working here **since** 2010.

Complete the sentences with the present perfect continuous form of the verbs in parentheses.

1. A: What _____have_____ you _____been doing_____ all day?
   B: I _____ (clean) the house, and Peter _____ (watch) TV. He _____ (not feel) very well lately.
   A: How _____ you _____ (feel) these days?
   B: I _____ (feel) great. I _____ (not eat) any junk food, and I _____ (exercise) a lot. I _____ (take) really good care of myself.

2. A: How long _____ you and Joe _____ (date)?
   B: We _____ (go out) together for almost a year. Can you believe it?
   A: Maya and I _____ (date) for even longer. I think it's time to get married. We _____ (talk) about it a lot lately.
   B: Joe and I _____ (not talk) about marriage, but I _____ (think) about it.

1 Participles as adjectives   page 87

> ■ Adjectives ending in *–ing* are present participles. They are things that *cause* a feeling.
> Adjectives ending in *–ed* are past participles. They *express* the feeling.

Complete the sentences with the correct participle.

1. Why are we watching this _____boring_____ movie? Aren't you _____bored_____ with it? (boring / bored)

2. Kristen Stewart is an _____ actress. I'm _____ by her talent. (amazing / amazed)

3. Are you _____ in computer-generated special effects? The latest 3-D movies are very _____. (interesting / interested)

4. I had an _____ experience the last time I went to the movies. I started to cough, and I couldn't stop. I was really _____. (embarrassing / embarrassed)

5. Julie and I saw an Italian comedy yesterday. I found it _____, but Julie didn't seem very _____ by it. (amusing / amused)

6. Oh, I'm really _____ with Jeremy right now. He took me to the most _____ movie last night. I wanted to walk out after half an hour, but he wouldn't leave! (disgusting / disgusted)

7. Do you think sci-fi movie directors make their films _____ intentionally? I get so _____ by the complicated storylines and weird characters. (confusing / confused)

8. I think that great books make great movies. If I find a book _____, I'm usually _____ by the movie, too. (fascinating / fascinated)

2 Relative pronouns for people and things   page 89

> ■ Relative clauses give information about nouns. Don't use a personal pronoun in a relative clause: He's an actor **that** won two Oscars. (NOT: He's an actor <u>that he won two Oscars</u>.)

Complete the conversations. Use *that* for things and *who* for people.

A: How did you like the movie last night? Was it any good?

B: It wasn't bad, but it's not the kind of movie _____that_____ makes you think. I like films _____ have a strong message and interesting storylines.

A: How about the acting? Did you like the actors _____ star in it?

B: Jessica Biel is pretty good, actually.

A: Oh, she's that beautiful actress _____ is married to Justin Timberlake.

B: Justin who? Who's that?

A: Oh, you know him. He's the one _____ was in the band 'NSync years ago. It was a "boy band" _____ was popular in the 1990s.

B: I remember 'NSync, but I don't remember the names of the guys _____ were in the band.

A: Well, I loved Justin Timberlake when I was a kid. And he's not a bad actor. Did you see the movie *The Social Network*?

B: I did see that. It's about the guys _____ started Facebook, right? I didn't realize Justin Timberlake was in it. Now I'll have to see it again!

1 Modals and adverbs page 93

■ Use the modals *might/may*, *could*, and *must* and the adverbs *maybe/perhaps*, *probably*, and *definitely* when you aren't sure about what you're saying:

Slight possibility: *might, may, maybe, perhaps*

Possibility: *could, probably*

Strong possibility: *must, definitely*

Rewrite each sentence in different ways, using the words in parentheses.

1. Perhaps it means she doesn't agree with you.
   a. (maybe) <u>Maybe it means she doesn't agree with you.</u>
   b. (might) _____
   c. (may) _____

2. That gesture could mean, "Come here."
   a. (probably) _____

3. That almost definitely means he doesn't understand you.
   a. (must) _____

2 Permission, obligation, and prohibition page 95

■ Use *have/has* with *got to*: You**'ve got to** keep the door closed. (NOT: You ~~got to~~ keep the door closed.)

Complete the conversations with the words and phrases in the box.
Use each word or phrase only once.

are allowed to	✓ can't
aren't allowed to	have to
can	have got to

1. **A:** Oh, no! That sign says, "No fishing." That means we
   _____<u>can't</u>_____ fish here.
   B: You're right. We _____ go somewhere else to fish. I
   think you _____ fish in the pond on Cedar Road. Let's go
   there.

2. **A:** What does that sign mean?
   B: It means bad news for us. It means you _____ bring dogs
   to the beach. We'd better take Buddy home.

3. **A:** Please don't leave your garbage here. You _____ put it
   in the trash room down the hall. That's one of the building's rules.
   B: I'm really sorry.

4. **A:** You _____ put your bike in the bike room downstairs, if
   you want. It's much safer than locking it up outside.
   B: Oh, that's great! I'll do that. I didn't know about the bike room.

UNIT 15

1 Unreal conditional sentences with *if* clauses [page 101]

■ The clauses in unreal conditional sentences can come in either order. Don't use a comma when the *if* clause comes second: **If** I won the lottery, I'd share the money with my family./I'd share the money with my family **if** I won the lottery.

Complete the conversation with the correct form of the verbs in parentheses.

1. **A:** If a friend _____ (ask) to borrow some money, what _____ you _____ (say)?

   B: Well, if I _____ (have) any extra money that month, I _____ probably _____ (give) it to her.

2. **A:** What _____ you _____ (do) if someone _____ (give) you a million dollars?

   B: Hmm, I'm not sure. I _____ (buy) a lot of nice clothes and jewelry, or I _____ (spend) some and _____ (give) some away, or I _____ (put) it all in the bank.

3. **A:** If you _____ (think) a friend was doing something dangerous, _____ you _____ (say) something to him, or _____ you _____ (keep) quiet?

   B: I _____ definitely _____ (talk) to my friend about it.

4. **A:** What _____ you _____ (do) if you _____ (have) a problem with your boss?

   B: That's a hard one. If that _____ (happen), I _____ (talk) to the human resources department about it, or I _____ just _____ (sit down) with my boss and _____ (talk) about the situation.

2 Past modals [page 103]

■ Use *should have* and *would have* for all subjects. They don't change form: He **should have called** sooner. (NOT: He should has called sooner.)

Read the situations. Use the words in parentheses to write opinions and suggestions.

1. My neighbor had a party last night. It was very loud, so I called the police.
   (you / speak / to your neighbor first)
   You should have spoken to your neighbor first.

2. The mail carrier put someone else's mail in my box. I threw it away.
   (you / write / a note and leave / the mail in your box)
   _____

3. My sister asked if I liked her new dress. It didn't look good on her, but I said it did.
   (I / tell her the truth)
   _____

4. A salesperson called me last night. I didn't want to buy anything, but I let her talk to me for almost half an hour.
   (I / tell her I'm not interested / hang up)
   _____

1 Reported speech: requests page 107

■ When a reported request is negative, *not* comes before *to*: Don't leave your wet towel on the floor. She told me **not to leave** my wet towel on the floor.
(NOT: She told me ~~to not~~ leave my wet towel on the floor.)

Harry's roommate, Tyler, is making some requests. Read what Tyler said to Harry. Write the requests with the verbs in parentheses and reported speech.

1. "Can you put away your clean clothes?" (ask)
   Tyler asked Harry to put away his clean clothes.

2. "Meet me in the cafeteria at school at noon." (say)

3. "Don't leave your shoes in the living room." (tell)

4. "Hang up your wet towels." (say)

5. "Could you stop using my phone?" (ask)

6. "Make your bed on weekdays." (tell)

7. "Don't eat my food." (say)

8. "Be a better roommate!" (tell)

2 Reported speech: statements page 109

■ The tense of the introducing verb (*ask, say, tell*) changes when the sentence is reported: simple present → simple past; present continuous → past continuous; present perfect → past perfect. Modals change, too: *can* → *could*; *will* → *would*; *may* → *might*.

Bill and Kathy are having a barbecue on Sunday. They're upset because a lot of their friends can't come. Read what their friends said. Change the excuses into reported speech.

1. Lori: "I have to visit my grandparents that day."
   Lori said that she had to visit her grandparents that day.

2. Mario: "I'm going to a play on Sunday."

3. Julia: "I've promised to take my brother to the movies that day."

4. Daniel: "I can't come. I have to study for a huge exam on Monday."

5. The neighbors: "We'll be out of town all weekend."

6. Alice: "I may have to babysit my nephew."

Grammar plus answer key

Unit 1

1 Past tense
2. did you grow up/are you from
3. Did you live
4. When did you move
5. did you go
6. when did you come/get

2 Used to
1. A: Hey, Dad. What kinds of clothes **did you use to** wear – you know, when you were a kid?
   B: Oh, we **used to** wear jeans and T-shirts – like you kids do now.
   A: Really? **Did** Mom **use to** dress like that, too?
   B: No, not really. She never **used to** like wearing pants. She always **used to** wear skirts and dresses.
2. A: **Did** you **use to** play a sport when you were a kid?
   B: Well, I **used to** be a swimmer. My sister and I **used to** swim on a team.
   A: Wow, that's cool! Were you good?
   B: Yeah. I **used to** win gold medals all the time. And my sister **used to** be the fastest swimmer on the team.

Unit 2

1 Expressions of quantity
1. A: There's **too much** traffic in this city. There should be **fewer** cars downtown.
   B: The problem is there **isn't** enough public transportation.
   A: You're right. We should have more **buses**. There **aren't** enough of them during rush hour.
2. A: How do you like your new neighborhood?
   B: It's terrible, actually. There's **too much** noise and **too little** parking.
   A: That's too bad. There **aren't** enough parking spaces in my neighborhood either.
3. A: Did you hear about the changes to the city center? Starting next month, there will be more bicycle **lanes** and **less** street parking.
   B: That's good. There **is too much** pollution downtown. I'm sure there will be **fewer** accidents, too.
   A: That's true.

2 Indirect questions from *Wh*-questions
Answers may vary. Some possible answers:
2. And could you **tell me where I can find a good restaurant**?
3. Do you **know what the name of the restaurant is**?
4. Can you **tell me what type of food they serve**?
5. Do you **know what time the restaurant opens**?

Unit 3

1 Evaluations and comparisons
A
Answers may vary. Some possible answers:
2. This street isn't quiet enough./This street is too noisy.
3. This house doesn't have enough bedrooms./This house is too small for us./This house has too few bedrooms for us.
4. This living room isn't spacious enough./This living room doesn't have enough space./This living room is too cramped/small.

B
Answers may vary. Some possible answers:
2. My old neighborhood isn't as safe as this one.
3. This apartment has (just) as much privacy as my old one.
4. My rent isn't as high as it used to be.

2 Wish
2. f   3. b   4. e   5. a   6. d

Unit 4

1 Simple past vs. present perfect
1. A: What **did you have** for dinner last night?
   B: I **tried** Indian food for the first time. **Have you ever had** it?
   A: A friend and I **ate** at an Indian restaurant just last week. It **was** delicious!
2. A: **Have you ever taken** a cooking class?
   B: No, **I haven't**. How about you?
   A: I **have taken** a few classes. My last class **was** in December. We **learned** how to make some wonderful Spanish dishes.
3. A: I **watched** a great cooking show on TV yesterday.
   B: Really? I **have never seen** a cooking show. **Was it** boring?
   A: No, it **wasn't**. It **was** very interesting!

2 Sequence adverbs
Step 1: First, put 2 pounds of chopped beef in a bowl.
Step 2: Then add salt and pepper to the meat in the bowl.
Step 3: Next, mix the meat and the salt and pepper together.
Step 4: After that, form the meat into four burgers with your hands.
Step 5: Finally, put the burgers in a pan and cook for 10 minutes.

Unit 5

1 Future with *be going to* and *will*
B: I'm not sure. I'm really tired, so I probably **won't do** anything exciting. Maybe I'**ll see** a movie on Saturday. How about you? How **are you going to spend** your weekend?
A: My wife and I **are going to do** some work on our house. We**'re going to paint** the living room on Saturday. On Sunday, we**'re going to clean** all the rugs.
B: **Are(n't) you going to do** anything fun?
A: Oh, I think we'**ll have/'re going to have** a lot of fun. We like working around the house. And Sunday's my birthday, so we**'re going to have** dinner at my favorite Italian restaurant.
B: Now that sounds like fun!

2 Modals for necessity and suggestions
1. You **must** show identification at the airport. They won't allow you on a plane without an official ID.
2. Your ID **needs to** have a picture of you on it. It's required.
3. The picture of you **has to** be recent. They won't accept an old photo.
4. Travelers **should** get to the airport at least two hours before their flight. It's not a good idea to get there later than that.
5. All travelers **have to** go through airport security. It's necessary for passenger safety.
6. Many airlines don't serve food, so passengers on long flights probably **ought to** buy something to eat at the airport.

Unit 6

1 Two-part verbs; *will* for responding to requests
2. A: Turn on the lights, please.
   B: OK. I'll turn them on.
3. A: Please turn down your music.
   B: OK. I'll turn it down.
4. A: Clean the kitchen up, please.
   B: OK. I'll clean it up.
5. A: Turn your phone off, please.
   B: OK. I'll turn it off.

2 Requests with modals and *Would you mind . . . ?*
2. Would you mind putting your shoes by the door?
3. Would you mind not leaving dishes in the sink?
4. Can you change the TV channel?
5. Would you mind not playing ball inside?
6. Would you mind cleaning up your mess?
7. Can you put away the clean towels?
8. Could you pick up your things?

Unit 7

1 Infinitives and gerunds for uses and purposes
2. a. I use my smartphone/it to take pictures.
   b. I use my smartphone/it for taking pictures.
3. a. You use a flash drive/it to back up files.
   b. You use a flash drive/it for backing up files.
4. a. He would only use a laptop/it to watch movies and play games.
   b. He would only use a laptop/it for watching movies and playing games.
5. a. I use my computer/it to shop online and do research.
   b. I use my computer/it for shopping online and doing research.

2 Imperatives and infinitives for giving suggestions
2. Try not to talk on the phone when you're in an elevator.
3. Be sure not to eat or drink anything when you're at the computer.
4. Remember to clean your computer screen and keyboard once a week.
5. Make sure not to use your tablet outside when it's raining.
6. When the bell rings to start class, be sure to put your music player away!

Unit 8

1 Relative clauses of time
2. It's a wonderful time when people give thanks for the good things in their lives.
3. It's a day when everyone eats much more than usual.
4. I remember one particular year when the whole family came to our house.
5. That year was very cold when it snowed all Thanksgiving day.
6. I remember another thing about that Thanksgiving when my brother and I baked eight pies.

2 Adverbial clauses of time
2. a. Before the ceremony starts, students gather to put on robes and special hats.
   b. Students gather to put on robes and special hats before the ceremony starts.
3. a. When music plays, the students walk in a line to their seats.
   b. The students walk in a line to their seats when music plays.
4. a. After school officials and teachers make speeches, students get their diplomas.
   b. Students get their diplomas after school officials and teachers make speeches.
5. a. When the ceremony is finished, students throw their hats into the air and cheer.
   b. Students throw their hats into the air and cheer when the ceremony is finished.

Unit 9

1 Time contrasts
A: I saw a fascinating program last night. It talked about the past, the present, and the future.
B: What kinds of things did it describe?
A: Well, for example, the normal work week in the 19th century **was/used to be** over 60 hours. Nowadays, many people **work/are working** around 40 hours a week.
B: Well, that sounds like progress.
A: You're right. But on the show, they said that most people **will work/might work** fewer hours in the future. They also talked about the way we shop. These days, many of us **shop** online. In the old days, there **were** no supermarkets, so people **had to go/used to have to go** to a lot of different stores. In the future, people **will do/might do/are going to do** all their shopping from their phones.
B: I don't believe that.
A: Me neither. What about cars? Do you think people **will still drive/are still going to drive** cars a hundred years from now?
B: What did they say on the show?
A: They said that before the car, people **walked/used to walk** everywhere. Nowadays, we **drive** everywhere. And that **won't change/isn't going to change/'s not going to change.**

2 Conditional sentences with if clauses
2. If you **join** a gym, exercise **will become** part of your routine.
3. You **won't have to** worry about staying in shape if you **work out** three or four times a week.
4. If you **ride** a bike or **run** a few times a week, you'**ll lose** weight and **gain** muscle.
5. You'**ll sleep** better at night if you **exercise** regularly.
6. If you **start** exercising, you **might not have** as many colds and other health problems.

Unit 10

1 Gerunds; short responses
2. A: I'm not interested in reading about politics or politicians.
   B: Neither am I.
3. A: I'm good at solving problems.
   B: So am I.
4. A: I don't mind working on weekends.
   B: Neither do I.
5. A: I enjoy learning new things.
   B: So do I.
6. A: I'm not good at developing new ideas.
   B: Neither am I.

2 Clauses with because
2. I wouldn't make a good high school teacher **because I'm not patient enough to work with kids**.
3. I wouldn't want to be a flight attendant **because I'm afraid of flying**.
4. I could never be an accountant **because I'm really bad with numbers**.
5. I would make a bad journalist **because I don't write very well**.
6. I'd be an excellent lawyer **because I love arguing with people**.

Unit 11

1 Passive with by (simple past)
2. Radium was discovered by Marie Curie in 1898.
3. The first aspirin was made by Dr. Felix Hoffmann in 1899.
4. The World Wide Web was developed by Tim Berners-Lee in 1989.
5. The planet Uranus was identified in 1781 by William Herschel.
6. The opera *Carmen* was written by Georges Bizet in the 1870s.

2 Passive without by (simple present)
2. Diamonds and gold from South Africa **are imported** by countries all over the world.
3. The U.S. dollar **is used** in Puerto Rico.
4. Colombia **is known** for its delicious coffee.
5. Many electronic products **are exported** by Japan and Korea. It's an important industry for these two countries.
6. The economy in many island countries, such as Jamaica, **is based** on tourism.

Unit 12

1 Past continuous vs. simple past
2. A: **Did** you **see** the storm yesterday?
   B: Yes! It **started** while I **was driving** to work.
3. A: We finally **moved** to a larger apartment.
   B: That's good. I know you **were living** in a tiny place when your daughter **was** born.
4. A: My sister **had** a bad accident. She **hurt** her back when she **was lifting** weights at the gym.
   B: That **happened** to me last year, but I **wasn't lifting** weights. I **was taking** a boxing class, and I **tripped**.

2 Present perfect continuous
1. A: What **have** you **been doing** all day?
   B: I'**ve been cleaning** the house, and Peter **has been watching** TV. He **hasn't been feeling** very well lately.
   A: How **have** you **been feeling** these days?
   B: I'**ve been feeling** great. I **haven't been eating** any junk food, and I'**ve been exercising** a lot. I'**ve been taking** really good care of myself.

2. A: How long **have** you and Joe **been dating**?
   B: We**'ve been going out** together for almost a year. Can you believe it?
   A: Maya and I **have been dating** for even longer. I think it's time to get married. We**'ve been talking** about it a lot lately.
   B: Joe and I **haven't been talking** about marriage, but I**'ve been thinking** about it.

Unit 13

1 Participles as adjectives

2. Kristen Stewart is an **amazing** actress. I'm **amazed** by her talent.
3. Are you **interested** in computer-generated special effects? The latest 3-D movies are very **interesting**.
4. I had an **embarrassing** experience the last time I went to the movies. I started to cough, and I couldn't stop. I was really **embarrassed**.
5. Julie and I saw an Italian comedy yesterday. I found it **amusing**, but Julie didn't seem very **amused** by it.
6. Oh, I'm really **disgusted** with Jeremy right now. He took me to the most **disgusting** movie last night. I wanted to walk out after half an hour, but he wouldn't leave!
7. Do you think sci-fi movie directors make their films **confusing** intentionally? I get so **confused** by the complicated storylines and weird characters.
8. I think that great books make great movies. If I find a book **fascinating**, I'm usually **fascinated** by the movie, too.

2 Relative pronouns for people and things

A: How did you like the movie last night? Was it any good?
B: It wasn't bad, but it's not the kind of movie **that** makes you think. I like films **that** have a strong message and interesting storylines.
A: How about the acting? Did you like the actors **who** star in it?
B: Jessica Biel is pretty good, actually.
A: Oh, she's that beautiful actress **who** is married to Justin Timberlake.
B: Justin who? Who's that?
A: Oh, you know him. He's the one **who** was in the band 'NSync years ago. It was a "boy band" **that** was popular in the 1990s.
B: I remember 'NSync, but I don't remember the names of the guys **who** were in the band.
A: Well, I loved Justin Timberlake when I was a kid. And he's not a bad actor. Did you see the movie *The Social Network*?
B: I did see that. It's about the guys **who** started Facebook, right? I didn't realize Justin Timberlake was in it. Now I'll have to see it again!

Unit 14

1 Modals and adverbs

1. a. Maybe it means she doesn't agree with you.
   b. It might mean she doesn't agree with you.
   c. It may mean she doesn't agree with you.
2. a. That gesture probably means, "Come here."
3. a. That must mean he doesn't understand you.

2 Permission, obligation, and prohibition

1. A: Oh, no! That sign says, "No fishing." That means we **can't** fish here.
   B: You're right. We**'ve got to/have to** go somewhere else to fish. I think you**'re allowed to/can** fish in the pond on Cedar Road. Let's go there.
2. A: What does that sign mean?
   B: It means bad news for us. It means you **aren't allowed to** bring dogs to the beach. We'd better take Buddy home.
3. A: Please don't leave your garbage here. You**'ve got to/ have to** put it in the trash room down the hall. That's one of the building's rules.
   B: I'm really sorry.
4. A: You **can** put your bike in the bike room downstairs, if you want. It's much safer than locking it up outside.
   B: Oh, that's great! I'll do that. I didn't know about the bike room.

Unit 15

1 Unreal conditional sentences with *if* clauses

1. A: If a friend **asked** to borrow some money, what **would** you **say**?
   B: Well, if I **had** any extra money that month, I **would** probably **give** it to her.
2. A: What **would/could** you **do** if someone **gave** you a million dollars?
   B: Hmm, I'm not sure. I **could/might buy** a lot of nice clothes and jewelry, or I **could/might spend** some and **give** some away, or I **could/might put** it all in the bank.
3. A: If you **thought** a friend was doing something dangerous, **would** you **say** something to him, or **would** you **keep** quiet?
   B: I **would** definitely **talk** to my friend about it.
4. A: What **would** you **do** if you **had** a problem with your boss?
   B: That's a hard one. If that **happened**, I **might/could talk** to the human resources department about it, or I **might/ could** just **sit down** with my boss and **talk** about the situation.

2 Past modals

2. You should have written a note and left the mail in your box.
3. I would have told her the truth.
4. I would have told her I wasn't interested and hung up (the phone).

Unit 16

1 Reported speech: requests

2. Tyler said to meet him in the cafeteria at school at noon.
3. Tyler told him/Harry not to leave his shoes in the living room.
4. Tyler said to hang up his wet towels.
5. Tyler asked him/Harry to stop using his/Tyler's phone.
6. Tyler told him/Harry to make his bed on weekdays.
7. Tyler said not to eat his/Tyler's food.
8. Tyler told him/Harry to be a better roommate.

2 Reported speech: statements

1. Lori said (that) she had to visit her grandparents that day. Lori told them (that) she had to visit her grandparents that day.
2. Mario said/told them (that) he was going to a play on Sunday.
3. Julia said/told them (that) she had promised to take her brother to the movies that day.
4. Daniel said/told them (that) he couldn't come because he had to study for a huge exam on Monday.
5. The neighbors said/told them (that) they would be out of town all weekend.
6. Alice said/told them (that) she might have to babysit her nephew.

Credits

The authors and publishers acknowledge the following sources of copyright material and are grateful for the permissions granted. While every effort has been made, it has not always been possible to identify the sources of all the material used, or to trace all copyright holders. If any omissions are brought to our notice, we will be happy to include the appropriate acknowledgements on reprinting and in the next update to the digital edition, as applicable.

Texts

Text on p. 13 adapted from "The 4 Happiest Cities on Earth" by Ford Cochran. Copyright © National Geographic Creative. Reproduced with permission; Mark Boyle for the text on p. 21 adapted from "Living without money changed my way of being." Reproduced with kind permission of Mark Boyle; Text on p. 41 adapted from "World's weirdest hotel requests and complaints" by James Teideman. Copyright © www.skyscanner.net. Reproduced with kind permission; Text on p. 83 adapted from "Deaf band 'Beethoven's Nightmare' feels the music" by Dennis McCarthy. Copyright © Los Angeles Daily News. Reproduced with permission.

Key: B = Below, BC = Below Centre, BL = Below Left, BR = Below Right, B/G = Background, C = Centre, CL = Centre Left, CR = Centre Right, L = Left, R = Right, T = Top, TC = Top Centre, TL = Top Left, TR = Top Right.

Illustrations

337 Jon (KJA Artists): 39, 92(B), 97; **Mark Duffi** : 18, 25(C), 37, 43(T); **Pablo Gallego** (Beehive Illustration): 43(B); **Thomas Girard** (Good Illustration): 2, 22, 41, 93; **John Goodwin** (Eye Candy Illustration): 40; **Daniel Gray**: 75, 118, 120; **Quino Marin** (The Organisation): 36, 80, 128; **Gavin Reece** (New Division): 58, 81, 119; **Paul Williams** (Sylvie Poggio Artists): 16, 114.

Photos

Back cover (woman with whiteboard): Jenny Acheson/Stockbyte/GettyImages; Back cover (whiteboard): Nemida/GettyImages; Back cover (man using phone): Betsie Van Der Meer/Taxi/GettyImages; Back cover (woman smiling): PeopleImages.com/DigitalVision/GettyImages; Back cover (name tag): Tetra Images/GettyImages; Back cover (handshake): David Lees/Taxi/GettyImages; p. v (TL): Hero Images/Getty Images; p. v (TR): Cultura RM Exclusive/dotdotred/Getty Images; p. v (CL): vitchanan/iStock/Getty Images Plus/Getty Images; p. v (CR): Svetlana Braun/iStock/Getty Images Plus/Getty Images; p. v (BL): Hero Images/Getty Images; p. v (BR): Cultura RM Exclusive/dotdotred/Getty Images; p. vi (Unit 1), p. 2 (header): Ekaterina Borner/Moment Open/Getty Images; p. 2 (TL): Juanmonino/E+/Getty Images; p. 2 (TR): Purestock/Getty Images; p. 6 (TR): GlobalStock/E+/Getty Images; p. 5 (T): JGI/Jamie Grill/Blend Images/Getty Images; p. 5 (T): Maskot/Maskot/Getty Images; p. 6 (CL): Alistair Berg/DigitalVision/Getty Images; p. 7 (TL): Bettmann/Getty Images; p. 7 (BR): Alberto Pizzoli/AFP/Getty Images; p. vi (Unit 2), p. 8 (header): Martin Polsson/Maskot/Getty Images; p. 8 (traffic jam): Roevin/Moment/Getty Images; p. 8 (green space): Yutthana Jantong/EyeEm/Getty Images; p. 8 (Ex 2a.a): Sergiy Serdyuk/Hemera/Getty Images Plus/Getty Images; p. 8 (Ex 2a.b): AvalancheZ/iStock/Getty Images Plus/Getty Images; p. 8 (Ex 2a.c): Peeterv/iStock/Getty Images Plus/Getty Images; p. 8 (microphone): Darryn van der Walt/Moment/Getty Images; p. 9: Kentaroo Tryman/Maskot/Getty Images; p. 10: arnaudbertrande/RooM/Getty Images; p. 11: Tim Bieber/Photodisc/Getty Images; p. 13 (photo 1): peder77/iStock/Getty Images Plus/Getty Images; p. 13 (photo 2): Sollina Images/The Image Bank/Getty Images; p. 13 (photo 3): Caiaimage/Paul Bradbury/Getty Images; p. 13 (photo 4): Jonathan Drake/Bloomberg/Getty Images; p. 14: Three Lions/Stringer/Getty Images; p. 15: Mark Edward Atkinson/Blend Images/Getty Images; p. vi (Unit 3), p. 16 (header): Hill Street Studios/Blend Images/Getty Images; p. 16 (BR): Lihee Avidan/Photonica World/Getty Images; p. 17 (L): Leren Lu/Taxi Japan/Getty Images; p. 17 (R): Aliyev Alexei Sergeevich/Blend Images/Getty Images; p. 18: Coneyl Jay/Stockbyte/Getty Images; p. 19 (T): laflor/iStock/Getty Images Plus/Getty Images; p. 19 (B): Westend61/Getty Images; p. 20: Jose Luis Pelaez Inc/Blend Images/Getty Images; p. 21: © Mark Boyle; p. vi (Unit 4), p. 22 (header): Yuri_Arcurs/DigitalVision/Getty Images; p. 22 (L): Anna Pustynnikova/iStock/Getty Images Plus/Getty Images; p. 22 (CL): John Ibarra Photography/Moment/Getty Images; p. 22 (CR): PuspaSwara/iStock/Getty Images Plus/Getty Images; p. 22 (R): trindade51/iStock/Getty Images Plus/Getty Images; p. 22 (B): David Stuart/Getty Images; p. 23: Dan Dalton/DigitalVision/Getty Images; p. 24 (TR): bdspn/iStock/Getty Images Plus/Getty Images; p. 24 (bake): Mark_KA/iStock/Getty Images Plus/Getty Images; p. 24 (boil): Dorling Kindersley/Getty Images; p. 24 (fry): Chris Everard/The Image Bank/Getty Images; p. 24 (grill): Dave Bradley Photography/The Image Bank/Getty Images; p. 24 (roast): Lew Robertson/Photographer's Choice/Getty Images; p. 24 (steam): Aberration Films Ltd/Science Photo Library/Getty Images; p. 25 (TR): Lauri Patterson/E+/Getty Images; p. 25 (photo 1): Simon Wheeler Ltd/Photolibrary/Getty Images; p. 25 (photo 2): jacktherabbit/iStock/Getty Images Plus/Getty Images; p. 25 (photo 3): Dave King/Dorling Kindersley/Getty Images; p. 25 (photo 4): Bruce James/StockFood Creative/Getty Images; p. 25 (photo 5): robdoss/iStock/Getty Images Plus/Getty Images; p. 26 (spaghetti): Lauri Patterson/E+/Getty Images; p. 26 (cookies): 4kodiak/E+/Getty Images; p. 26 (salsa): Douglas Johns/StockFood Creative/Getty Images; p. 26 (toast): DebbiSmirnoff/iStock/Getty Images Plus/Getty Images; p. 26 (popcorn): Michael Deuson/Photolibrary/Getty Images; p. 26 (CR): Plattform/Getty Images; p. 26 (BL): AD077/iStock/Getty Images Plus/Getty Images; p. 27 (TR): stevecoleimages/E+/Getty Images; p. 27 (BL): Lombardis Pizza of New York City; p. 29 (CR): Lauri Patterson/E+/Getty Images; p. 29 (BR): Echo/Cultura/Getty Images; p. vi (Unit 5), p. 30 (header): Hero Images/Getty Images; p. 30 (Ex 1: photo 1): Gary John Norman/Cultura Exclusive/Getty Images; p. 30 (Ex 1: photo 2): Yuri_Arcurs/DigitalVision/Getty Images; p. 30 (Ex 1: photo 3): LuckyBusiness/iStock/Getty Images Plus/Getty Images; p. 30 (Ex 1: photo 4): Yellow Dog Productions/The Image Bank/Getty Images; p. 30 (BR): AID/a.collectionRF/Getty Images; p. 31: Ed Freeman/The Image Bank/Getty Images; p. 33: AngiePhotos/E+/Getty Images; p. 34 (CR): John W Banagan/Photographer's Choice/Getty Images; p. 34 (BR): annebaek/iStock/Getty Images Plus/Getty Images; p. 35 (photo 1): Brian Bailey/The Image Bank/Getty Images; p. 35 (photo 2): Matteo Colombo/Moment/Getty Images; p. 35 (photo 3): Adam Woolfitt/robertharding/Getty Images; p. vi (Unit 6), p. 36 (header): B and G Images/Photographer's Choice/Getty Images; p. 36 (TL): Westend61/Getty Images; p. 38 (CR): Stockbyte/Getty Images; p. 38 (BR): DragonImages/iStock/Getty Images Plus/Getty Images; p. 42: Rudi Von Briel/Photolibrary/Getty Images; p. vi (Unit 7), p. 44 (header): anyaivanova/iStock/Getty Images Plus/Getty Images; p. 44 (TR): MixAll Studio/Blend Images/Getty Images; p. 45: monkeybusinessimages/iStock/Getty Images Plus/Getty Images; p. 46 (CR): scyther5/iStock/Getty Images Plus/Getty Images; p. 46 (BR): Michele Falzone/AWL Images/Getty Images; p. 47: Maskot/Getty Images; p. 48 (speaker): Atsadej0819/iStock/Getty Images Plus/Getty Images; p. 48 (GPS): Peter Dazeley/Photographer's Choice/Getty Images; p. 48 (flash drive): Westend61/Getty Images; p. 48 (smartphone): milindri/iStock/Getty Images Plus/Getty Images; p. 48 (ATM): Volodymyr Krasyuk/iStock/Getty Images Plus/Getty Images; p. 49: Daren Woodward/iStock/Getty Images Plus/Getty Images; p. vi (Unit 8), p. 50 (header): ferrantraite/E+/Getty Images; p. 50 (Saint Patrick's Day): Sachin Polassery/Moment Editorial/Getty Images; p. 50 (Day of the Dead): Darryl Leniuk/Photographer's Choice/Getty Images; p. 50 (Chinese New year): WILLIAM WEST/AFP/Getty Images; p. 50 (Thanksgiving): Kathryn Russell Studios/Photolibrary/Getty Images; p. 51 (L): Hero Images/Getty Images; p. 51 (C): JGI/Jamie Grill/Blend Images/Getty Images; p. 51 (R): Blend Images – JGI/Jamie Grill/Brand X Pictures/Getty Images; p. 52 (TL): altrendo images/Getty Images; p. 52 (CR): Thinkstock Images/Stockbyte/Getty Images; p. 52 (B): huzu1959/Moment Open/Getty Images; p. 53 (Julia): Tara Moore/Stone/Getty Images; p. 53 (Anusha): Carlina Teteris/Moment/Getty Images; p. 53 (TR): Blend Images/Getty Images; p. 54: Tetra Images/Getty Images; p. 55 (TL): oversnap/iStock/Getty Images Plus/Getty Images; p. 55 (BR): ruslan117/iStock/Getty Images Plus/Getty Images; p. 56 (CR): vgajic/iStock/Getty Images Plus/Getty Images; p. 57 (TL): Dezein/iStock/Getty Images Plus/Getty Images; p. 57 (TC): artpartner-images/Photographer's Choice/Getty Images; p. 57 (TR): André Rieck/EyeEmGetty Images; p. 57 (BR): Satoshi Kawase/Moment/Getty Images; p. vi (Unit 9), p. 58 (header): Artur Debat/Moment/Getty Images; p. 58 (TL): Michael Fresco/Evening Standard/Hulton Archive/Getty Images; p. 58 (TC): Car Culture/Car Culture ® Collection/Getty Images; p. 58 (TR): Javier Pierini/The Image Bank/Getty Images; p. 59: Hero Images/Getty Images; p. 60 (CR): Jordan Siemens/Iconica/Getty Images; p. 60 (BR): RoBeDeRo/E+/Getty Images; p. 61: GH-Photography/iStock/Getty Images Plus/Getty Images; p. 62 (TR): Barry Austin Photography/Iconica/Getty Images; p. 62 (Ex 11a: photo 1): Hill Street Studios/Blend Images/Getty Images; p. 62 (Ex 11a: photo 2): Hill Street Studios/Blend Images/Getty Images; p. 62 (Ex 11a: photo 3): Hill Street Studios/Blend Images/Getty Images; p. 62 (Ex 11a: photo 4): Aziz Ary Neto/Cultura/Getty Images; p. 62 (Ex 11a: photo 5): Blend Images-Mike Kemp/Brand X Pictures/Getty Images; p. 63: Daniel Schoenen/LOOK-foto/LOOK/Getty Images; p. vi (Unit 10), p. 64 (header): Hero Images/Getty Images; p. 64 (BR): BJI/Blue Jean Images/Getty Images; p. 65: Caiaimage/Paul Bradbury/Caiaimage/Getty Images; p. 67 (disorganised): Stuart McCall/Photographer's Choice/Getty Images; p. 67 (hardworking): Dave and Les Jacobs/Blend Images/Getty Images; p. 67 (Ex 9a): adventtr/E+/Getty Images; p. 67 (Paula): Portra Images/Taxi/Getty Images; p. 67 (Shawn): PeopleImages/DigitalVision/Getty Images; p. 67 (Dalia): Jetta Productions/Blend Images/Getty Images; p. 68: Hill Street Studios/Getty Images; p. 69: Image Source/Getty Images; p. 71: monkeybusinessimages/iStock/Getty Images Plus/Getty Images; p. vi (Unit 11), p. 72 (header): d3sign/Moment/Getty Images; p. 72 (Eiffel Tower): Kart Thomas/Photolibrary/Getty Images; p. 72 (Machu Picchu): mimmopellicola.com/Moment/Getty Images; p. 72 (Neuschwanstein Castle): Brian Lawrence/Getty Images; p. 72 (Mount Fuji): Christian Kober/robertharding/Getty Images; p. 72 (Statue of Liberty): Brian Lawrence/Getty Images; p. 72 (Big Ben): Joe Fox/Photographer's Choice/Getty Images; p. 73: Print Collector/Hulton Fine Art Collection/Getty Images; p. 74 (L): JTB Photo/Universal Images Group/Getty Images; p. 74 (C): PIERRE VERDY/AFP Creative/Getty Images; p. 74 (R): JLGutierrez/iStock/Getty Images Plus/Getty Images; p. 76 (TR): Radius Images/Getty Images Plus/Getty Images; p. 76 (CR): Jodi Jacobson/E+/Getty Images; p. 76 (BR): Photography Aubrey Stoll/Moment/Getty Images; p. 77 (TL): Hemant Chawla/The India Today Group/Getty Images; p. 77 (CR): Luis Javier Sandoval/Oxford Scientific/Getty Images; p. 77 (BL): EPA european pressphoto agency b.v./Alamy; p. vi (Unit 12), p. 78 (header): Timur Emek/Getty Images Europe/Getty Images; p. 78 (TL): JasnaXX/RooM/Getty Images; p. 78 (TR): Rodrigo Alvarez-Icaza/Moment Open/Getty Images; p. 78 (BR): James Woodson/Photodisc/Getty Images; p. 79 (TR): Michael Krinke/Vetta/Getty Images; p. 79 (BR): biglike/iStock/Getty Images Plus/Getty Images; p. 82: David Lees/Taxi/Getty Images; p. 83: Rachel Murray/WireImage/Getty Images; p. 84: Ben Pruchnie/Getty Images Europe/Getty Images; p. vi (Unit 13), p. 86 (header): spawns/iStock/Getty Images Plus/Getty Images; p. 86 (TL): Jim Spellman/WireImage/Getty Images; p. 86 (TR): Pictorial Press Ltd/Alamy; p. 86 (BR): Murray Close/Contributor/Moviepix/GettyImages; p. 87: Araya Diaz/WireImage/Getty Image; p. 89: Jon Kopaloff/FilmMagic/Getty Images; p. 90 (TR): Daniel Zuchnik/WireImage/Getty Images; p. 90 (BR): Valerie Macon/Getty Images North America/Getty Images; p. 91 (BL): Paul Hawthorne/Getty Images North America/Getty Images; p. 91 (TR): Alberto E. Rodriguez/Getty Images North America/Getty Images; p. vi (Unit 14), p. 92 (header): Joe Drivas/Photographer's Choice/Getty Images; p. 93 (Ex 4: photo 1): champja/iStock/Getty Images Plus/Getty Images; p. 93 (Ex 4: photo 2): Dahl Per/Getty Images; p. 93 (Ex 4: photo 3): Seymour Hewitt/The Image Bank/Getty Images; p. 93 (Ex 4: photo 4): Merbe/E+/Getty Images; p. 93 (Ex 4: photo 5): BJI/Blue Jean Images/Getty Images; p. 93 (Ex 4: photo 6): m-imagephotography/iStock/Getty Images Plus/Getty Images; p. 94: BJI/Blue Jean Images/Getty Images; p. 98: uniquely india/Getty Images; p. 99: GlobalStock/E+/Getty Images; p. vi (Unit 15), p. 100 (header): Tetra Images/Getty Images; p. 100 (TL): moodboard/Brand X Pictures/Getty Images; p. 100 (CL): Marcin Balcerzak/Hemera/Getty Images Plus/Getty Images; p. 100 (C): Erik Dreyer/The Image Bank/Getty Images; p. 100 (BR): Thomas_EyeDesign/E+/Getty Images; p. 102: pp76/iStock/Getty Images Plus/Getty Images; p. 104 (TR): Wavebreakmedia Ltd/Wavebreak Media/Getty Images Plus/Getty Images; p. 104 (CR): Ariel Skelley/Blend Images/Getty Images Plus/Getty Images; p. 105 (Jack): Frank Herholdt/The Image Bank/Getty Images; p. 105 (Sarah): Betsie Van Der Meer/Taxi/Getty Images; p. 105 (Maya): Caiaimage/Sam Edwards/Caiaimage/Getty Images; p. 105 (Dag): Dimitri Otis/Taxi/Getty Images; p. 105 (Andres): Ridofranz/iStock/Getty Images Plus/Getty Images; p. 105 (Marta): Mark Edward Atkinson/Tracey Lee/Blend Images/Getty Images; p. vi (Unit 16), p. 106 (header): Dan Dumitru Comaniciu/iStock/Getty Images Plus/Getty Images; p. 106 (TR): GK Hart/Vikki Hart/Stone/Getty Images; p. 107: ajr_images/iStock/Getty Images Plus/Getty Images; p. 108 (Gabriel): gradyreese/E+/Getty Images; p. 108 (Craig): Leland Bobbe/Image Source/Getty Images; p. 109 (Grant): Ezra Bailey/Taxi/Getty Images; p. 109 (Sayo): Sappington Todd/Getty Images; p. 109 (Diego): Fuse/Getty Images; p. 109 (Carrie): Jordan Siemens/Getty Images; p. 110: Jamie Grill/Photodisc/Getty Images; p. 111 (TR): Tom Le Goff/DigitalVision/Getty Images; p. 111 (CR): Ugurhan Betin/iStock/Getty Images Plus/Getty Images; p. 112:

interchange

FIFTH EDITION

2

Video Activity Worksheets

Jack C. Richards
Revised by Lynne Robertson

Credits

Illustration credits

Andrezzinho: 22 (*bottom*), 36, 50; Ilias Arahovitis: 14 (*bottom*), 16 (*center*), 30; Ralph Butler: 4, 16 (*top*), 29, 49, 54; Carlos Diaz: 28, 48 (*top*), 52, 58; Chuck Gonzales: 12, 34 (*top*), 38 (*top*), 46 (*top*), 56 (*bottom*), 64; Jim Haynes: 24, 30, 41, 57, 62 (*bottom*); Trevor Keen: 10 (*bottom*), 20, 40, 48 (*bottom*), 56 (*top*); Joanna Kerr: 18, 34 (*bottom*); KJA-artists.com: 14 (*top*), 22 (*top*), 38 (*center*), 45, 62 (*top*); Karen Minot: 6; Ortelius Design: 42; James Yamasaki: 17

Photo Acknowledgements

The authors and publishers acknowledge the following sources of copyright material and are grateful for the permissions granted. While every effort has been made, it has not always been possible to identify the sources of all the material used, or to trace all copyright holders. If any omissions are brought to our notice, we will be happy to include the appropriate acknowledgements on reprinting and in the next update to the digital edition, as applicable.

Key: T = Top, L = Left, R = Right, B = Below, CL = Centre Left, C = Centre, CR = Centre Right.

p. 2: © Radius Images/Alamy; p. 6: Glenn Van Der Knijff/Lonely Planet Images/Getty Images; p. 8 (L): Mark Gibson/DanitaDelimont.com; p. 8 (CL): © Joel W. Rogers/Corbis; p. 8 (CR): © Wendy White/Alamy; p. 8 (R): Chris Cheadle/All Canada Photos/Getty Images; p. 18: Barry Winiker/Photolibrary/Getty Images; p. 20 (L): Sportstock/iStock/Getty Images; p. 20 (C): © RosalreneBetancourt 9/Alamy; p. 20 (R): dschnarrs/Getty Images; p. 26 (T): © Paula Solloway/Alamy; p. 31 (B): Jiang Hongyan/Shutterstock; p. 50 (T): © Philip Scalia/Alamy.

Video credits

Unit 7 courtesy of Allrecipes.com. Used with permission. Unit 11 courtesy of Paul Rose. Used with permission. Unit 14 courtesy of bnet.com. Used with permission.

Plan of Video 2

1 What do you miss most? Immigrants to the United States from four continents talk about their lives.
Functional Focus Finding out about someone; talking about oneself
Grammar Past tense questions
Vocabulary Words to talk about immigration

2 Victoria, British Columbia Some tourists take a guided tour of Victoria, British Columbia.
Functional Focus Asking for information about places
Grammar Indirect questions
Vocabulary Locations

3 The right apartment Three roommates debate which new apartment to move into.
Functional Focus Giving opinions; making comparisons and evaluations
Grammar Too . . . and not . . . enough; as . . . as
Vocabulary Words for apartment hunting

4 What's Cooking? A sports reporter hosts a cooking show when the chef gets sick.
Functional Focus Giving instructions
Grammar Sequence adverbs
Vocabulary Cooking words

5 The great outdoors A family goes on a camping trip.
Functional Focus Making suggestions
Grammar Modals for suggestion
Vocabulary Camping words

6 What a mess! A father and daughter tidy up the house and the computer.
Functional Focus Making requests
Grammar Requests with imperatives and modals; two-part verbs
Vocabulary Language for requests

7 How to frost a cake A pastry chef demonstrates the basics of cake decorating.
Functional Focus Explaining uses and purposes of things
Grammar Imperatives and infinitives for giving suggestions
Vocabulary Cake decorating tools

8 Thanksgiving People describe what they eat at Thanksgiving dinner.
Functional Focus Describing an event
Grammar Relative clauses of time
Vocabulary Thanksgiving foods

9 Car, bike, or bus? Friends discuss the best way to get around.
Functional Focus Talking about the past, present, and future.
Grammar Time contrasts – past, present, and future
Vocabulary Transportation

10 The job interview Two candidates interview for an internship position.
Functional Focus Interviewing for a job; describing one's qualifications
Grammar Gerunds; clauses with *because*
Vocabulary Common interview questions and answers; personality traits

11 Two brothers in Peru Two brothers visit Machu Picchu.
Functional Focus Giving factual information
Grammar The passive with and without *by*
Vocabulary Sightseeing words

12 Profile: A TV reporter A TV reporter, Kai Nagata, talks about his life and career.
Functional Focus Talking about the past and present
Grammar Verb tenses: past continuous, simple past; present perfect continuous
Vocabulary Language related to news reporting

13 Street performers People give their opinions of street performers in Boston, Massachusetts.
Functional Focus Giving opinions
Grammar Present and past participles
Vocabulary Types of street performers

14 The body language of business An expert describes how body language can affect a job interview.
Functional Focus Explaining gestures and meaning
Grammar Modals and adverbs for probability
Vocabulary Body language terms; personality attributes

15 Sticky situations People talk about what they would have done in embarrassing situations with guests.
Functional Focus Talking about problems; giving suggestions
Grammar Past modals (*would have* and *should have*)
Vocabulary Verbs and nouns to discuss problems with guests

16 It's my birthday! Tim's friends all have excuses for missing his birthday party. But then, "Surprise!"
Functional Focus Reporting what people say
Grammar Reported speech
Vocabulary Adjectives for feelings

1 What do you miss most?

☰ Preview

1 CULTURE

The United States is a country of immigrants. Until the 1960s, most immigrants came from Europe. Today, most come from Latin America and Asia, but there are some immigrants from almost every country in the world. In Virginia, one high school has students from 85 countries. In Sacramento, California, at one elementary school over 50% of the students speak a language other than English at home. In both schools, the school lunch program offers foods from many countries, and most students have friends from different cultures. Still, students get homesick. "I like it here, but sometimes I miss what I left behind," says Ji Eun Park, a South Korean immigrant to New York.

Are there immigrants in your country? Where are they from?
Do you have friends in other countries? Which countries?
What do you think immigrants miss? Name two things.

2 VOCABULARY *Life in a new place*

PAIR WORK Put three more items in each column. (Many can go in both columns.) Then compare around the class.

architecture	friends	nature	sports
✓ family gatherings	holidays	professions	traditions
food	music and dance	✓ skills	

Things immigrants bring with them	Things immigrants miss
skills	family gatherings

3 GUESS THE FACTS

Watch the video with the sound off. Where are these people from? What is it like there?

4 GET THE PICTURE

Complete the chart. Fill in each person's country of origin. Then add one more piece of information. Compare with a partner.

First name:
Nami

Country:
Syria

Other:
used to play soccer

First name:
Patricia

Country:

Other:

First name:
Rolando

Country:

Other:

First name:
Mihoko

Country:

Other:

5 WATCH FOR DETAILS

Check (✓) **True** or **False**. Then correct the false statements. Compare with a partner.

	True	False	
1. Joon was born in North America.	☐	✓	Joon was born in South Korea.
2. Joon moved when she was 18.	☐	☐	
3. Nami used to play soccer in Syria.	☐	☐	
4. Nami misses spending time with his brother.	☐	☐	
5. Patricia came to the U.S. when she was 19.	☐	☐	
6. Patricia's parents miss having family around.	☐	☐	
7. Rolando used to listen to music in English.	☐	☐	
8. Rolando used to work for a record company.	☐	☐	
9. Mihoko has been in the U.S. for 6 years.	☐	☐	
10. Mihoko studied art in New York.	☐	☐	

6 WHAT DO THEY REMEMBER?

What do these people remember most about their home countries?
Check (✓) all the correct answers. Then compare with a partner.

	Nami	Patricia	Rolando	Mihoko
family	✓	☐	☐	☐
food	☐	☐	☐	☐
going to the beach	☐	☐	☐	☐
listening to music in English	☐	☐	☐	☐
parties	☐	☐	☐	☐
picnics	☐	☐	☐	☐
playing soccer	✓	☐	☐	☐
restaurants	☐	☐	☐	☐

Follow-up

7 DIFFICULT CHOICES

A **GROUP WORK** Imagine you're going to move to a
new country. Add two questions to the list. Then
interview three classmates and complete the chart.

I'd like to move to Australia.

	Classmate 1	Classmate 2	Classmate 3
1. Which country will you choose?	....	....	....
2. What will you miss most?	....	....	....
3. What will your biggest problem be?	....	....	....
4.			
....	....	....	....
5.			
....	....	....	....

B **CLASS ACTIVITY** Compare answers as a class.

Language close-up

8 WHAT DID THEY SAY?

Watch the video and complete the conversation. Then practice it.

Joon Park is interviewing Rolando, an immigrant from Mexico.

Joon: When you ...._were_........ a kid, what did you ....
to do for fun?

Rolando: Most of the .... , I have to say, that I used
.... listen to .... in English. I used to
listen to .... over and over and over.

Joon: What .... you use to do for .... in
Mexico?

Rolando: I used to work for a record ....

Joon: What was it .... , moving to the United States?

Rolando: In the beginning, it was .... not to be able to
communicate and .... to people and make
.... understood, and .... I felt, um,
frustrated a .... of times. But once my English
.... , I was able to communicate ....

Joon: What do you .... most about your .... country?

Rolando: Besides my .... , the food. The food is .... in
Mexico. It's .... colorful.

9 PAST TENSE QUESTIONS *Finding out about someone*

A Complete the questions with the phrases in the box. Then add two
questions of your own.

1. Where _were you born_ .... ?

2. How many .... ?

3. Did you play .... ?

4. Where did you .... ?

5. Did you study .... ?

6. Did you work .... ?

7. .... ?

8. .... ?

> any sports in high school
> English in high school
> go to high school
> ✓ were you born
> part-time after school
> people are in your family

B (PAIR WORK) Interview a classmate. Take turns asking and answering the questions.

VIDEO ACTIVITIES

Victoria, British Columbia

Preview

1 CULTURE

Victoria, British Columbia, is located on the tip of Vancouver Island. It is the capital city of the province of British Columbia, Canada. Victoria started as a port in the 1800s. There were many beautiful buildings then, and most of them are still standing today. Victoria has a mild climate and is very sunny – good conditions for growing a wide variety of plants. Its nickname is "The City of Gardens." Victoria is a popular place for tourists now. Many people take the ferry from the city of Vancouver (which is not on the island) to visit Victoria. Popular sites include the Empress Hotel and Beacon Hill Park.

Would you like to visit Victoria?
What other interesting facts do you know about Canada?

2 VOCABULARY *Locations*

PAIR WORK Imagine that you are visiting Victoria. Ask about the location of places to see. Use the map and some of these words.

across from	between	near	straight ahead
behind	just past	not far from	to the right/left

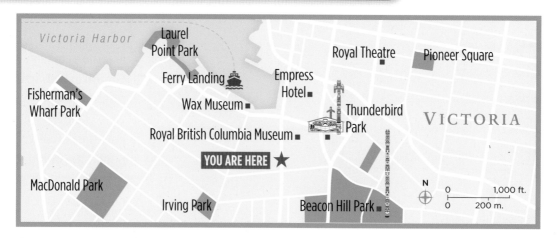

A: Excuse me. Do you know where Thunderbird Park is?
B: It's not far from the Empress Hotel.

Interchange VRB 2 © Cambridge University Press 2012   Photocopiable

GUESS THE STORY

Watch the first two minutes of the video with the sound off.
These people are taking a tour of Victoria. What do you think
the problem is? Check (✓) your answer.

- ☐ The tour guide gets lost.
- ☐ Someone on the tour is too talkative.
- ☐ The tour guide doesn't know the answers to questions.
- ☒ One of the tourists falls asleep.
- ☐ The tourists don't like Victoria.

▤ Watch the video

GET THE PICTURE

A Look at your answer to Exercise 3. Did you guess correctly?

B Check (✓) the things the tour group did. Then compare
with a partner.

- ☑ They took pictures of the Empress Hotel.
- ☐ They took a tour inside the Royal British Columbia Museum.
- ☑ They went to Thunderbird Park.
- ☐ They ate lunch in Vancouver.
- ☑ They visited Craigdarroch Castle.
- ☑ They stopped at Beacon Hill Park.

5 WATCH FOR DETAILS

What did you learn about Victoria? Check (✓) the
correct answers. Then compare with a partner.

1. A room at the Empress Hotel
   - ☐ opened in 1907.
   - ☑ costs more than 300 Canadian dollars.

2. The totem poles at Thunderbird Park are from
   - ☑ the first people who lived in the area.
   - ☐ Vancouver.

3. Craigdarroch Castle is known for
   - ☐ its famous guests.
   - ☑ its stained-glass windows.

4. The totem pole in Beacon Hill Park is
   - ☐ not the original one.
   - ☑ the fourth tallest in the world.

6 WHAT'S YOUR OPINION?

A PAIR WORK Check (✓) the words that describe Ted.
Can you add two words of your own?

annoying	outgoing	talkative	unfriendly	....
enthusiastic	smart	tired	whiny	....

B Do you like tour groups? What are the advantages? the disadvantages?

Follow-up

7 A DAY IN VICTORIA

A PAIR WORK Which of these things would you like to do in Victoria? Number
them from 1 (most interesting) to 4 (least interesting). Compare answers with a partner.

**Stay at the
Empress Hotel**

**Tour the Royal British
Columbia Museum**

**Visit Craigdarroch
Castle**

**Ride through
Beacon Hill Park**

B GROUP WORK Plan a morning in Victoria. Choose two things to do.

8 TOURIST INFORMATION

A GROUP WORK You work for the Tourist Information Center in your city.
Fill in the name of your city. Then complete the chart for visitors.

A BRIEF GUIDE TO .... (name of city)	Some interesting facts	Buildings and landmarks ....
	Local foods	Interesting things to do ....

B Now one student in your group will play the role of a curious tourist. The tourist
will ask lots of questions about the information in your chart. Try to answer all of them!

9 WHAT DID THEY SAY?

Watch the video and complete the conversation. Then practice it.

A tour group is sightseeing in Victoria.

Rita: This ......*historic*...... landmark is the Fairmont Empress ....HOTEL.... . Many ....FAMOUS.... guests ....HAVE.... ....STAYED.... here, from writers, ...KINGS.... and queens, to ....ACTORS.... and actresses, to ....POLITICIANS.... .

Ken: ....CAN.... ....YOU.... ....TELL.... us ....WHEN.... the hotel opened?

Rita: Yes, it ....OPENED.... in 1907.

Yuka: ....DO.... ....YOU.... ....KNOW.... how much a room ....COSTS.... for one night?

Rita: Well, the Empress is a ....LUXURY.... hotel, so a room ....SHOULD.... run over ....300.... ....CANADIAN.... ....DOLARS.... .

10 INDIRECT QUESTIONS Asking for information

A Change these sentences to indirect questions. Begin with **Could you tell me . . . ?** or **Do you know . . . ?**

1. What time does the tour end?   Could you tell me what time the tour ends?

2. Where is the Empress Hotel?   ....

3. Where do the totem poles come from?   ....

4. How late does the museum stay open?   ....

5. When does the next ferry to Vancouver leave?   ....

B **PAIR WORK** Take turns asking and answering the questions using the information from the video.

C **GROUP WORK** Now take turns asking indirect questions about other cities. How many questions can your group answer?

3 The right apartment

1 CULTURE

Colleges and universities in the United States and Canada usually provide dormitories for students on campus, but almost 60 percent prefer to live in apartments with friends. In a recent survey, most students said that dormitories have too many rules. Even more said that it was just easier to live with friends. But even friends can have problems when they rent an apartment together. The biggest problems: deciding who's going to cook and clean, getting things fixed when they don't work, and living with other people's bad habits.

Where do university students usually live in your country? Why? What do you think are some advantages and disadvantages of sharing an apartment with friends?

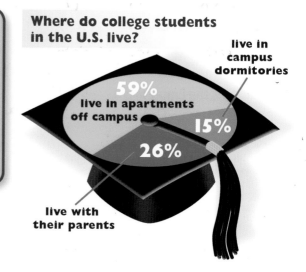

Where do college students in the U.S. live?

59% live in apartments off campus

15% live in campus dormitories

26% live with their parents

2 VOCABULARY *Apartment hunting* MANUEL

PAIR WORK What do you think are the most important factors in renting an apartment? Number the items below from 1 (most important) to 8 (least important).

appliances

location

noise

rent

security

size

view

other ....

3 GUESS THE STORY

Watch the first minute of the video with the sound off.

What don't the young women like about their apartment? Choose an answer from Exercise 2.

They don't like the ~~S I Z E~~ .

HOTEL

≡ Watch the video

4 GET THE PICTURE

What is each apartment like? Circle the correct answers. Then compare with a partner.

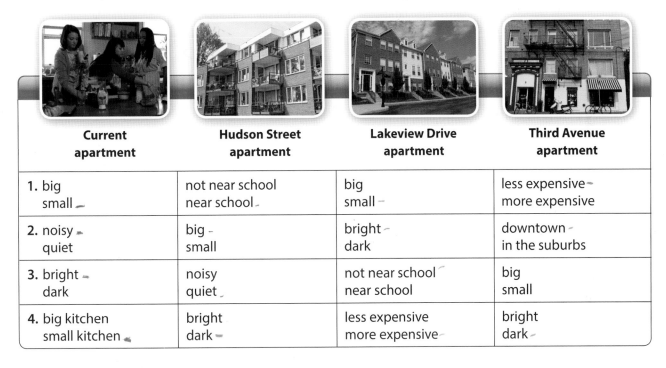

Current apartment	Hudson Street apartment	Lakeview Drive apartment	Third Avenue apartment
1. big / small —	not near school / near school —	big / small —	less expensive — / more expensive
2. noisy — / quiet	big — / small	bright — / dark	downtown — / in the suburbs
3. bright — / dark	noisy / quiet —	not near school — / near school	big / small
4. big kitchen / small kitchen —	bright / dark —	less expensive / more expensive —	bright / dark —

5 WATCH FOR DETAILS

Correct the mistakes below. Then compare with a partner.

Amber, Molly, and Ellen ~~work~~ *are students* at a university, and they want to find

a new apartment. They look in the ~~newspaper~~ *INTERNET*. There is a ~~noisier~~ *QUIETER*

apartment for rent on Hudson Street. There is a more expensive

apartment on Lakeview Drive that has a ~~dingy~~ *BIG* kitchen.

The apartment on Third Avenue is less expensive and has ~~three~~ *ONE*

bedrooms. The girls decide to choose the second apartment.

6 A MATTER OF OPINION

A Who holds these opinions? Check (✓) all the correct answers. Then compare with a partner.

	Ellen	Amber	Molly
Hudson Street apartment			
good location	☐	☐	☐
too small	☐	☐	☐
too close to school	☐	☐	☐
Lakeview Drive apartment			
too expensive	☐	☐	☐
too far from school	☐	☐	☐
much brighter	☐	☐	☐
Third Avenue apartment			
the nicest	☐	☐	☐
good location	☐	☐	☐
too small/no privacy	☐	☐	☐

B **PAIR WORK** Which apartment do you think Ellen, Amber, and Molly will choose? Why?

▤ Follow-up

7 ROLE PLAY *Renting an apartment*

A **PAIR WORK** Imagine that you want to rent an apartment with two friends. What questions will you need to ask? Make a list.

1. How much is the rent?

2. How many bedrooms does it have?

3. ....

4. ....

5. ....

6. ....

B **GROUP WORK** Now join another pair. Three of you are friends. The fourth person is a rental agent.

Agent: Describe two different apartments. Make them sound as different as possible.

Friends: Ask lots of questions about the two apartments.

Start like this:

Friend 1: We're looking for an apartment in
  (name of neighborhood).
Agent: Well, I have two great apartments to show you.
Friend 2: How big are they?

8 WHAT DID THEY SAY?

Watch the video and complete the conversation. Then practice it.

The three roommates debate which apartment to choose.

Amber: I know it isn't ....much.... ....bigger.... than this place, but I like the
...APARTMENT... on Hudson Street. The location is ...GREAT...... ;
we can .... to school.

Molly: Yeah. There are three .... , but I ....
it was ....

Amber: But it's so .... ! We can walk to the ...LIBRARY...
to study – and that .... money, too.

Ellen: But .... we .... a bigger apartment,
we .... study at the library. We
.... study at home. The apartment on Hudson Street
is .... to school. It's like .... in
a dormitory.

Molly: Yeah, that's true. But it .... noisy ....
this place, and I .... when it's ....

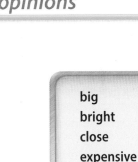

9 EVALUATIONS AND COMPARISONS *Giving opinions*

A Complete the sentences using **is too** . . . or **isn't** . . . **enough**, choosing
words from the box. Then compare with a partner. Make sure your sentences
are true in the video!

1. The roommates think their apartment ....*is too small*...... for three people.
2. Ellen thinks the apartment on Hudson Street .... to school.
3. Ellen thinks one tiny window ....
4. Amber thinks the Lakeview Drive apartment .... from school.
5. Molly thinks the Lakeview Drive apartment ....
6. Ellen and Amber think the Third Avenue apartment ....

> big
> bright
> close
> expensive
> far
> ✓ small

B Now compare two of the apartments using **as . . . as**. Share your sentences
with a partner.

1. The old apartment isn't as big as the one on Hudson Street.
2. ....
3. ....
4. ....
5. ....

C PAIR WORK Now compare your own house or apartment to one of the
apartments the roommates looked at. Do you think you would like to live there?

What's Cooking?

1 CULTURE

Cooking in the United States and Canada is popular with both men and women. There are best-selling cookbooks and popular TV cooking shows to help people learn to cook almost every kind of food. But cooking shows appeal to people who don't like to cook, too. Some cooking shows feature chefs competing against each other (like *Iron Chef*) or exploring new foods in different countries (like *No Reservations*). And many people film their own cooking demonstrations and post them online. For North Americans, watching cooking shows isn't just educational – it's entertaining!

What do you think the programs Iron Chef *and* No Reservations *are about?*
Would you like to be on a cooking show? Why or why not?
Who likes to cook in your family?

2 VOCABULARY *Cooking*

PAIR WORK What things can you use to cook chicken? Put the words in the chart. Can you add four more words?

Kitchen appliances	Cooking utensils	Cooking ingredients
a refrigerator	a baking dish	salt
a STOVE	A FRYING PAN	BREAD CRUMBS
an OVEN	A KNIFE	BUTTER

bread crumbs   butter

flour   ✓a baking dish

a stove   ✓salt   ✓a refrigerator   a frying pan   an oven   oil   a knife

3 GUESS THE STORY

Answer these questions.

1. What do you think the text message says? Who do you think it's from?

2. What do the producer and the cameraman decide to do?

3. Who do you think this man is?

▤ Watch the video

4 GET THE PICTURE

Check (✓) the correct answers. Then compare with a partner.

1. Why is Hank doing the cooking show today?
   - ☐ He has changed jobs.
   - ☑ The chef is sick.
   - ☐ He's learning to cook.

2. What does Hank usually do?
   - ☐ He's a news reporter.
   - ☑ He's a sports reporter.
   - ☐ He's a producer.

3. How successful was Hank as a chef?
   - ☐ He was very successful.
   - ☐ He was just OK.
   - ☑ He was not very successful.

5 MAKING INFERENCES

Which statements are probably true? Which are probably false?
Check (✓) your answers. Then compare with a partner.

	True	False
1. Olivia was surprised by Juliana's text message.	☑	☐
2. Hank wants to do the cooking show.	☐	☑
3. Hank has cooked Chicken con Mozzarella before.	☐	☑
4. Hank knows the difference between the microwave and the oven.	☑	☑
5. The oven is too hot.	☑	☐
6. Hank pounds the chicken correctly.	☐	☑
7. Hank uses the correct amount of salt and pepper.	☐	☑
8. Hank adds too much butter.	☑	☐
9. The producers think Hank should always host the cooking show.	☐	☑
10. Juliana will do the show next week.	☑	☐

6 A SIMPLE MEAL

A **PAIR WORK** Do you know how to make a grilled cheese sandwich?
Number the steps (1 to 6). Then practice giving instructions like this:

This is how you make a grilled cheese sandwich.

.... Finally, take the hot sandwich out of the pan, and you have a grilled cheese sandwich.

.... Next, put some cheese between the slices of bread.

.... First, take two slices of bread.

.... After that, put the sandwich in the hot frying pan.

.... When the first side is cooked, flip the sandwich with a spatula.

.... Then heat up a frying pan with some butter or oil.

B Now write out instructions for your own simple snack, but
put the steps in the wrong order. Read the steps out loud.
Your partner will put them in the correct order.

A Quick Snack

7 HOW ABOUT YOU?

PAIR WORK Answer these questions.

1. Do you ever cook at home? Why or why not?
2. What are three dishes that you know how to make?
3. Have you ever had an accident in the kitchen? What happened?

8 WHAT'S THE RECIPE?

Watch the video and complete the recipe. Then compare with a partner.

Here is the recipe Hank Walker tried to follow.

Chicken con Mozzarella

First turn the ..OVEN.. to 350 degrees Fahrenheit.

Next, ..POUND.. the chicken.

Then ..SPRINKLE. the chicken with a little salt and pepper.

Next, ..SPREAD.. butter on the chicken.

After that, ..ROLL.. a strip of mozzarella cheese ..INSIDE.. each piece of chicken. ..SECURE.. with a toothpick.

Now, for the coating on the ..CHICKEN.. .

First, ..BEAT.. two eggs.

After that, ..ROLL.. the chicken in flour, the eggs, and bread crumbs.

Place in a ..BAKING.. dish.

After that, sprinkle ..WITH.. rosemary.

Finally, ..PUT.. the chicken in the oven and ..BAKE.. for 20 minutes.

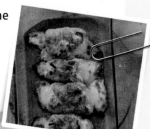

9 SEQUENCE ADVERBS *Giving instructions*

Put the pictures in order (1 to 8). Then give the correct instructions for each photo, choosing from the verbs in the box. Use the sequence adverbs **first, then, next, after that,** and **finally.**

bake	roll
beat	spread
✓pound	sprinkle
roll	sprinkle

.....BEAT.....

.....Roll.....

Finally,

.....Roll.....

First, pound the chicken.

.....SPREAD.....

.....SPRINKLE.....

.....SPRINKLE.....

5 The great outdoors

1 CULTURE

Every year, millions of people in the United States and Canada go camping. Many bring tents and sleeping bags and go to a park campsite. Some go to quiet wilderness areas with few people. Others go to private campgrounds. Most people say they camp to get away from everything and everyone. But this is not always possible. At popular parks like Yellowstone National Park and the Grand Canyon, you have to make a reservation for a campsite months in advance – and be prepared for traffic jams!

Have you ever gone camping? Where? When?
What do you think are two enjoyable things and two difficult things about camping?

2 VOCABULARY Camping

PAIR WORK What would you take on a camping trip? Put the words in the chart. Can you add three more words?

Camping equipment	Food and drink	Things to enjoy
a backpack		

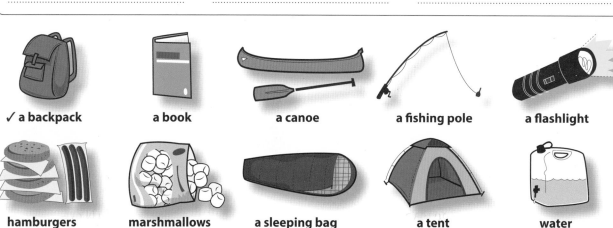

✓ a backpack	a book	a canoe	a fishing pole	a flashlight
hamburgers and hot dogs	marshmallows	a sleeping bag	a tent	water

3 GUESS THE STORY

A *Watch the video with the sound off.*
What things does the family take on the camping trip? Circle
them in Exercise 2.

B The family arrives at the campsite. What do you think each
family member wants to do first?

☰ Watch the video

4 GET THE PICTURE

Check (✓) **True** or **False**. Correct the false statements. Then compare with a partner.

	True	False	
1. Ed is looking forward to reading his book.	☐	☐	....
2. Ben is planning on going swimming.	☐	☐	....
3. The family is going to roast chicken later.	☐	☐	....

5 WATCH FOR DETAILS

Check (✓) the correct answers. Then compare with a partner.

1. Ed had a hard week and is looking forward
   - ☑ to peace and quiet.
   - ☐ to roasting peanuts.

2. Lisa wants
   - ☐ to go fishing.
   - ☐ to set up the tent.

3. Ben isn't excited
   - ☐ to go fishing.
   - ☐ to set up the tent.

4. Michelle puts Lisa's leaf
   - ☐ on her door.
   - ☐ in Ed's book.

5. Ben is not
   - ☐ inside the tent.
   - ☐ going to go fishing.

6. In the end, Ed says he's
   - ☐ not going to waste time reading.
   - ☐ not going to roast marshmallows.

6 GOING CAMPING

A GROUP WORK Plan a weekend camping trip. First, choose one of the places below or another place that you know.

Now agree on answers to these questions.

1. When are we going to go?
2. How are we going to get there?
3. What are we going to take?
4. How long are we going to stay?
5. What are we going to do each day?

B CLASS ACTIVITY Compare your plans around the class. Which group planned the most interesting trip?

7 ROLE PLAY

A GROUP WORK Imagine you are a family on a camping trip. In groups of four, take the role of mother, father, or one of the two children. What would you like to do? List at least four possibilities for your character.

My character: ....

I'd like to . . .

go fishing

....

....

....

....

I'd like to take it easy.

B Now take turns acting out the trip: arriving at the campsite, setting up camp, and doing what you want to do. How do you get along? Who wants to do the same things? Who decides what you do?

Language close-up

8 WHAT DID THEY SAY?

Watch the video and complete the conversation. Then practice it.

Ed and Michelle arrive at the campsite with their children Ben and Lisa.

Ed: Ah, finally, some ....*peace*........ and . . .

Ben/Lisa: Sweet!! Yeah!! Cool! Awesome!

Ed: . . . .

Ben: I'm .... to .... fishing!

Lisa: I'm .... go .... the tent!

Michelle: Don't worry, Ed. .... keep an eye on them. You've had a hard week. .... don't .... grab a .... and

your .... and take it easy? .... get things set up.

Ed: No, it's fine. .... I .... Lisa with the .... , and you .... go fishing with Ben.

Michelle: Uh-uh. No fishing .... camp is .... Ben!

Ben: Yeah?

Michelle: Ben, honey, ... to help your sister and father set up the .... Then you .... go fishing, OK?

Ben: Aw, Mom!

9 MODALS FOR SUGGESTION

A What suggestions did Michelle and Ed make? Match the phrases from columns A and B and write the sentences. Then compare with a partner.

A	B
Why don't you	read right away.
You have to	think about tonight.
Don't you think you should	help your sister and father set up the tent.
You ought to	get your sleeping bag out and get yourself set up in there?
You don't have to	grab a chair and your book and take it easy?

1. Why don't you grab a chair and your book and take it easy?

2. ....

3. ....

4. ....

5. ....

Why don't you take it easy?

B **PAIR WORK** Imagine that you are about to leave on a camping trip. Give five more suggestions of your own, using the expressions in column A above.

1. ....

2. ....

3. ....

4. ....

5. ....

6 What a mess!

Preview

1 CULTURE

In the United States, chores are usually divided among the members of a household. However, in a survey of married couples, 65 percent of women said that they did most of the household work. But the men did not agree. Only 5 percent of men said that the women did more work. The majority of men thought that the chores were split evenly. And what chores did men like to do? Men liked to cook dinner and clear the table. Women complained about the amount of laundry.

Who does the chores at your house? How do you decide who does what?
Do you feel everyone does the same amount of work?

2 VOCABULARY *Requests*

A **PAIR WORK** What are they saying? Write one request below each picture.

> Would you take out the trash?   ✓ Can I use the computer now?
>
> Could you hang up your coat, please?   Would you mind turning down the TV?
>
> Why don't you clean up your room?   Please tell me when you're off the phone.

1. <u>Can I use the computer now?</u>   2. ....   3. ....

4. ....   5. ....   6. ....

B Now you make the requests. Have conversations like these:

A: Can I use the computer now?   A: Would you take out the trash?
B: Just a minute.   B: Sure. No problem.

3 GUESS THE STORY

Watch the first minute of the video with the sound off. Answer these questions.

1. What does the daughter want?
2. What do you think her father says to her?

Watch the video

4 GET THE PICTURE

A Alexis's father asks her to do several things. Complete the sentences. Then compare with a partner.

go clean up your room	✓ take out the trash
hang up your coat	tell me what you're doing

1. Would you mind <u>taking out the trash</u> ?

2. Would you mind _____ , please?

3. Would you mind _____ ?

4. Why don't you _____ ?

5 WATCH FOR DETAILS

Correct the mistakes below. Then compare with a partner.

Alexis comes home and greets her ~~mother~~ *father*. She asks if she can use the telephone. Her father has to finish what he's doing, so he asks her to cook dinner. Then he asks Alexis to order a pizza. Finally, he gives her the computer, but he hasn't vacuumed his bookmarks or emailed the trash. He asks Alexis to clean up the living room while he orders a salad.

6 WHAT'S YOUR OPINION?

A (PAIR WORK) Check (✓) the tasks you like and don't like to do.
Then compare with a partner.

	Like	Don't like
1. hang up coats	☐	☐
2. take out trash	☐	☐
3. empty trash on the computer	☐	☐
4. clean up room	☐	☐
5. put away laundry	☐	☐
6. heat up leftovers	☐	☐

B Do you sometimes get annoyed when someone you live with doesn't do
his or her chores? What kinds of things irritate you? Give opinions like this:

A: I get annoyed when my roommate turns up the TV too loud.
B: It bothers me when my brother . . .

☰ Follow-up

7 ROLE PLAY *Roommates*

A (PAIR WORK) Imagine you have a roommate. What would you ask
him or her to do? Complete the list.

1. Would you mind vacuuming the rug? ....

2. ....

3. ....

B Now act out your questions with a partner.
Start like this:

A: Would you mind vacuuming the rug?
B: OK. But could you pick up your books, please?
   They're all over the floor.

8 WHAT DID THEY SAY?

Watch the video and complete the conversation. Then practice it.

Dad is working when Alexis approaches him with a request.

Dad: Would you mind ...<u>telling</u>..... ....<u>me</u>..... what you're doing?

Alexis: Nothing.... .... the computer now?

Dad: .... it as soon as I'm finished with it.

Alexis: OK, well . . . I'm just going to .... here and wait for a while, then.

Dad: Ugh! I've got an idea: .... go clean up your room?

Alexis: I'll clean it up tonight ....

Dad: Uh-uh. You clean up your room, you .... the laptop. That's the deal.

Alexis: OK. I'll go .... now. But after that . . . ?

Dad: You can use the ....

9 TWO-PART VERBS *Making requests*

A Match each item below with at least two of the verbs in the box. Then add three things of your own. Which of these verbs do they go with?

1. the trash	<u>pick up the trash</u>	<u>take out the trash</u>
2. your jacket	....	....
3. the TV	....	....
4. those magazines	....	....
5. the laundry	....	....
6.	....	....
7.	....	....
8.	....	....

> clean up
> hang up
> pick up
> put away
> take off
> take out
> turn off
> turn on

B **PAIR WORK** Now have conversations like these. First, use the items in part A. Then practice the conversations again using things of your own.

A: Would you mind picking up the trash?
B: Sure, no problem.

A: Could you take off your shoes, please?
B: Yes, of course.

Interchange VRB 2 © Cambridge University Press 2012   Photocopiable

Unit 6 ■ **25**

How to frost a cake

≡ Preview

1 CULTURE

Many cultures celebrate important occasions, like weddings or birthdays, by eating cake. The early Romans made flat round cakes sweetened with nuts and honey. In China, mooncakes are traditionally eaten during the Mid-Autumn Festival. The Portuguese brought a sponge cake, *kasutera*, to Japan in the 16th century, and it is now a popular food at festivals. It seems no matter where you go, there's always an occasion for cake.

When do you eat cake? What is your favorite kind of cake?
Do you know how to make a cake?

2 VOCABULARY *Cake decorating tools*

PAIR WORK Match the words in the box with their description below. Then write the correct word under each picture.

cake plate	✓frosting	offset spatula	pastry brush	simple syrup	waxed paper

frosting............................ a sweet coating used on cakes

.... a cooking tool with a bent blade used for spreading toppings

.... a small flat brush used for coating baked goods

.... a plate raised up on a platform

.... a sweet sugar liquid used to moisten cakes

.... a nonstick paper used in baking

1. ....

2. frosting..............................

3. ....

4. ....

5. ....

6. ....

3 GUESS THE FACTS

What steps are in the pictures? Choose the correct description and write it below each picture.

Make flat tops. ✓

Cut into pieces.

Spread a thin layer of frosting on the cake.

Frost, put on the top layer, and frost again.

Spread the final layer of frosting.

Apply simple syrup.

1

Make flat tops.

Place the cake on waxed paper.

Chill the cake.

Smooth the frosting.

Brush crumbs off the cake.

Smooth frosting from between the layers.

Brush on simple syrup.

Watch the video

4 GET THE PICTURE

A Look at your answers to Exercise 3. Did you guess correctly? Correct your answers. Then compare with a partner.

B Put the pictures in Exercise 3 in order (1 to 6). Write the numbers in the boxes.

5 WATCH FOR DETAILS

Check (✓) **True** or **False**. Then correct the false statements. Compare with a partner.

	True	False	
1. You need to trim a rounded cake layer.	✓	☐	
2. You use the serrated knife to spread frosting.	☐	✓	TO CUT THE CAKE
3. You use waxed paper to frost the cake.	☐	✓	TO KEEP THE CAKE PLATE CLEAN
4. You use simple syrup to add moisture.	✓	☐	
5. Use a spatula to apply simple syrup.	☐	✓	TO SPREAD THE FROSTING
6. It's best to try to align the cake layers.	✓	☐	
7. A "crumb coat" is the final coat of frosting.	✓	✓	THE FIRST COAT OF FROSTING
8. You should put the cake in the oven to chill.	☐	✓	IN THE REFRIGERATOR
9. You can use the cake plate to rotate the cake.	✓	☐	
10. A cold spatula helps smooth the frosting.	☐	✓	A HOT SPATULA

6 HOW DOES IT WORK?

PAIR WORK Take turns describing the decorating tools shown in the video. Have conversations like this:

A: What's this?
B: It's called an offset spatula. It's used to . . .

Follow-up

7 HOW TO . . .

A What is something you know how to make?
What equipment do you use? What are these things used for?
Complete the chart.

My favorite thing to make:

Things I use to make it	What they're used for

B **PAIR WORK** Take turns asking and answering questions about your chart.
Start like this:

A: What can you make?
B: I can make my own clothes.

A: What tools do you need to make them?
B: To make clothes, you need some fabric, a pattern, scissors, . . .

Interchange VRB 2 © Cambridge University Press 2012   Photocopiable

☰ Language close-up

8 WHAT DID SHE SAY?

Watch the video and complete the instructions. Then compare with a partner.

An expert gives instructions on how to frost a cake.

Step 1: Make flat tops. If the cake ......*layers*...... have domed-shaped tops, you'll ...*NEED*... ...*TO*... ...*TRIM*... them to make the tops flat. Place a cooled cake layer ......*ON*...... a sheet of ...*WAXED*... ...*PAPER*... . This will make it ...*EASIER*...... to maneuver. Rest your .....*PALM*...... on the domed top, and ...*HOLD*..... the ...*SERRATED*... ...*KNIFE*..... parallel to the top of the cake. Lightly score the edge .....*WHERE*...... you'll make the cut. ...*GENTLY*......... begin sawing .....*BACK*..... ...*AND*... ...*FORTH*..... into the cake. ...*WHEN*.............. you've made one cut, ...*ROTATE*......... the cake and make another cut.

9 IMPERATIVES AND INFINITIVES *Giving suggestions*

A Complete each sentence with **be sure to**, **don't forget to**, or **remember to** and one of the verbs in the box. One of the verbs can be used twice. Then compare with a partner.

| align |
| brush |
| chill |
| hold |

1. To make flat cake tops, ...*remember to hold*... the knife parallel to the top of the cake.

2. When you prepare to frost, ... any loose crumbs off the cake.

3. .... a layer of simple syrup on before you frost.

4. When you place the top layer on, ... the two layers.

5. After you make the "crumb coat," .... the cake in the fridge.

B **PAIR WORK** Now describe something you are going to do. Your partner will give suggestions.

A: I'm going on a trip to Venezuela.
B: Don't forget to bring a camera.

Thanksgiving

1 CULTURE

On the fourth Thursday in November, people in the United States celebrate Thanksgiving. They get together with family and friends, share a special meal, and "give thanks" for what they have. The tradition goes back to 1620, when the first group of Europeans, called Pilgrims, settled in North America. The Pilgrims didn't know how to grow crops in the New World, so the Native Americans helped them. Later, they celebrated the good harvest with a special meal. Today on Thanksgiving Day, families and friends do the very same thing.

How did the tradition of Thanksgiving begin?
Is there a similar holiday in your country? What is it?

In Canada, Thanksgiving is celebrated on the second Monday in October.

2 VOCABULARY *Thanksgiving foods*

A **PAIR WORK** Put the words in the chart. Check (✓) the ones you think are special Thanksgiving foods.

Main dishes	Side dishes	Dessert
	corn	

corn

cranberry sauce

green beans

B *Watch the first two minutes of the video with the sound off.* How many of these foods do you see? Circle them.

sweet potatoes

rolls

roast turkey with stuffing

pumpkin pie

mashed potatoes with gravy

3 GUESS THE FACTS

What do you think are the most popular Thanksgiving foods?
What do you think people do after the Thanksgiving meal?

☰ Watch the video

4 GET THE PICTURE

Write two new things you learned about Thanksgiving.
Then compare with a partner.

NOTES

1. ....

2. ....

5 WATCH FOR DETAILS

What do these people eat on Thanksgiving? Check (✓) all the correct
answers. Then compare with a partner.

	Joe	Alisa	Susan	Juan Carlos
cranberry sauce	✓	☐	☐	☐
gravy	✓	☐	☐	☐
kimchi	☐	☐	✓	☐
maracuchitos	☐	☐	☐	☐
mashed potatoes	✓	✓	✓	☐
rice	☐	☐	✓	☐
stuffing	☐	✓	✓	☐
sweet potatoes	☐	✓	☐	☐
turkey	✓	✓	✓	☐

6 UNTRADITIONAL FOODS

Complete the sentences. Then compare with a partner.

1. Kimchi is a traditional dish from ......KOREA...... .
2. Maracuchitos are a tradition from ......VENEZUELA...... . They are
   plantains with ...CHEESE... , fried.
3. One Venezuelan dessert is made from pineapple and ...PAPAYA... ,
   served with ...ICE CREAM... .

7 AFTER DINNER

Do Joe and Susan have these things in common? Check (✓) **True** or **False**.
Correct the false sentences. Then compare with a partner.

	True	False	
1. Joe and Susan both watch football on Thanksgiving.	☐	☑	JOE CLEANING / SUSAN CARDS-MOVIE
2. They both spend the holiday with friends.	☐	☑	FAMILY
3. They both eat turkey, mashed potatoes, and gravy.	☐	☑	GRAVY NOT

8 WHAT DOES THANKSGIVING MEAN TO THEM?

What did these people say about Thanksgiving? Complete the sentences.
Then compare with a partner.

It's kind of a time to ....
....
....

My favorite part of Thanksgiving
is ....
....

It is a ....
....
....

Follow-up

9 SPECIAL HOLIDAYS

CLASS ACTIVITY   What is your favorite holiday? Complete the chart. Then
compare answers as a class. How many holidays did your class list?

Name of holiday: ....

1. When is it? ....

2. What special foods do you eat? ....

3. What else do you do? ....

4. What does the holiday mean to you? ....

10 WHAT DID THEY SAY?

Watch the video and complete the conversation. Then practice it.

A host is asking people about Thanksgiving in North America.

Host: Hello and welcome to this week's ....*episode*........ of *Dinner*
.... , the show .... food. My ....
is Anthony Russo. And .... we're ....
to be talking about Thanksgiving. As you know, North America is
a huge .... Do you think everyone
.... Thanksgiving in the same way? ....
you .... they eat the same foods? Let's ask some
people and ....

* * *

Host: How would you .... Thanksgiving to someone
.... of North America?

Bernie: Well, you know, Thanksgiving's a .... holiday. It's kind of
a time to sit back, ... , and . . . a little reflection on how
you .... be .... for what you have.

11 RELATIVE CLAUSES OF TIME *Describing an event*

A Rewrite these sentences with relative clauses of time. Begin with
Thanksgiving is a time when . . . Then compare with a partner.

1. Alisa's family watches football.

   Thanksgiving is a time when Alisa's family watches football.

2. Joe helps with the clean-up.

   ....

3. Juan Carlos prepares a special Venezuelan dish called maracuchitos.

   ....

4. Susan goes out to a movie with her family.

   ....

5. Bernie gives thanks for the things that he has.

   ....

B **PAIR WORK** Take turns making statements about special days in your country,
like this:

"New Year's Eve is a time when people dance in the streets."

9 Car, bike, or bus?

Preview

1 CULTURE

The first vehicle similar to a bicycle was built in 1690 in France. It was called a hobbyhorse. In Scotland, in 1840, pedals were added and it became the first real bicycle. Today there are twice as many bicycles as cars. There are over a billion bicycles in the world, with 400 million of them in China alone. In the U.S., almost 90 universities now have a campus bike program. Students "check out" the bikes to get around campus. This helps cut down on traffic, reduce pollution, and improve campus safety, but students need to remember: The bikes still need to be locked!

Do people ride bicycles in your country? How about 25 years ago?
How do people travel now?
Do most people own a car? How about a bicycle?

2 VOCABULARY *Transportation costs*

A **PAIR WORK** Do you know all of these words? Circle the word in each item that doesn't belong.

1. car   insurance   parking ticket   ~~sidewalk~~
2. tires   expense   bicycle   helmet
3. job   loan   credit   debt
4. repairs   bus   route   public transportation
5. lend   commute   borrow   manage

B Now choose two words from each item and use them in a sentence, like this:

"I bought a new car, but then I couldn't afford the insurance!"

3 GUESS THE STORY

Look at the characters. Which form of transportation do you think each one prefers? Write it on the line.

bike	car	bus

1. Luis
   CAR

2. Jessica
   BUS

3. Will
   BIKE

4. Emi
   CAR

Watch the video

4 GET THE PICTURE

A Look at your answers to Exercise 3. Did you guess correctly? Write the transportation each person prefers in the chart.

	Luis	Jessica	Will	Emi
Transportation:	car			
Other:	can take out a car loan			

B Now write one more piece of information about each person. Compare with a partner.

5 WATCH FOR DETAILS

Check (✓) **True** or **False**. Then correct the false statements. Compare with a partner.

	True	False	
1. Luis rides a bike now.	☐	✓	Luis takes the bus now.
2. Luis has already told his wife about the car.	☐	✓	I MAY HAVE TO TALK CARMEN
3. Will rode his bike through a puddle.	✓	☐	
4. Jessica will drive to work after graduation.	☐	✓	SHE WILL TAKE THE BUS
5. A car loan can help someone establish credit.	✓	☐	
6. Someone else bought the car Luis wants.	✓	☐	

6 WHAT'S YOUR OPINION?

A Complete the sentences with the consequences you think will happen.

1. If you buy a car before you have a job, ...

2. If you take out a car loan, ...

3. If you ride a bike instead of driving, ...

4. If you take the bus to work, ...

5. If you walk everywhere you go, ...

6. If you're not careful where you park your car, ...

B **PAIR WORK** Choose three sentences from part A and share your opinions.

Follow-up

7 YOUR CITY

A **PAIR WORK** In your city or town, what are the advantages and disadvantages of these forms of transportation? Complete the chart. Then compare around the class.

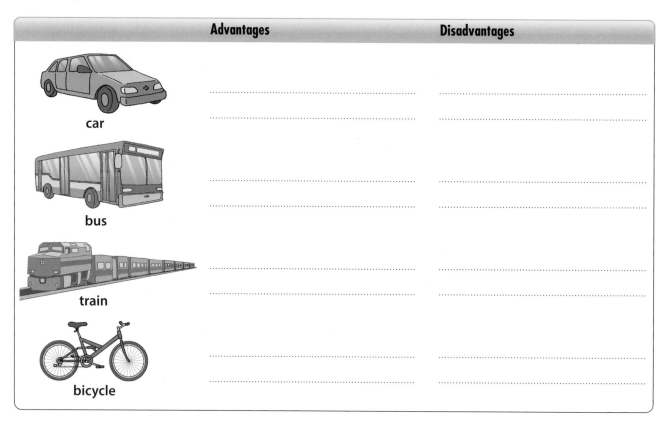

	Advantages	Disadvantages
car		
bus		
train		
bicycle		

B Convince another pair to leave their cars at home. Give as many reasons as you can why another form of transportation is better.

"If you drive a car every day, you're going to spend a lot of money on gas."

8 *WHAT DID THEY SAY?*

Watch the video and complete the conversation. Then practice it.

Jessica and Will warn Luis about the expenses of owning a car.

Jessica: People ....*used*.... ....*to*.... pay for things with cash. They
didn't buy on credit. ....
money to buy the car, you're ....
.... that debt for years.

Will: And even .... you .... the debt,
you're going to have to spend a lot of .... on the car.
You're going to .... to pay for ....
insurance, and you're going to .... to pay for
....

Jessica: Yeah, and you're going to have to pay for ....
And, if you're not .... , you're going to pay
parking .... It all ....

Luis: You're right. I didn't think .... the expenses.

Jessica: After graduation, I'm still going to ....
.... to work. But that's OK with me. Public transportation
in .... city is .... efficient.

9 *TALKING ABOUT THE PAST, PRESENT, AND FUTURE*

A Complete each sentence with at least two of the phrases
in the box. Then compare with a partner.

In the past, people used to . . .

1. ....
2. ....

Today, many people . . .

3. ....
4. ....

In the future, people will . . .

5. ....
6. ....

> think it's safer to get a job before
>   you buy a car
> pay for things with cash
> take the bus to work
> not buy things on credit
> establish credit through loans
> walk or bike to work more often

B Write two more sentences of your own about transportation in the
past, present, and future. Take turns reading them to a partner.

1. ....
2. ....

10 The job interview

1 CULTURE

Nearly 50 percent of North American college students have an internship at some point during college. In Canada, internships are called *co-ops*. A co-op, or internship, is like a temporary job, usually related to the student's major. Internships often take place during the summer when students are not in school. Others may be part-time during the school year. Some colleges offer course credit for doing an internship, and some employers pay interns a small wage. All internships allow students to gain experience in a new field. Interning is a great way to break into a company because employers often hire the former interns after they graduate.

Have you ever had a part-time job or internship? What did you do? Where would you like to work?

2 VOCABULARY *Getting a job*

PAIR WORK What questions would a job interviewer ask at a fast-food restaurant? Match the parts of the sentences. Then add two questions of your own.

1. Where did you   want to work here?
2. What are your   find out about this job?
3. Why do you   well with children?
4. Do you like   qualifications?
5. Do you get along   good with money?
6. Are you   working with people?

7. ....

8. ....

3 GUESS THE STORY

PAIR WORK What do you think each job candidate is like? Write a few words for each person.

Susan   Scott

.....professional....   ....

....

                                         Susan   Scott

4 GET THE PICTURE

Complete the sentences. Then compare with a partner.

1. Mario Verdi is the ....
2. Danielle Derby is the ....
3. Susan and Scott are applying for an ....
4. Susan is quite skilled with ....
5. Scott enjoys working with ....
6. Mario likes .... Danielle prefers ....

5 WHO SAID WHAT?

A Who said the sentences below? Check (✓) the correct answers. Then compare with a partner.

	Danielle	Susan	Scott	Mario
1. I know all of the main design programs.	☐	✓	☐	☐
2. Would you be able to create a banner ad for a web page?	☐	☐	☐	☐
3. I love sports, and I love marketing.	☐	☐	☐	☐
4. I see you're quite skilled with computers.	☐	☐	☐	☐
5. Do you have any sales experience?	☐	☐	☐	☐
6. I can sell anything.	☐	☐	☐	☐
7. I love being busy.	☐	☐	☐	☐
8. I don't mind trying new things because I'm a very fast learner.	☐	☐	☐	☐

6 WHAT'S YOUR OPINION?

A What skills does the internship require? Write two more skills in the chart.

Job skills	Susan	Scott
Design skills	☐	☐
Computer skills	☐	☐
Other:	☐	☐
Other:	☐	☐

B Does Susan have the skills? Does Scott have the skills? Check (✓) the correct answers.

C PAIR WORK Discuss who you think is best for the job and why.

A: I think Scott has more of the skills the job needs. He said he's good with numbers.
B: Oh, I don't think so. I think when he says he's good at computers, he's exaggerating.

Follow-up

7 INTERVIEW

PAIR WORK Interview a classmate for an internship. Use the questions in Exercise 2 and in the video to help you. Start like this:

A: Why do you want an internship here?
B: Well, I'm very creative. . . .

8 JOB SKILLS

A PAIR WORK What do a salesperson and a graphic designer need to be good at? Choose from these phrases and add other ideas of your own.

managing money   using their visual sense
solving problems   getting along with people
using computers

B GROUP WORK Now play a game. What skills do people with these jobs need? Take turns giving your ideas. Think of as many things as you can. The person with the most ideas wins.

a chef   a firefighter   a teacher

C What are you good at? Tell your group. Your classmates will suggest an appropriate career for you!

A manager needs to be good at managing money.

☰ Language close-up

9 WHAT DID THEY SAY?

Watch the video and complete the conversation. Then practice it.

Danielle and Mario interview an internship candidate.

Mario: You have a very ….*impressive*…. résumé, Susan. …………………… us about …………………… .

Susan: Well, Mr. Verdi, I'm …………………… and I …………………… that my artistic …………………… would …………………… …………………… well here.

Danielle: I see you're quite …………………… with …………………… .

Susan: Yes. I …………………… all the …………………… design …………………… . And I'm actually …………………… a …………………… for my father's …………………… , and I'm …………………… a 3-D software …………………… this …………………… .

Danielle: Excellent! But won't you be …………………… …………………… for an internship?

Susan: Oh, no. I …………………… …………………… busy.

10 SHORT RESPONSES *Giving personal information*

A Write personal responses to these statements, choosing from the expressions below. Then compare with a partner.

So am I.	Neither am I.	I am.	I'm not.
So do I.	Neither do I.	I do.	I don't.
So can I.	Neither can I.	I can.	I can't.

1. I like working with numbers. ……………………………………

2. I enjoy working with computers. ……………………………………

3. I'm not good at managing money. ……………………………………

4. I don't like doing office work. ……………………………………

5. I can sell anything. ……………………………………

6. I can't type very fast. ……………………………………

I can design an ad.

So can I.

B Now write four new statements about yourself and read them to your partner. Your partner will respond with one of the expressions above.

1. …………………………………………………… 3. ……………………………………………………

2. …………………………………………………… 4. ……………………………………………………

Two brothers in Peru

1 CULTURE

Peru is located in western South America. It is bordered by the Pacific coast, divided by the Andes Mountains, and is partly covered by the Amazon Rain Forest. Nearly 30 million people live in this diverse land. Spanish is the official language, but many people speak the native language, Quechua. Peru is the home of Machu Picchu, an archaeological site that once was a busy Incan city. It was abandoned about 500 years ago but is now a popular destination for tourists, historians, and hikers. Machu Picchu is a UNESCO World Heritage site and an important cultural attraction.

Would you like to visit Machu Picchu? Why or why not?
What do you enjoy most about traveling?

2 VOCABULARY Sightseeing

A PAIR WORK What can you do when you travel to a historic site? Put the words in the chart. Can you add two more words?

✓ancient ruins	go hiking	join a tour group	temples
eat at restaurants	hot springs	shop at local markets	

Things to see	Things to do
ancient ruins	

B Which things in your chart do you like to do the most?

3 GUESS THE FACTS

Watch the first 30 seconds of the video with the sound off.
Answer these questions.

Who are the people in the video?
What do you think the video is going to show?

4 GET THE PICTURE

A These are the things that Derek and Paul did in Peru. Put the pictures in order (1 to 5).

B Now write the correct sentence under each picture. Compare with a partner.

They climbed Huayna Picchu for a different view.
They saw the Incas'"riding lawnmower," the llama.
They ate fruits and vegetables from local markets.

They took the train back to Cusco.
✓ They hiked the Inca Trail to Machu Picchu.

....

....

....

....

They hiked the Inca Trail to
Machu Picchu.

....

....

....

....

5 WHAT'S YOUR OPINION?

A What do you think of Derek and Paul's trip? Rate each part of the trip from 1 (very interesting) to 5 (not interesting). Circle the numbers.

1. Exploring Machu Picchu	1	2	3	4	5
2. Visiting the town of Aguas Calientes	1	2	3	4	5
3. Seeing the open market with fruits and vegetables	1	2	3	4	5
4. Learning about the history of Machu Picchu	1	2	3	4	5
5. Climbing Huayna Picchu	1	2	3	4	5

B PAIR WORK Compare opinions.

A: What did you think of exploring Machu Picchu?   B: It looked fun. I gave it a 1. How about you? . . .

6 WATCH FOR DETAILS

Write one thing that you learned about the people, places, or things below. Then compare with a partner.

1. Machu Picchu ....

2. The Inca ....

3. Aguas Calientes ....

4. Huayna Picchu ....

5. Paul and Derek ....

☰ Follow-up

7 A DAY AT MACHU PICCHU

A GROUP WORK Use your knowledge of Machu Picchu to plan three things to do. Choose from the suggestions in the tourist brochure below.

Bus or hike to Machu Picchu.

Join a tour of Machu Picchu.

Learn about the history of Hiram Bingham and the site.

See llamas.

Explore and shop in the local markets.

Hike to Huayna Picchu.

Start like this:

A: I'd like to learn about Hiram Bingham.
B: So would I. I wonder what year he was born. . . .

B CLASS ACTIVITY Compare answers as a class.

8 WHAT DID HE SAY?

Watch the video and complete the description. Then compare with a partner.

Paul talks about the construction of Machu Picchu.

Machu Picchu, which means "Old Peak," ......was...... ...constructed...

around 1450. .... , as the empire collapsed ....

the Spanish, it .... abandoned, roughly 100 years

.... Machu Picchu ....

the outside ....

In 1911, the site .... explorer

and historian Hiram Bingham .... the ....

of some .... residents. He .... the

.... job of clearing .... hundreds of

.... of .... growth from the ....

9 THE PASSIVE *Giving factual information*

A Imagine that Paul and Derek said these things about Machu Picchu.
Complete the sentences using the verbs in parentheses.
Then compare with a partner.

1. The historic site of Machu Picchu ....is located...........
   in Peru. (locate)
2. Tourists .... all the comforts of home in
   Aguas Calientes. (offer)
3. This entire hotel .... out by tourists. (rent)
4. Ancient techniques .... still ....
   by craftsmen in this town. (use)
5. The buildings .... out of blocks of stone. (build)
6. The site .... by half a million people a year! (visit)

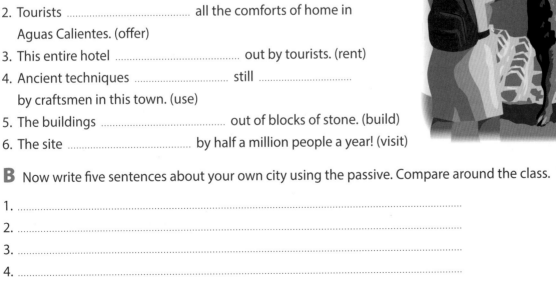

B Now write five sentences about your own city using the passive. Compare around the class.

1. ....
2. ....
3. ....
4. ....
5. ....

12 Profile: A TV reporter

1 CULTURE

Changes in technology have changed journalism. News media have shifted from the printed word of newspapers and magazines to the Internet. Reporters still report on current events, but on the Internet, stories often include photos, videos, and frequent updates throughout the day. Today, a reporter can carry his or her own video camera or even report using a cell phone. And as more readers are posting their own news stories and opinions online, the face of journalism is changing.

Where do you get your news?
What do you think is the biggest change to journalism today?
How do you think journalism will change in the next 10 years?

2 VOCABULARY *The life of a reporter*

PAIR WORK Put the words in the word map.

✓ car accident	house fire	learning a language	radio reporter	TV reporter
corruption	laptop computer	organized crime	riding a bike	video camera

Types of reporters
....
....

Technology to produce stories
....
....

The Life of a Reporter

Story assignments
car accident
....
....
....

Hobbies
....
....

3 GUESS THE FACTS

Watch the first minute and a half of the video with the sound off.
Answer these questions.

1. Where do you think this person works?

   ....

2. Where do you think he lives?

   ....

3. What hobbies do you think he has?

   ....

☰ Watch the video

4 GET THE PICTURE

Look at your answers to Exercise 3. Did you guess correctly? Correct your
answers. Then compare with a partner.

5 WATCH FOR DETAILS

Check (✓) **True** or **False**. Then correct the false statements. Compare with a partner.

	True	False	
1. Kai Nagata owns the Canadian Broadcasting Company (CBC).	☐	✓	*Kai works for the CBC.*
2. The CBC news network is in Canada.	☐	☐	....
3. When Kai first moved to Montreal, he spoke French very well.	☐	☐	....
4. Kai started out as a TV reporter.	☐	☐	....
5. Kai tells his stories in words.	☐	☐	....
6. Kai uses a laptop computer to produce stories.	☐	☐	....
7. Kai wants to tell stories about other countries.	☐	☐	....
8. Lately, Kai has been assigned to stories about corruption.	☐	☐	....
9. Kai likes knowing what stories he'll be assigned.	☐	☐	....
10. Kai thinks he will be a journalist for a short time.	☐	☐	....

6 WHAT'S YOUR OPINION?

A PAIR WORK What stories has Kai Nagata covered? Check (✓) your answers. Can you add one or two more stories that you heard mentioned? Then compare with a partner.

☐ corruption

☐ demonstration

☐ house fire

☐ ....

☐ inflation

☐ ....

B If you were a reporter, which stories in part A would you like to cover? Which wouldn't you like to cover? Think of two more stories you would like to cover. Write them below. Discuss with a partner.

1. ....   2. ....

☰ Follow-up

7 ROLE PLAY *How long have you been . . . ?*

A PAIR WORK Imagine that you are a reporter interviewing your partner for a profile story. Ask questions about past and current interests. Then switch places. Start like this:

A: What things did you like when you were a kid?
B: When I was little, I liked . . .
A: What are you interested in now?
B: Well, lately I've been . . .

B GROUP WORK Take turns telling your group about what your partner has been doing. Try to use some of the phrases in the box below.

began as	has been able to	moved to
first started	has been thinking about	plans to
had	has been working on	wanted to

Language close-up

8 WHAT DID HE SAY?

Watch the video and complete the commentary. Then compare with a partner.

Kai Nagata talks about his career as a reporter.

When I first ......started...... off at the CBC, I

.... on the radio side. I went out as a radio

reporter, and I .... all the same news stories

as the TV reporters, but only for audio. Then I ....

.... and moved over to television, and so, for the

last year, I've .... all my stories visually.

In the .... , TV reporters ....

.... rely on a big crew, a big team .... lots of .... ,

complicated equipment. But with .... technology, I ....

.... a whole TV story on my own. I've .... stories for

TV .... just a video camera in my backpack .... a laptop

computer.

9 VERB TENSES *Talking about the past and present*

A Match phrases from A and B and write four sentences. Then compare with a partner.

A
Kai has been learning French
Kai was promoted to the TV side
Kai has been riding his bike
Kai's ancestors immigrated to Canada
Kai reported simple stories

B
since he was a kid.
since he arrived in Montreal.
after working as a radio reporter.
when he first joined the CBC.
more than a hundred years ago.

1. Kai has been learning French since he arrived in Montreal.
2. ....
3. ....
4. ....
5. ....

B Now complete these sentences with information about yourself. Compare with a partner.

1. I was .... when I ....

2. While I was .... , I became interested in ....

3. I've been .... for the last ....

13 Street performers

1 *CULTURE*

Visitors to Boston, Massachusetts should not miss Faneuil (*fan-yule*) Hall Marketplace. It is one of the United States' top tourist sites. This historic marketplace opened in 1742 and was a market and the site of famous meetings. It is near the water, and there are many restaurants and shops for people to enjoy. What makes the marketplace really exciting, though, is the free entertainment. Every day the marketplace fills with street performers and the people who come to watch them.

Faneuil Hall Marketplace

Are street performers popular in your country?
Would you stop to watch a street performer?
Do you think people should give money to street performers?
* Why or why not?*

2 VOCABULARY *Street performers*

A **PAIR WORK** Write the correct word(s) under each picture.

> ✓an acrobat   an accordion player   a balloon man   a clown   a dance troupe   a magician

1. ....

2. an acrobat ....

3. ....

4. ....

5. ....

6. ....

B Can you think of four more types of street performers? Write them below.

1. .... 2. .... 3. .... 4. ....

3 GUESS THE FACTS

Watch the first minute of the video with the sound off. Who is the host?

a reporter   a tour guide   a tourist

☰ Watch the video

4 GET THE PICTURE

Write the type of performer under each picture. Which performers did the host talk
to or talk about? Check (✓) the correct answers. Then compare with a partner.

....

....

....

....

5 WATCH FOR DETAILS

What are these people's opinions of the performers? Write at least two words.
Then compare with a partner.

....
....
....

....
....
....

....
....
....

A What do you think of the performers? Rate each performance from 1 (very good) to 5 (poor). Circle the numbers.

1	1	1	1
2	2	2	2
3	3	3	3
4	4	4	4
5	5	5	5

B **PAIR WORK** Compare opinions. Choose words from the box or use words of your own.

amazing	energetic	great	surprised
amusing	entertaining	interesting	talented
boring	excellent	fascinating	unbelievable
creative	fun	silly	

A: What did you think of the balloon man?
B: I thought he was creative. I gave him a 2. How about you? . . .

Follow-up

7 HIRE A PERFORMER

GROUP WORK Imagine you are planning a party and want to hire a performer or group of performers. Which of these performers would you like to hire? Why?

A: I think it would be great to hire a magician.
B: Why?
A: Well, because magicians are entertaining. . . .

| a mime | a guitarist | a magician | a pianist | a rock band |

☰ Language close-up

8 WHAT DID THEY SAY?

Watch the video and complete the interview. Then compare with a partner.

The host asks a woman what she thought of a street performer.

Host: So what did you .... *think* .... about his .... ?

Woman: I .... by what he could do, and all the things he .... make

out of balloons! This man is .... It .... you feel like you're a

.... again. I think .... both really ....

what he's doing. It's .... to .... by someone on the street, and

.... , they're just making something .... out of a ....

9 PARTICIPLES *Giving opinions*

A Rewrite these sentences using present and past participles.
Then compare with a partner.

1. The balloon man entertained me.

   The balloon man was entertaining.

   I was entertained by the balloon man.

2. The musician surprised me.

   ....

   ....

3. The dance troupe energized me.

   ....

   ....

4. The host amused me.

   ....

   ....

B Now change your sentences to give your true opinions. Read them to a partner.

C Complete the chart. Then compare with a partner.

Something you find entertaining	Something you find boring
I find .... entertaining.	....
Something you find amusing	**Something you find surprising**
....	....

The body language of business

Preview

1 CULTURE

Picture yourself riding in an elevator alone. What happens when someone else enters the elevator? Where do you both stand? Do you make eye contact? Where do people stand when there are four people? Imagine that you enter a crowded elevator, face everyone, make eye contact, and smile. What would people do? What would they think about you? There are unspoken rules for riding in an elevator, just as there are cultural rules for how close we stand to people, the gestures we use, and how much eye contact is polite. But there is one gesture that is universally understood: a smile.

In your country, what gesture do you use when you meet someone for the first time? How do you greet an old friend?
What gestures are considered rude?

2 VOCABULARY *Body language*

PAIR WORK Which word do you think best describes the people below?
Check (✓) the correct word.

1. ✓ friendly
   ☐ nervous

2. ☐ bored
   ☐ interested

3. ☐ confident
   ☐ lazy

4. ☐ approachable
   ☐ surprised

5. ☐ confused
   ☐ sincere

3 GUESS THE FACTS

Watch the first 30 seconds of the video with the sound off.
What is your first impression of the woman in the job interview?
Write down a few words that describe her body language.

....

☰ Watch the video

4 GET THE PICTURE

Check (✓) the correct answers. Then compare with a partner.

1. The host says you can make a good
   first impression with . . .
   ☐ what you say.
   ☐ your body language.

2. The host says you have seven seconds
   to show . . .
   ☐ your credibility, confidence, and competence.
   ☐ your job skills and professional experience.

5 WATCH FOR DETAILS

Write the correct sentence under each picture. Then compare with a partner.

✓Adjust your attitude.	Make eye contact.	Shake hands.	Stand tall.
Lean in slightly.	Raise your eyebrows.	Smile.	

1. ....

2. ....

3. ....

4. ....

5. ....

6. ....

7. Adjust your attitude.

6 WHAT DOES IT MEAN?

What gestures can you use to convey these attitudes? Check (✓) all the correct answers.
Then compare with a partner.

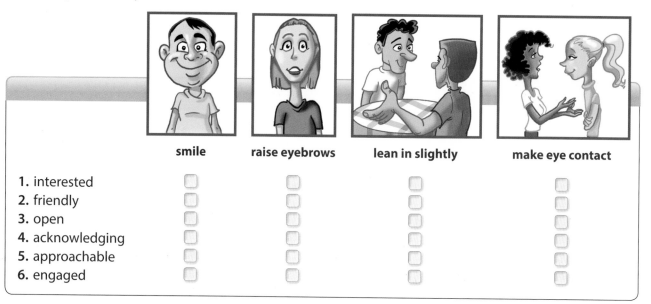

	smile	raise eyebrows	lean in slightly	make eye contact
1. interested	☐	☐	☐	☐
2. friendly	☐	☐	☐	☐
3. open	☐	☐	☐	☐
4. acknowledging	☐	☐	☐	☐
5. approachable	☐	☐	☐	☐
6. engaged	☐	☐	☐	☐

Follow-up

7 GESTURES

A PAIR WORK What are some other gestures you might make during
a job interview? Add two gestures to the list. Then compare with a partner.

1. Adjust your attitude.
2. Stand tall.
3. Smile.
4. Make eye contact.
5. Raise your eyebrows.
6. Lean in slightly.
7. Shake hands.
8. ....
9. ....

B Act out each gesture from part A and have your partner
guess which one it is.

8 ROLE PLAY

PAIR WORK Practice making good first impressions.
Take turns acting as the interviewer and interviewee.
Remember to use gestures from the video. Start like this:

A: Hello, I'm (name). (shakes hands)
B: I'm (name). Thank you for coming in. (smiles)

Interchange VRB 2 © Cambridge University Press 2012   Photocopiable

Language close-up

9 WHAT DID SHE SAY?

Watch the video and complete the descriptions. Then compare with a partner.

The host explains some ways to make a positive first impression.

First, adjust your attitude. ..... Don't ..... wait ..... until you ....
the interview room to .... Before you ....
through the door, ... about the situation and ....
a conscious choice about the .... you want to embody.
.... that attract .... include .... ,
.... , approachable, and ....

           *   *   *

Make eye contact. .... at someone's .... transmits
energy and indicates .... and ....
.... the interviewer's eyes .... enough to notice
what .... they are. With this one ....
technique, ... dramatically increase ....
likeability factor.

10 MODALS AND ADVERBS *Expressing probability*

A Complete each conversation with a logical answer. Then compare with a partner.

1. A: I just had a job interview. The interviewer didn't offer to shake my hand.
   B: Maybe it means ....

2. A: I sent my friend three text messages, but she didn't respond.
   B: It could mean ....

3. A: My boss was late for our meeting. And she didn't make eye contact at first.
   B: It may mean ....

4. A: I just got this new coat, and I really like it. But sometimes I see people whispering.
   B: Perhaps it means ....

B (PAIR WORK) Now have similar conversations about
real or imaginary situations in your own life.

A: My friend Steve doesn't answer my text messages.
B: Maybe it means . . .

15 Sticky situations

1 CULTURE

In a recent survey, people in the United States were asked to describe their most embarrassing moments during a visit to someone's home. Here are the top answers:

- Dressing incorrectly for the occasion.
- Arriving on the wrong day or wrong time.
- Spilling something or breaking something valuable.
- Saying something by mistake that offended the host.
- Forgetting someone's name.

Would the same things be embarrassing in your culture?
   Why or why not?
What was your most embarrassing moment during a visit to
   someone's home?

**Almost everyone has dressed the
wrong way at least once!**

2 VOCABULARY *Problems with guests*

PAIR WORK   Do you know these nouns and verbs? Complete the chart.
(If you don't know a word, look it up in your dictionary.) Then take
turns answering the questions below.

Verb	Noun	Verb	Noun
apologize	*apology*	misunderstand	
	approval		offer
invite			realization
	lie		reminder

1. Have you apologized for anything recently?
2. What's something a person might lie about?
3. Have you had a problem because someone misunderstood you recently?
4. Has someone offered you something nice recently?
5. Have you had to remind someone to do something lately?

GUESS THE FACTS

Watch the video with the sound off. What three embarrassing situations do you see?

☰ Watch the video

4 **GET THE PICTURE**

A What happened to these people? Write the correct sentence under each picture.

This person didn't like what the host served for dinner.
This person arrived too early for a party.
A dinner guest stayed too late at this person's house.
This person served food her guest didn't like.

A dinner guest stayed too late at this person's house.

Her husband fell asleep at the table.

....

....

....

....

....

....

B Now write one more piece of information under each picture. Compare with a partner.

C (PAIR WORK) Take turns. Describe what happened to each person.

"This woman invited her boss over for dinner. They had a good time, but her boss wouldn't leave. Her husband fell asleep. . . ."

A What are these people's opinions about the situations? Write the correct number in each box. Then compare with a partner.

Situation 1

The guest should have . . .   The host should have . . .

1. apologized and offered to help.   1. asked the guest to run an errand.
2. pretended to have an errand to run.   2. put the guest to work.
3. left quickly and come back later.

Situation 2

The host should have . . .

1. lied and said she had to get up early.
2. pretended she wasn't tired.
3. reminded her boss it was late.
4. asked her boss to do the dishes.

Situation 3

The guest should have . . .   The host should have . . .

1. gone home before eating.   1. asked her guests if they had food allergies.
2. lied and said she was allergic to seafood.   2. asked her guests to bring food.
3. eaten it anyway.   3. eaten it anyway.

B PAIR WORK Which people do you agree with? Take turns sharing your opinions.

A: I agree with her *(points to photo)*. The guest should have . . .
B: I think his suggestion is better *(points)*. The guest should have . . .

                    Interchange VRB 2 © Cambridge University Press 2012 Photocopiable

Follow-up

6 WHAT WOULD YOU HAVE DONE?

GROUP WORK Take turns describing awkward or embarrassing situations you've been in. Say what you did. Your classmates will tell you what they would have done.

A: I realized I forgot my best friend's birthday, so I gave her some flowers two weeks later and apologized. What would you have done?

B: Well, I think I would have . . .

Language close-up

7 WHAT DID THEY SAY?

People are describing difficult situations involving guests.

A Watch the first situation. Complete the guest's description.

I was ....invited........ to a ...., and I .... an hour

.... I thought it would .... me .... to get

there. Well, Rebecca .... to the door .... sweatpants

and an old T-shirt. . . . I could .... the shower .... in the

background, and of course, ... a single guest was ....

B Now watch the second situation. Complete the host's description.

I .... my boss and her husband to .... the other

.... We had a .... time, but she just wouldn't

.... By .... , my .... and I were so

.... Finally, my husband fell .... at the table. My boss

was very .... when she .... it was so ....

I just .... know what to do when a guest won't go ....

8 WOULD HAVE AND SHOULD HAVE *Giving suggestions*

A **PAIR WORK** Can you think of suggestions for these situations? Write statements using **would have** and **should have**. Then compare around the class. Who has the best suggestions?

1. A guest arrived on the wrong day for the party.
   The guest <u>should have apologized and gone home</u> .
   If I were the host, I <u>would have . . .</u> .

2. A dinner guest broke a valuable dish.
   If I were the guest, I ....
   The host ....

3. Two dinner guests got into a big argument.
   The guests ....
   If I were the host, I ....

4. The host discovered she didn't have enough food.
   The guests ....
   If I were the host, I ....

16 It's my birthday!

≡ Preview

1 *CULTURE*

In the United States and Canada, birthdays are celebrated at all ages and in different ways. There is no typical party; some are large and others are small. For children, parents throw parties at home or at a child-themed restaurant. Guests are expected to bring presents. For adults, parties are held at home or at a restaurant or club. Presents aren't usually expected, but for parties at home, it's always good to bring some food or drink for the host. Two things you can expect at all birthday parties: a cake with candles and people singing "Happy Birthday to You."

How do people in your country celebrate birthdays?
Are certain birthdays more important to celebrate than others?
What are guests expected to do for a birthday?

2 **VOCABULARY** *Adjectives*

PAIR WORK How would you feel in the situations below? Choose adjectives from the box.

amused	delighted	enthusiastic	nervous	shy
angry	disappointed	excited	pleased	upset
bored	embarrassed	interested	relaxed	worried

1. You are a dinner guest at someone's house. Your host offers you food you don't like.

   A: I think I'd feel worried. How can I avoid eating it and not offend my host?

   B: Really? I'd be relaxed. Just eat a little bit and say you had a big lunch.

2. Your best friend gives you a gift that you really don't like.

3. Someone forgets an appointment with you.

4. You meet someone you like at a party. The next day you run into the person at the supermarket.

5. Someone talks to you at the store. You realize it's someone you've met before, but you can't remember the person's name.

3 GUESS THE STORY

Watch the first two minutes of the video with the sound off.
What do you think Tim is doing? Check (✓) your answer.

- ☐ trying to make plans
- ☐ trying to get out of plans
- ☐ trying to find someone

Watch the video

4 GET THE PICTURE

How do you think these people really felt? Check (✓) the best answers.
Then compare with a partner.

1. How did Sofia act when she told Tim everyone was busy?
   - ☐ angry
   - ☐ sympathetic

2. How did Tim feel when Steve said he was busy Saturday?
   - ☐ disappointed
   - ☐ pleased

3. Was Sofia pleased with Steve's text message?
   - ☐ definitely
   - ☐ probably not

4. How did Tim feel when he arrived at Sofia's house?
   - ☐ happy to see her, but disappointed that no one else could come
   - ☐ confused that Sofia was the only person there

5. What was Tim's reaction when Sofia turned on the video?
   - ☐ He was angry that his friends surprised him.
   - ☐ He was delighted that his friends surprised him.

5 MAKING INFERENCES

Who said what? Check (✓) the person who said each sentence.
Was the person lying, or being sincere? On the line,
write **L** for lying or **S** for sincere. Compare with a partner.

1. Everyone told me they were busy. ☐ .... ✓ ....L.... ☐ .... ☐ ....

2. I didn't know you were into salsa dancing. ☐ .... ☐ .... ☐ .... ☐ ....

3. We're on a conference call. ☐ .... ☐ .... ☐ .... ☐ ....

4. John can't come to your dinner Saturday. ☐ .... ☐ .... ☐ .... ☐ ....

5. Maybe you guys can stop by the club afterwards. ☐ .... ☐ .... ☐ .... ☐ ....

6. I guess you'll miss my birthday. Too bad. ☐ .... ☐ .... ☐ .... ☐ ....

☰ Follow-up

6 POLITE RESPONSES

A **PAIR WORK** Imagine you're talking with friends. Complete the conversations below with polite responses or excuses. Then act them out.

1. A: Why don't we play chess? It's one of my favorite games!

   B: It's one of my favorite games, too.

2. A: Do you want to go see the new science fiction movie on Saturday?

   B: ....

3. A: We're having something special for dinner. I hope you like spicy food!

   B: ....

4. A: What do you think of this poem I wrote?

   B: ....

B Now act out at least two new conversations of your own. You can make them long or short. Make sure not to hurt your partner's feelings!

☰ Language close-up

7 WHAT DID THEY SAY?

Watch the video and complete the conversation. Then practice it.

Jessica and John make excuses not to come to Tim's birthday party.

Jessica: John can't come to .....your..... ...dinner... Saturday. I just asked him. And .... that he has other plans.

John: I did?

Jessica: Yeah, you .... that you were playing guitar with your .... , uh, someplace. In fact, I was very .... that you .... playing. Very *surprised*.

John: Oh, yeah. .... , I'm busy . . . playing . . . on Saturday. ....

Tim: .... you weren't in the band anymore.

John: This is my farewell concert. I .... do it.

Tim: I guess you'll miss my birthday. ....

John: Yeah, but I can't .... You know .... it is. Maybe .... can stop by the club ....

Tim: Sure. Yeah. Thanks. That sounds ....

8 REPORTED SPEECH *He said, she said*

A Report what each person said. Then compare with a partner.

1. "Maybe they can change their plans." (Tim)
   Tim said maybe they could change their plans.

2. "I'm salsa dancing." (Steve)
   ....

3. "I'll make it up to you." (Steve to Tim)
   ....

4. "We're on a conference call." (Jessica)
   ....

5. "John can't come to dinner." (Jessica)
   ....

"I'm salsa dancing."

B CLASS ACTIVITY Ask several classmates what they think of the things in the box. Write down their answers. Then report their opinions to the class.

A: What do you think of wrestling?
B: I think it's awful.
A: Tina said she thought wrestling was awful. . . .

jazz music
motorcycles
old movies
pet costumes
vegetarian food
wrestling

This page is intentionally left blank

interchange

FIFTH EDITION

2

Workbook

Jack C. Richards

with Jonathan Hull and Susan Proctor

CAMBRIDGE
UNIVERSITY PRESS

This page is intentionally left blank

Contents

Credits

The authors and publishers acknowledge the following sources of copyright material and are grateful for the permissions granted. While every effort has been made, it has not always been possible to identify the sources of all the material used, or to trace all copyright holders. If any omissions are brought to our notice, we will be happy to include the appropriate acknowledgements on reprinting and in the next update to the digital edition, as applicable.

Key: B = Below, BL = Below Left, BR = Below Right, C = Centre, CL = Centre Left, CR = Centre Right, Ex = Exercise, L = Left, R = Right, T = Top, TL = Top Left, TR = Top Right.

Illustrations

337 Jon (KJA Artists): 4, 22; **417 Neal** (KJA Artists): 1, 16, 67, 84, 90; **Mark Duffi** : 39 (Victrola, telephone), 51; **Thomas Girard** (Good Illustration): 32, 87; **John Goodwin** (Eye Candy Illustration): 36, 94; **Gary Venn** (Lemonade Illustration Agency): 30, 64; **Quino Marin** (The Organisation): 79, 91; **Gavin Reece** (New Division): 85; **Paul Williams** (Sylvie Poggio Artists): 42.

Photos

Back cover (woman with whiteboard): Jenny Acheson/Stockbyte/GettyImages; Back cover (whiteboard): Nemida/GettyImages; Back cover (man using phone): Betsie Van Der Meer/Taxi/GettyImages; Back cover (woman smiling): PeopleImages.com/DigitalVision/GettyImages; Back cover (name tag): Tetra Images/GettyImages; Back cover (handshake): David Lees/Taxi/GettyImages; p. 2: JackF/iStock/Getty Images Plus/GettyImages; p. 3: Slaven Vlasic/Getty Images Entertainment/GettyImages; p. 5: Baar/ullstein bild/GettyImages; p. 6: Jetta Productions/Stone/GettyImages; p. 7 (TL): Vasilii Kosarev/EyeEm/GettyImages; p. 7 (TR): skynesher/E+/GettyImages; p. 7 (CL): Richard Newstead/Moment/GettyImages; p. 7 (CR): Scott Olson/Getty Images News/GettyImages; p. 7 (BL): Cultura RM Exclusive/Dan Dunkley/Cultura Exclusive/GettyImages; p. 7 (BR): ALAN SCHEIN/GettyImages; p. 8: Daniel Allan/Photodisc/GettyImages; p. 10 (cable railway): Anthony Collins/Photodisc/GettyImages; p. 10 (ferry): Michael Coyne/Lonely Planet Images/GettyImages; p. 10 (subway): GILLARDI Jacques/hemis.fr/GettyImages; p. 10 (tram): marco wong/Moment/GettyImages; p. 11: Jack Hollingsworth/Stockbyte/GettyImages; p. 12: Sven Hagolani/GettyImages; p. 13: Stewart Cohen/The Image Bank/GettyImages; p. 14 (CR): H. Armstrong Roberts/ClassicStock/Archive Photos/GettyImages; p. 14 (BR): Johner Images/Brand X Pictures/GettyImages; p. 17: Jake Fitzjones/Dorling Kindersley/GettyImages; p. 18 (TR): Goodluz/iStock/Getty Images Plus/GettyImages; p. 18 (CL): KingWu/iStock/Getty Images Plus/GettyImages; p. 18 (BR): Coprid/iStock/Getty Images Plus/GettyImages; p. 19: Ethan Daniels/WaterFrame/GettyImages; p. 20: Thinkstock/Stockbyte/GettyImages; p. 21 (BL): 4FR/iStock/Getty Images Plus/GettyImages; p. 21 (T): Bolot/E+/GettyImages; p. 21 (BR): Lise Metzger/The Image Bank/GettyImages; p. 22: Lartal/Photolibrary/GettyImages; p. 23: Tony Robins/Photolibrary/GettyImages; p. 24 (CR): Anthony Lee/OJO Images/GettyImages; p. 24 (BR): Steve Brown Photography/Photolibrary/GettyImages; p. 25: Xavier Arnau/Vetta/GettyImages; p. 27 (C): Leonardo Martins/Moment/GettyImages; p. 27 (T): Michele Falzone/AWL Images/GettyImages; p. 27 (B): Michele Falzone/AWL Images/GettyImages; p. 28: FRED DUFOUR/AFP/GettyImages; p. 29: Hero Images/GettyImages; p. 30 (L): Tomasz Konczuk/EyeEm/GettyImages; p. 30 (R): OcusFocus/iStock/Getty Images Plus/GettyImages; p. 31: John Howard/DigitalVision/GettyImages; p. 33 (R): Blend Images-KidStock/Brand X Pictures/GettyImages; p. 33 (L): Laoshi/E+/GettyImages; p. 34: Rich Legg/E+/GettyImages; p. 35: DreamPictures/Blend Images/GettyImages; p. 37 (Ex 1.2): altrendo images/GettyImages; p. 37 (Ex 1.2): Maximilian Stock Ltd./Oxford Scientific/GettyImages; p. 37 (Ex 1.3): Tony Cordoza/Photographer's Choice/GettyImages; p. 37 (Ex 1.4): Tetra Images/GettyImages; p. 37 (Ex 1.5): Peter Dazeley/Photographer's Choice/GettyImages; p. 38: VCG/Visual China Group/GettyImages; p. 39 (TL): Stock Montage/GettyImages; p. 39 (TR): Roberto Machado Noa/LightRocket/GettyImages; p. 39 (CR): Ivan Stevanovic/E+/GettyImages; p. 39 (BR): Justin Sullivan/Getty Images News/GettyImages; p. 41 (Ex 8.1): Westend61/GettyImages; p. 41 (Ex 8.2): Prykhodov/iStock/Getty Images Plus/GettyImages; p. 41 (Ex 8.3): Jeffrey Hamilton/Stockbyte/GettyImages; p. 41 (Ex 8.4): Paul Bradbury/Caiaimage/GettyImages; p. 41 (Ex 8.5): sputnikos/iStock/Getty Images Plus/GettyImages; p. 41 (Ex 8.6): Image Source/GettyImages; p. 43 (TR): Charles Ommanney/The Washington Post/GettyImages; p. 43 (BR): Tetra Images/GettyImages; p. 44 (Ex 1.2): altrendo images/GettyImages; p. 45 (Martin Luther): FPG/Hulton Archive/GettyImages; p. 45 (Valentine's Day): Dorling Kindersley/GettyImages; p. 45 (April Fools' Day): Wodicka/ullstein bild/GettyImages; p. 45 (Mother's Day): Ariel Skelley/Blend Images/GettyImages; p. 45 (Father's Day): Ariel Skelley/Blend Images/GettyImages; p. 45 (Independence Day): Tetra Images/GettyImages; p. 45 (Labor Day): Blend Images-Ronnie Kaufman/Larry Hirshowitz/Brand X Pictures/GettyImages; p. 45 (Thanksgiving): Paul Poplis/Photolibrary/GettyImages; p. 46 (TR): PeopleImages/DigitalVision/GettyImages; p. 46 (CR): Floresco Productions/OJO Images/GettyImages; p. 47 (Japan): Eriko Koga/Taxi Japan/GettyImages; p. 47 (Morocco): Hisham Ibrahim/Photographer's Choice/GettyImages; p. 47 (Scotland): Education Images/Universal Images Group/GettyImages; p. 47 (India): Jihan Abdalla/Blend Images/GettyImages; p. 48: RubberBall Productions/Brand X Pictures/GettyImages; p. 49: Dan Dalton/Caiaimage/GettyImages; p. 50 (Ex 3.1 photo 1): JTB Photo/Universal Images Group/GettyImages; p. 50 (Ex 3.1 photo 2): fST Images - Caspar Benson/Brand X Pictures/GettyImages; p. 50 (Ex 3.2 photo 1): Glow Images/GettyImages; p. 50 (Ex 3.2 photo 2): Jason Homa/Blend Images/GettyImages; p. 50 (Ex 3.3 photo 1): David Caudery/PC Format Magazine/GettyImages; p. 50 (Ex 3.3 photo 2): David Caudery/Apple Bookazine/GettyImages; p. 50 (Ex 3.4 photo 1): H. Armstrong Roberts/ClassicStock/Archive Photos/GettyImages; p. 50 (Ex 3.4 photo 2): Sydney Roberts/DigitalVision/GettyImages; p. 50 (Ex 3.5 photo 1): Thomas Trutschel/Photothek/GettyImages; p. 50 (Ex 3.5 photo 2): Justin Sullivan/Getty Images News/GettyImages; p. 52: Westend61/GettyImages; p. 54: H. Armstrong Roberts/ClassicStock/Archive Photos/GettyImages; p. 55: JGI/Jamie Grill/Blend Images/GettyImages; p. 58 (Ex 7.1): Roberto Westbrook/Blend Images/GettyImages; p. 58 (Ex 7.2): Marc Romanelli/Blend Images/GettyImages; p. 58 (Ex 7.3): PeopleImages.com/DigitalVision/GettyImages; p. 58 (Ex 7.4): Rick Gomez/Blend Images/GettyImages; p. 58 (Ex 7.5): Ezra Bailey/Taxi/GettyImages; p. 59 (TR): Sam Diephuis/Blend Images/GettyImages; p. 59 (CR): Betsie Van Der Meer/Taxi/GettyImages; p. 60: JGI/Jamie Grill/Blend Images/GettyImages; p. 61: Arcaid/Universal Images Group/GettyImages; p. 62 (Ex 3.1): Matteo Colombo/Moment/GettyImages; p. 62 (Ex 3.2): Alan Copson/Photographer's Choice/GettyImages; p. 62 (Ex 3.3): John Lawson, Belhaven/Moment/GettyImages; p. 62 (Ex 3.4): Lily Chou/Moment/GettyImages; p. 62 (Ex 3.5): De Agostini/W. Buss/De Agostini Picture Library/GettyImages; p. 62 (Ex 3.6): Avatarmin/Moment/GettyImages; p. 63 (CR): Oliver J Davis Photography/Moment/GettyImages; p. 63 (TR): kimrawicz/iStock/Getty Images Plus/GettyImages; p. 64: John Elk III/Lonely Planet Images/GettyImages; p. 65 (C): Christian Adams/Photographer's Choice/GettyImages; p. 65 (BR): Erika Satta/EyeEm/GettyImages; p. 66: Yongyuan Dai/Moment/GettyImages; p. 68 (Ex 4.1): Redrockschool/E+/GettyImages; p. 68 (Ex 4.2): Milenko Bokan/iStock/Getty Images Plus/GettyImages; p. 68 (Ex 4.3): Jetta Productions/Iconica/GettyImages; p. 68 (Ex 4.4): Deklofenak/iStock/Getty Images Plus/GettyImages; p. 69: Rick Diamond/WireImage/GettyImages; p. 70: Marc Romanelli/Blend Images/GettyImages; p. 71: PeopleImages/DigitalVision/GettyImages; p. 72: Jamie Grill/The Image Bank/GettyImages; p. 73: Kris Connor/Getty Images Entertainment/GettyImages; p. 74 (TL): Monica Schipper/FilmMagic/GettyImages; p. 74 (BR): fotoMonkee/E+/GettyImages; p. 75 (TR): Popperfoto/Moviepix/GettyImages; p. 75 (BR): Metro-Goldwyn-Mayer/Archive Photos/GettyImages; p. 76: Buyenlarge/Archive Photos/GettyImages; p. 77: Ernst Haas/Ernst Haas/GettyImages; p. 78: Â©Lions Gate/Courtesy Everett Co/REX/Shutterstock; p. 80: Alan Copson/AWL Images/GettyImages; p. 82: Karl Johaentges/LOOK-foto/Look/GettyImages; p. 83 (T): YinYang/E+/GettyImages; p. 83 (Ex 7.1): Marcio Silva/iStock/Getty Images Plus/GettyImages; p. 83 (Ex 7.2): Gary D'Ercole/Stockbyte/GettyImages; p. 83 (Ex 7.3): Illiano/iStock/Getty Images Plus/GettyImages; p. 83 (Ex 7.4): Silvrshootr/iStock/Getty Images Plus/GettyImages; p. 83 (Ex 7.5): Danita Delimont/Gallo Images/GettyImages; p. 86: BrianAJackson/iStock/Getty Images Plus/GettyImages; p. 88: Monkey Business Images/Monkey Business/Getty Images Plus/GettyImages; p. 92: Sam Edwards/OJO Images/GettyImages; p. 93 (TL), p. 93 (BR): Simon Winnall/Iconica/GettyImages; p. 95: BananaStock/Getty Images Plus/GettyImages; p. 96: Sporrer/Rupp/Cultura/GettyImages.

1 Good memories

1 Past tense

A Write the past tense of these verbs.

Verb	Past tense	Verb	Past tense
be	_was/were_	hide	
become		laugh	
do		lose	
email		move	
get		open	
have		scream	

B Complete this paragraph. Use the past tense of each of the verbs in part A.

My best friend in school _____was_____ Michael. He and I _____ in Mrs. Gilbert's third-grade class, and we _____ friends. We often _____ crazy things in class, but I don't think Mrs. Gilbert ever really _____ mad at us. For example, Michael _____ a pet lizard named Peanut. Sometimes he _____ it in Mrs. Gilbert's desk drawer. Later, when she _____ the drawer, she always _____ loudly, and the class _____. After two years, Michael's family _____ to another town. We _____ each other for a few years, but then we _____ contact. I often wonder what he's doing now.

2 **Complete the questions in this conversation.**

Sarah: Welcome to the building. My name's Sarah Walker.

Benedito: Hello. I'm Benedito Peres. It's nice to meet you.

Sarah: Nice to meet you, too. Are you from around here?

Benedito: No, I'm from Brazil.

Sarah: Oh, really? _Were you born_ in Brazil?

Benedito: No, I wasn't born there, actually. I'm originally from Portugal.

Sarah: That's interesting. So, when _____ to Brazil?

Benedito: I moved to Brazil when I was in elementary school.

Sarah: Where _____?

Benedito: We lived in Recife. It's a beautiful city in northeast Brazil. Then I went to college.

Sarah: _____ to school in Recife?

Benedito: No, I went to school in São Paulo.

Sarah: And what _____?

Benedito: Oh, I studied engineering. But I'm here to go to graduate school.

Sarah: Great! When _____?

Benedito: I arrived last week. I start school in three days.

Sarah: Well, good luck. And sorry for all the questions!

3 **Answer these questions.**

1. Where were you born?

_____

2. Did your family move when you were a child?

_____

3. Did you have a favorite teacher in elementary school?

_____

4. What hobbies did you have when you were a kid?

_____

5. When did you begin to study English?

_____

4 Gael García Bernal

A Scan the article about Gael García Bernal. Where is he from? What does he do?

Gael García Bernal was born in 1978 in Guadalajara, Mexico. As a child, he began to act, and when he was a teenager, he became a star in television soap operas. He decided to go to London to study acting when he was 19. While he was in London, Mexican director Alejandro González Iñárritu invited him to act in the film *Amores Perros*. When it was released in 2000, *Amores Perros* immediately made Gael García Bernal known to the world.

Gael later made many other successful films. With the Mexican actor Diego Luna, he co-starred in *Y tu mamá también* in 2001, a film about two upper-class Mexican teenagers. In 2002, he won the Ariel, Mexico's most important film award, for *El Crimen del Padre Amaro*, the story of a young priest in a small town. Two years later, he worked with the Brazilian director Walter Salles on *The Motorcycle Diaries*, the story of a young Ernesto "Che" Guevara's journey by motorcycle through South America. That same year, Gael worked with the Spanish director Pedro Almodóvar on *Bad Education*. In 2007, Gael directed his first film, *Déficit*, which was about people at a weekend party in Mexico.

As you can see, Gael García Bernal is an international star who works on films in different languages. One of Gael's more recent projects is *Mozart in the Jungle*, an American TV show mostly in English. Gael won a Golden Globe Award in 2016 for playing the lead role, the talented conductor Rodrigo.

Despite his busy career, Gael spends as much time as possible with his son Lázaro and his daughter Libertad. He also likes to sing and make music when he is not acting.

B Check (✓) True or False. For statements that are false, write the correct information.

	True	False
1. Gael García Bernal studied acting in Paris.	☐	☐
2. A Brazilian director directed the film that made him famous.	☐	☐
3. He won an award for his role in *El Crimen del Padre Amaro*.	☐	☐
4. He has never directed a film.	☐	☐
5. He plays a singer in *Mozart in the Jungle*.	☐	☐
6. Gael prefers not to work in foreign language films.	☐	☐

5 Choose the correct word or phrase.

1. I used to collect _____comic books_____ (hobbies / scrapbooks / comic books) when I was a kid.

2. My favorite _____ (pet / hobby / place) was a cat called Felix.

3. We used to go to _____ (the playground / summer camp / school) for two weeks during our summer vacations. It was really fun.

4. There was a great _____ (amusement park / playground / beach) on my street. We used to go there every afternoon to play.

6 Look at these childhood pictures of Allie and her brother Robert. Complete the sentences using *used to*.

1. In the summer, Allie and Robert sometimes
   _____used to go to summer camp_____.

2. They also _____.
   Their dog Bruno always used to follow them.

3. Allie _____ every weekend during summer vacation. She hardly ever goes now.

4. Robert _____.
   Now they're worth a lot of money.

5. They _____.
   They don't have any pets now.

7 Look at the answers. Write the questions using *used to*.

1. **A:** _What did you use to do in the summer?_

    B: We used to go to the beach.

2. **A:** _____

    B: No, we didn't collect shells. We used to build sand castles.

3. **A:** _____

    B: Yes, we did. We used to swim for hours. Then we played all kinds of sports.

4. **A:** Really? What _____

    B: Well, we used to play beach volleyball with some other kids.

5. **A:** _____

    B: No, we didn't. We used to win!

8 How have you changed in the last five years? Write answers to these questions.

1. What hobbies did you use to have five years ago?
    What hobbies do you have now?

    _I used to . . ._____

    _Now, . . ._____

2. What kind of music did you use to like then?
    What kind of music do you like now?

    _____

    _____

3. What kinds of clothes did you use to like to wear?
    What kinds of clothes do you like to wear now?

    _____

    _____

9 Complete the sentences. Use the past tense of the verbs given.

Paola: I'm an immigrant here. I _____was_____ (be) born in Chile and _____ (grow up) there. I _____ (come) here in 2011. I _____ (not be) very happy at first. Things _____ (be) difficult for me. I _____ (not speak) English, so I _____ (go) to a community college and _____ (study) English there. My English _____ (get) better, and I _____ (find) this job. What about you?

10 Choose the correct responses.

1. **A:** Are you from Toronto?

   B: _No, I'm originally from Morocco._

   • No, I'm originally from Morocco.
   • Neither am I.

2. **A:** Tell me a little about yourself.

   B: _____

   • Sure. Nice to meet you.
   • What do you want to know?

3. **A:** How old were you when you moved here?

   B: _____

   • About 16.
   • About 16 years ago.

4. **A:** Did you learn English here?

   B: _____

   • Yes, I was 10 years old.
   • No, I studied it in Morocco.

5. **A:** By the way, I'm Lucy.

   B: _____

   • What's your name?
   • Glad to meet you.

2 Life in the city

1 Choose the correct compound noun for each picture.

- [ ] bicycle lane
- [ ] subway station
- [ ] taxi stand
- [ ] bus stop
- [✓] streetlights
- [ ] traffic jam

1. streetlights

2. _____

3. _____

4. _____

5. _____

6. _____

2 Problems, problems

A Choose a solution for each problem.

Problems

1. no more parking spaces: _build a public parking garage_

2. dark streets: _____

3. no places to take children: _____

4. crime: _____

5. car accidents: _____

6. traffic jams: _____

Solutions

☐ install modern streetlights
☐ build a subway system
☐ install more traffic lights
☐ hire more police officers
☐ build more parks
☑ build a public parking garage

B Look at these solutions. Write sentences explaining the problems.
Use *too much*, *too many*, or *not enough* and the problems in part A.

1. _There aren't enough parking spaces._

   The city should build a public parking garage.

2. _____

   The city should install more traffic lights.

3. _____

   The city should build a subway system.

4. _____

   The city should hire more police officers.

5. _____

   The city should build more parks.

6. _____

   The city should install modern streetlights.

C Find another way to say the problems in part B. Begin each sentence
with *There should be more/less/fewer . . .*

1. _There should be more parking spaces._
   _____

2. _____
   _____

3. _____
   _____

4. _____
   _____

5. _____
   _____

6. _____
   _____

3 City blues

A Match the words in columns A and B. Write the compound nouns.

A	B
☑ air	☐ district
☐ business	☐ garages
☐ green	☐ hour
☐ parking	☐ spaces
☐ bicycle	☐ lanes
☐ public	☑ pollution
☐ rush	☐ transportation

1. _air pollution_
2. _____
3. _____
4. _____
5. _____
6. _____
7. _____

B Complete this online post using the compound nouns in part A.

● ● ● ‹ ›

CITY FORUM   HOME | HEADLINES | LOCAL NEWS | INTERNATIONAL | BUSINESS | SPORTS | CONTACT US

Life in this city needs to be improved. For one thing, there are too many cars, and there is too much bad air, especially during _____rush hour_____. The _____ is terrible. This problem is particularly bad downtown in the _____. Too many people drive their cars to work. Also, the city doesn't spend enough money on _____. There should be more buses and subway trains so people don't have to drive.

We also need fewer _____ downtown. It's so easy to park that too many people drive to work. Instead, the city should create more parks and _____ so people can relax and get some fresh air when they're downtown. There should also be more _____ so people can ride to work and get some exercise.

C Write two paragraphs about a problem in a city you know.
First describe the problem and then suggest solutions.

_____
_____
_____
_____
_____
_____
_____
_____
_____
_____

4 Transportation in Hong Kong

A Read about transportation in Hong Kong. Write the correct types of transportation in the article.

GETTING AROUND HONG KONG

Hong Kong has an excellent transportation system. If you fly there, you will arrive at one of the most modern airports in the world. And during your visit, there are many ways to get around Hong Kong.

tram

subway

cable railway

ferry

1. _____

These have run in the streets of Hong Kong Island since 1904. They have two decks, and they carry more than 180,000 passengers a day. You can travel on six routes, totaling 30 kilometers (about 19 miles). You can also hire one for a private party with up to 25 guests – a great way to enjoy Hong Kong!

2. _____

Take one of these to cross from Hong Kong Island to Kowloon or to visit one of the other islands. You can also use them to travel to Macau and Guangdong. They are very safe and comfortable, and they are one of the cheapest boat rides in the world.

3. _____

Hong Kong's underground railway is called the MTR – the Mass Transit Railway. It is the fastest way to get around. You can take the MTR from the airport to all the major centers in Hong Kong. The MTR carries over four million passengers a day!

4. _____

This is found on Hong Kong Island. It pulls you up Victoria Peak, which is 552 meters (about 1,800 feet) above sea level, the highest mountain on the island. The system is nearly 130 years old. In that time, there has never been an accident. Two cars carry up to 120 passengers each.

B Complete the chart about each type of transportation. Where you cannot find the information, write *NG* (not given).

	cable railway	ferry	subway	tram
1. How old is it?				
2. How many people use it?				
3. How safe is it?				
4. Where can you go?				

5 Complete these conversations. Use the words in the box.

☐ ATM   ☑ duty-free shop   ☐ sign   ☐ hotel   ☐ schedule

1. **A:** Could you tell me where I can buy some perfume?

   B: You should try the _duty-free shop_.

2. **A:** Can you tell me where I can find a good place to stay?

   B: Yeah, there is a nice _____
   on the next street.

3. **A:** Do you know where I can change money?

   B: There's a money exchange on the second floor.
   There's also an _____ over there.

4. **A:** Do you know what time the last train leaves for
   the city?

   B: No, but I can check the _____.

5. **A:** Could you tell me where the taxi stand is?

   B: Sure. Just follow that _____.

6 Complete the questions in this conversation at a hotel.

Guest: Could you _tell me where the gym is_____?

Clerk: Sure, the gym is on the nineteenth floor.

Guest: OK. And can you _____?

Clerk: Yes, the coffee shop is next to the gift shop.

Guest: The gift shop? Hmm. I need to buy something for my wife.
Do you _____?

Clerk: It closes at 6:00 P.M. I'm sorry, but you'll have to wait until tomorrow.
It's already 6:15.

Guest: OK. Oh, I'm expecting a package.
Could you _____?

Clerk: Don't worry. I'll call you when it arrives.

Guest: Thanks. Just one more thing.
Do you _____?

Clerk: The airport bus leaves every half hour. Anything else?

Guest: No, I don't think so. Thanks.

7 Rewrite these sentences. Find another way to say each sentence using the words given.

1. There are too many cars in this city. (fewer)

There should be fewer cars in this city.

2. We need fewer buses and cars downtown. (traffic)

3. Where's the subway station? (Could you)

4. There isn't enough public parking. (parking garages)

5. How often does the bus come? (Do you)

6. What time does the last train leave? (Can you)

8 Answer these questions about your city or another city you know.

The streets are closed to traffic in a traffic-free zone.

1. Are there any traffic-free zones? If so, where are they located?

2. How do most people travel to and from work?

3. What's the rush hour like?

4. What's the city's biggest problem?

5. What has the city done about it?

6. Is there anything else the city could do?

3 Making changes

1 Opposites

A Write the opposites. Use the words in the box.

☐ dark	☐ old
☐ expensive	☐ safe
☑ inconvenient	☐ small
☐ noisy	☐ spacious

1. convenient / <u>inconvenient</u>
2. cramped / _____
3. dangerous / _____
4. big / _____

5. bright / _____
6. modern / _____
7. quiet / _____
8. cheap / _____

B Rewrite these sentences. Find another way to say each sentence using *not . . . enough* or *too* and the words in part A.

1. The house is too expensive.

   <u>The house isn't cheap enough.</u>

2. The rooms aren't bright enough.

   _____

3. The living room isn't spacious enough for the family.

   _____

   _____

4. The bathroom is too old.

   _____

5. The yard isn't big enough for our pets.

   _____

6. The street is too noisy for us.

   _____

7. The neighborhood is too dangerous.

   _____

8. The location isn't convenient enough.

   _____

2 Add the word *enough* to these sentences.

> **Grammar note: *enough***
>
> ***Enough* comes <u>after</u> adjectives but <u>before</u> nouns.**
>
> **adjective + *enough***
> It isn't *spacious enough*.
> The rooms aren't *light enough*.
>
> ***enough* + noun**
> There isn't *enough space*.
> It doesn't have *enough light*.

1. The apartment isn't comfortable ˄. *enough*
2. There aren't bedrooms.
3. It's not modern.
4. There aren't parking spaces.

5. The neighborhood doesn't have streetlights.
6. There aren't closets.
7. It's not private.
8. The living room isn't spacious.

3 Complete this conversation. Use the words given and the comparisons in the box. (Some of the comparisons in the box can be used more than once.)

> almost as . . . as   just as many . . . as
> as many . . . as   not as . . . as

Realtor: How did you like the house on Twelfth Street?

Client: Well, it's _____not as convenient as_____ the apartment on Main Street. (convenient)

Realtor: That's true, the house is less convenient.

Client: But the apartment doesn't have _____ the house. (rooms)

Realtor: Yes, the house is more spacious.

Client: But I think there are _____ in the apartment. (closets)

Realtor: You're right. The closet space is the same.

Client: The wallpaper in the apartment is _____ the wallpaper in the house. (dingy)

Realtor: I know, but you could change the wallpaper in the house.

Client: Hmm, the rent on the apartment is _____ the rent on the house, but the house is much bigger. (expensive) Oh, I can't decide. Can you show me something else?

A Complete this questionnaire about where you live, and find your score below.

How does your home measure up?

The outside

		Yes	No
1.	Are you close enough to shopping?	☐	☐
2.	Is there enough public transportation nearby?	☐	☐
3.	Are the sidewalks clean?	☐	☐
4.	Are there good restaurants in the neighborhood?	☐	☐
5.	Is there a park nearby?	☐	☐
6.	Is the neighborhood quiet?	☐	☐
7.	Is the neighborhood safe?	☐	☐
8.	Is there enough parking nearby?	☐	☐
9.	Does the outside of your home look good?	☐	☐

The inside

		Yes	No
10.	Are there enough bedrooms?	☐	☐
11.	Is there enough closet space?	☐	☐
12.	Is the bathroom modern?	☐	☐
13.	Is there a washing machine?	☐	☐
14.	Is there enough space in the kitchen?	☐	☐
15.	Do the stove and refrigerator work well?	☐	☐
16.	Is the living room comfortable enough?	☐	☐
17.	Is the dining area big enough?	☐	☐
18.	Are the walls newly painted?	☐	☐
19.	Are the rooms bright enough?	☐	☐
20.	Is the building warm enough in cold weather?	☐	☐

To score:
How many "Yes" answers do you have?

16–20
It sounds like a dream home!

11–15
Great! All you need now is a swimming pool!

6–10
Well, at least guests won't want to stay long!

0–5
It's time to look for a better place to live!

B Write two short paragraphs about where you live. In the first paragraph describe your neighborhood, and in the second paragraph describe your home. Use the information in part A or your own information.

_____

_____

_____

_____

_____

_____

_____

_____

5 | Wishes

A Which words or phrases often go with which verbs? Complete the chart.

☐ guitar	☐ happier	☐ my own room	☐ soccer
☐ more free time	☑ healthy	☐ somewhere else	☐ to a new place

be	play	have	move
healthy	_____	_____	_____
_____	_____	_____	_____

B Describe what these people would like to change. Use *I wish* and words or phrases in part A.

1. I wish I were healthy.

2. _____

3. _____

4. _____

5. _____

6. _____

6 Choose the correct responses.

1. **A:** I wish I had a bigger apartment.

   B: _Why?_____
   - Why?
   - I don't like my neighbors, either.

2. **A:** I wish I could retire.

   B: _____
   - I don't like it anymore.
   - I know what you mean.

3. **A:** Where do you want to move?

   B: _____
   - Somewhere else.
   - Something else.

4. **A:** I wish I could find a bigger house.

   B: _____
   - Is it too large?
   - It's very nice, though.

7 Rewrite these sentences. Find another way to say each sentence using the words given.

1. There should be more bedrooms in my apartment. (enough)

   _There aren't enough bedrooms in my apartment._____

2. This neighborhood is safe enough. (dangerous)

   _____

3. My apartment doesn't have enough privacy. (private)

   _____

4. Our house has the same number of bedrooms as yours. (just as many)

   _____

5. I don't have enough closet space. (wish)

   _____

6. We wish we could move to a new place. (somewhere else)

   _____

7. That apartment is too small. (big)

   _____

8. I wish housework were easy. (not difficult)

   _____

8 Best wishes

A Scan the article about making wishes. Which three countries does it refer to?

MAKING WISHES

All over the world, people have always wished for things such as peace, love, good health, and money. Over hundreds of years, people in different countries have found different ways to make wishes. Here are some interesting examples.

The Trevi Fountain in Rome, Italy, is a place where many people go to make a wish. The water from the fountain flows into a large pool of water below. To make a wish, visitors stand facing away from the fountain. Then, they use their right hand to throw a coin into the pool over their left shoulder. They believe this will bring them luck and bring them back to Rome one day. The coins in the fountain, several thousand euros each day, are given to poor people.

A very different way of making wishes happens in Anhui province in eastern China. Huangshan (which means "Yellow Mountain") is famous for its beautiful sunrises and sunsets. That's why people think it is a very romantic place. Couples go there to make a wish that they will stay together forever. Each couple buys a "love lock," or padlock, with a key. Next, they lock their padlock to a chain at the top of the mountain. Then they throw the key down the mountain so that their lock can never be opened.

In Turkey and some neighboring countries, May 5th is a special day for making wishes. People believe that each year on that day two wise men return to Earth. They come to help people and give them good health. In the evening, there are street food markets selling different kinds of seasonal food and musicians playing traditional music. People write their wishes on pieces of paper and then attach the paper to a tree. Nowadays, however, some people go online and send their wishes to special websites.

B Read the article. Check (✓) the statements that are true for each place.

	Rome	Huangshan	Turkey
1. People make wishes only once a year.	☐	☐	☐
2. You need a lock and key.	☐	☐	☐
3. You put your wish on a tree.	☐	☐	☐
4. You need a coin to make your wish.	☐	☐	☐
5. Wish-making is only for couples.	☐	☐	☐
6. The money from the wishes goes to poor people.	☐	☐	☐
7. Some people make their wishes on the Internet.	☐	☐	☐

4 Have you ever tried it?

1 Complete the conversation with the correct tense.

Margo: I went to Sunrise Beach last week.

Have you ever been
(Did you ever go / Have you ever been)

to Sunrise Beach, Chris?

Chris: Yes, _____. It's beautiful.
(I did / I have)

_____
(Did you go / Have you gone)

to the restaurant on the beach?

Margo: Yeah, I _____.
(did / have)

I _____ on Saturday.
(went / have gone)

_____ the sea snails.
(I had / I've had)

Chris: Wow! _____ sea snails!
(I never ate / I've never eaten)

Margo: Oh, they were delicious. On Sunday

I _____
(got / have gotten)

to the beach early to see the sun come up.

_____ a sunrise on a beach, Chris?
(Did you ever see / Have you ever seen)

Chris: No, _____.
(I didn't / I haven't)

Margo: Then I _____ swimming around 6:00,
(went / have gone)

but there were some strange dark shadows in the water.

_____ of sharks at Sunrise Beach?
(Did you ever hear / Have you ever heard)

Chris: Yes, _____. I _____ a news report about sharks last summer.
(I did / I have)   (heard / have heard)

Margo: Wow! Maybe I _____ a lucky escape on Sunday morning!
(had / have had)

Why don't you come with me next time?

Chris: Are you kidding?

2 Have you ever . . . ?

A Look at this list and check (✓) five things you have done. Add other activities if necessary.

- ☐ ride a motorcycle
- ☐ go horseback riding
- ☐ cook for over 10 people
- ☐ eat raw fish
- ☐ go to a classical music concert
- ✓ have green tea ice cream
- ☐ read a novel in English
- ☐ take a cruise
- ☐ travel abroad
- ☐ try Indian food
- ☐ _____
- ☐ _____
- ☐ _____
- ☐ _____

B Write questions about the things you checked in part A. Use *Have you ever . . . ?*

1. Have you ever had green tea ice cream? _____

2. _____

3. _____

4. _____

5. _____

C Answer the questions you wrote in part B. Then use the past tense to give more information.

1. Yes, I have. I had some in a Japanese restaurant. It was delicious! _____

2. _____

3. _____

4. _____

5. _____

3 Do I have an allergy?

A Scan the article. What can cause allergies?

ALLERGIES

ANDREW was sneezing all of the time. He took an aspirin every morning for a week before he decided to see a doctor. She told him that he had hay fever, an allergy to the pollen from the juniper trees that grew in the area where Andrew lived. The doctor suggested an anti-allergy medicine that he had to take three times a day. But Andrew didn't get completely well until he also bought an air filter to clean the air in his apartment.

MARIANA loved her cat Lucy very much, but her eyes were always red and irritated. She discovered she had an allergy to her cat! She tried to pet Lucy less, but that didn't work. Her friends advised her to give Lucy away, but Mariana couldn't do that. Instead she changed where Lucy could go. Lucy was no longer allowed in Mariana's bedroom. Mariana made a little bed for Lucy in the garage. Mariana played with her cat outside because fresh air is best for cat allergies.

It was a very sad day when **ERIC'S** mother told him he shouldn't eat his favorite food anymore. He had a food allergy, she said, and peanut butter was the problem. Peanuts made his skin very red with a painful itch. Eric tried to eat less peanut butter, but he still itched. Now Eric eats almond butter, cashew butter, and tahini, which is also called sesame butter. A lot of his friends also eat these foods since Eric's school no longer serves peanut butter because of peanut allergies.

B Read the article. What problem did each person have? Complete the first column of the chart.

	Problem	What didn't work	What worked
Andrew			
Mariana			
Eric			

C Read the article again. What didn't work? What worked? Complete the rest of the chart.

4 Eggs, anyone?

A Here's a recipe for a mushroom omelet. Look at the pictures and number the sentences from 1 to 5.

_____ After that, pour the eggs into a frying pan. Add the mushrooms and cook.

_____ Then beat the eggs in a bowl.

__1__ First, slice the mushrooms.

_____ Next, add salt and pepper to the egg mixture.

_____ Finally, fold the omelet in half. Your omelet is ready. Enjoy!

B Describe your favorite way to cook eggs. Use sequence adverbs.

HOW TO COOK EGGS:

5 Complete the conversation. Use the past tense or the present perfect of the verbs given.

Alexa: I _____went_____ (go) to a Thai restaurant last night.

Pedro: Really? I _____ (never eat) Thai food.

Alexa: Oh, you should try it. It's delicious!

Pedro: What _____ you _____ (order)?

Alexa: First, I _____ (have) soup with green curry and rice. Then I _____ (try) pad thai. It's noodles, shrimp, and vegetables in a spicy sauce.

Pedro: I _____ (not taste) pad thai before. _____ (be) it very hot?

Alexa: No. It _____ (be) just spicy enough. And after that, I _____ (eat) bananas in coconut milk for dessert.

Pedro: Mmm! That sounds good.

Alexa: It was.

6 Choose the correct word.

1. We had delicious guacamole dip and chips on Saturday night while we watched TV.
   It was a great _____snack_____ (dinner / snack / meal).

2. I had a huge lunch, so I _____ (ordered / skipped / tried) dinner.

3. What _____ (appetizers / ingredients / skewers) do
   you need to cook crispy fried noodles?

4. First, fry the beef in oil and curry powder, and then _____ (pour / mix / toast)
   the coconut milk over the beef.

5. We need to leave the restaurant now. Could we have the
   _____ (check / recipe / menu), please?

7 **Choose the correct responses.**

☐ Yuck! That sounds awful.　☐ That sounds wrong.　☐ Mmm! That sounds good.

1. A: Have you ever tried barbecued chicken? You marinate the meat in
barbecue sauce for about an hour and then cook it on the grill.

B: _____

2. A: Here's a recipe called Baked Eggplant Delight. I usually bake eggplant
for an hour, but this says you bake it for only five minutes!

B: _____

3. A: Look at this dish – frogs' legs with bananas! I've never seen that before.

B: _____

8 **Use the simple past or present perfect of these verbs to complete the sentences.**

☑ ride　☐ take　☐ bring　☐ do

1. Have you ever ____ridden____ a horse? It's great!

2. I _____ all the ingredients with me.

3. _____ you eat a huge dinner last night?

4. We _____ my mother to the new Chilean restaurant.

☐ give　☐ decide　☐ eat　☐ be

5. I haven't _____ a birthday gift to my father yet.

6. We have never _____ to a Chinese restaurant.

7. I have never _____ snails. What are they like?

8. Have you _____ what kind of pizza you would like?

☐ make　☐ break　☐ buy　☐ skip

9. I _____ this chicken sandwich for $5.

10. Oh, I'm sorry. I just _____ a glass. What a mess!

11. Victor _____ gogi gui for dinner.

12. I wasn't hungry this morning, so I _____ breakfast.

☐ fall　☐ forget　☐ drive　☐ try

13. Oh, no! I _____ to buy rice.

14. Have you ever _____ a sports car?

15. I _____ Greek food for the first time last night.

16. Have you ever _____ asleep at the movies? It's really embarrassing.

5 Hit the road!

1 Vacation plans

A Which words or phrases often go with which verbs? Complete the chart.
Use each word or phrase only once.

☐ a camper   ☐ a condominium
☐ camping   ☐ on vacation
☐ something exciting   ☐ sailing lessons
☑ long walks   ☐ a car
☐ a lot of hiking   ☐ swimming
☐ some fishing   ☐ a vacation

take	do	go	rent
long walks			

B Write four things you plan to do on your next vacation. Use *be going to* and the information in part A or your own information.

Vacation plans

1. _____
2. _____
3. _____
4. _____

C Write four sentences about your possible vacation plans. Use *will* with *maybe*, *probably*, *I guess*, or *I think*. Use the information in part A or your own information.

Possible plans

1. _____
2. _____
3. _____
4. _____

2 **Complete the conversation. Use *be going to* or *will* and the information on the notepads.**

Scott: So, Elena, do you have any vacation plans?

Elena: Well, ___I'm going to paint my apartment___ because the walls are a really ugly color. What about you?

Scott: _____ and take a long drive.

Elena: Where are you going to go?

Scott: I'm not sure. _____. I haven't seen her in a long time.

Elena: That sounds nice. I like to visit my family, too.

Scott: Yes, and _____ for a few days. I haven't been hiking in months. How about you? Are you going to do anything else on your vacation?

Elena: _____. I have a lot of work to do before school starts.

Scott: That doesn't sound like much fun.

Elena: Oh, I am planning to have some fun, too. _____. I love to go surfing!

> ## Elena
>
> paint my apartment – yes
> catch up on my studying – probably
> relax on the beach – yes

> ## Scott
>
> rent a car – yes
> visit my sister Jeanne – probably
> go to the mountains – maybe

3 **Travel plans**

A Look at these answers. Write questions using *be going to*.

1. A: _Where are you going to go?_____

  B: I'm going to go someplace nice and quiet.

2. A: _____

  B: I'm going to drive.

3. A: _____

  B: I'm going to stay in a condominium. My friend has one near the beach.

4. A: _____

  B: No, I'm going to travel by myself.

B Use the cues to write other answers to the questions in part A. Use *be going to* or *will*.

1. _I'm not going to go to a busy place._____ (not go / busy place)

2. _____ (maybe / take the train)

3. _____ (not stay / hotel)

4. _____ (I think / ask a friend)

4 Travel ads

A Scan the travel ad. Where can tourists see beautiful nature scenes?

● ● ● ‹ ›
http://www.holidayofalifetime.com

THE PERFECT SOUTH AMERICAN VACATION ● **SEE TWO EXCITING CITIES AND ONE OF SOUTH AMERICA'S NATURAL WONDERS** ● **11 DAYS FOR $1,199 + AIRFARE!**

BUENOS AIRES

In this unique city of art, culture, and history, there are over 150 parks, 42 theaters, and museums and shops everywhere. You must visit Avenida 9 de Julio, the widest avenue in the world. The food is excellent, and you simply have to try the steaks! The home of the tango also offers great nightlife – all night long!

RIO DE JANEIRO

There's a lot to do in this exciting city! There's opera and ballet as well as museums, churches, parks, and great beaches. Just outside of the city, there are the Sugarloaf and Corcovado Mountains. Dining starts late in Rio, around 9:00 P.M., and dancing in the clubs begins around 11:00 P.M.

IGUAÇU FALLS

Bigger than Niagara Falls, this is truly an unforgettable wonder. For a real adventure, you ought to take a boat ride. And you must explore the national parks near the falls.

Book with FLIGHT and SAVE!
Reserve online, or call **1-800-555-TRIP** for more information.

B Read the ad. Check (✓) True or False. For the statements that are false, write the correct information.

	True	False
1. People have dinner late in Rio de Janeiro.	☐	☐
2. Buenos Aires has the longest avenue in the world.	☐	☐
3. Niagara Falls is bigger than Iguaçu Falls.	☐	☐
4. Both Rio de Janeiro and Buenos Aires have exciting nightlife.	☐	☐
5. Buenos Aires and Iguaçu Falls have great beaches.	☐	☐

5 Circle the correct word or words to give advice to travelers.

1. You ought (check / (to check)) the weather.
2. You should never (leave / to leave) cash in your hotel room.
3. You need (take / to take) your credit card with you.
4. You have (pay / to pay) an airport tax.
5. You should (let / to let) your family know where they can contact you.
6. You'd better not (go / to go) out alone late at night.
7. You must (get / to get) a vaccination if you go to some countries.

6 Take it or leave it?

A Check (✓) the most important item to have in each situation.

1. A vacation to a foreign country
   - ☐ a carry-on bag
   - ✓ a passport
   - ☐ a driver's license

2. A mountain-climbing vacation
   - ☐ a suitcase
   - ☐ a visa
   - ☐ hiking boots

3. A sailing trip
   - ☐ a hotel reservation
   - ☐ a first-aid kit
   - ☐ an ATM card

4. A visit to a beach
   - ☐ a credit card
   - ☐ a swimsuit
   - ☐ a plane ticket

B Give advice to these people. Use the words or phrases in the box and the items in part A. Use each word or phrase only once.

☐ ought to	☐ need to	☐ should	✓ had better ('d better)

1. Martina is going on a vacation to a foreign country.
   She'd better take a passport.

2. Robin and Evan are going on a mountain-climbing vacation.
   _____

3. Kevin and Susie are planning a sailing trip.
   _____

4. Eddie is going to visit a beach.
   _____

7 You don't need to take that!

Your friends are planning to drive across North America and camp along the way. What advice can you give them? Write sentences using the expressions in the box and some of the cues below.

You don't have to . . .	You ought to . . .
You have to . . .	You should . . .
You must . . .	You shouldn't . . .
You need to . . .	You'd better . . .

bring cooking equipment

buy good quality camping equipment

buy maps and travel guides

forget a first-aid kit

forget your passport or identification

get a GPS system for your car

pack a lot of luggage

remember to bring insect spray

remember to bring a jacket

take a credit card

take a lot of cash

take your driver's license

1. _You have to bring cooking equipment._

2. _____

3. _____

4. _____

5. _____

6. _____

7. _____

8. _____

9. _____

10. _____

8 Rewrite these sentences. Find another way to say each sentence using the words given.

1. I'm not going to go on vacation on my own. (alone)

_____

2. I don't want to travel with anyone. (by myself)

_____

3. You ought to travel with a friend. (should)

_____

4. It's necessary to get a vaccination. (must)

_____

9 I'm going on vacation!

A Read these notes, and then write a description of your vacation.
Use *be going to* for the plans you've decided on. Use *will* with *maybe*,
probably, *I guess*, or *I think* for the plans you're not sure about.

- arrive in Lisbon, Portugal, on July 6
- check in at the Tivoli Hotel
- go shopping (not sure)
- spend three days in Lisbon sightseeing
- take a tour bus across the border to Seville in Spain
- visit the cathedral (not sure)
- see some flamenco dancing in the evening
- rent a car and drive to Málaga on the Costa del Sol
- visit the old city center (not sure)
- spend time on the beach (not sure)
- fly to Madrid on July 19
- visit some museums (not sure)
- take a tour of the city and see the sights
- go home on July 22

I'm going to arrive in Lisbon, Portugal, on July 6 and check in at the Tivoli Hotel.
Then maybe I'll go shopping. . . .

B Write four more things you need to remember before you go on vacation.

1. I have to check the weather.

2.

3.

4.

5.

6 Sure! I'll do it.

1 Write responses to these requests. Use *it* or *them*.

1. Please take out the trash.

   OK, I'll take it out.

2. Please put the dishes away.

_____

3. Hang up the towels.

_____

4. Turn off the lights, please.

_____

5. Turn on the radio.

_____

2 Two-part verbs

A Use the words in the box to make two-part verbs. (You may use words more than once.)

away	down	off	on	out	up

1. clean _____up_____

2. hang _____

3. let _____

4. pick _____

5. put _____

6. take _____

7. take _____

8. throw _____

9. turn _____

10. turn _____

B Make requests with the two-part verbs in part A. Then give a reason for making the request.

1. Please clean up your room. It's a mess.

2. _____

3. _____

4. _____

5. _____

6. _____

3 Choose the correct word.

1. Hang up your _____coat_____. (books / coat / trash)

2. Take out the _____. (groceries / trash / yard)

3. Turn down the _____. (garbage / TV / toys)

4. Pick up your _____. (lights / things / yard)

5. Put away your _____. (clothes / microwave / dog)

6. Turn on the _____. (magazines / mess / radio)

4 What's your excuse?

A Complete these requests. Use the sentences in the box.

☐ It's a mess.   ☑ They shouldn't be on the floor.
☐ It's too loud.   ☐ The milk is getting warm.
☐ The bag is almost full.

1. Pick up your clothes, please. _They shouldn't be on the floor._____

2. Please put the groceries away. _____

3. Take the garbage out. _____

4. Clean up the kitchen, please. _____

5. Turn down the music. _____

B Write an excuse for each request in part A.

1. _Sorry, but there isn't enough room in my closet._

2. _____

3. _____

4. _____

5. _____

5 Two ways to get chores done

A Scan this article. What is different about the two computer apps for children's chores?

ChoreMonster is an app that allows parents to set up a chart of chores on a computer or cell phone for their children. When the kids complete their chores, they win cute little monsters that can be added up for a reward that their parents have agreed upon. For chores like cleaning their room, vacuuming the house, or washing the car, kids can earn a toy or something fun to do.

But wait! Will the cute little monsters that satisfy children between the ages of four and twelve satisfy a teenager? Let's take a look at another app to see what can happen when children become teenagers.

VexBox is not an app based on rewards. Instead, it is designed to frustrate, or vex, teenagers who don't do their chores. VexBox slows down computer connections until the teen completes a chore. It can take teenagers ten minutes to download their favorite song! The idea is that teens will do anything, even their chores, so they can get back to using the Internet at full speed.

Most teens do not like VexBox. That's the idea, of course. If they do their chores, then their parents won't use it!

B Read the article. Then answer these questions in your own words.

1. Do you think computer apps for chores are a good idea? Why or why not?

_____

_____

2. Would you use ChoreMonster for a young child? Why or why not?

_____

_____

3. Smartphones are not affected by VexBox. Would that be a problem for parents with teenagers where you live? Why?

_____

_____

6 Rewrite these sentences. Find another way to say each sentence using the words given.

1. Turn off your cell phone, please. (Can)

   Can you turn off your cell phone, please?

2. Take this form to the office. (Would you mind)

   _____

3. Please turn the TV down. (Could)

   _____

4. Don't leave wet towels on the floor. (Would you mind)

   _____

5. Text me today's homework assignment. (Would)

   _____

6. Pass me that book, please. (Can)

   _____

7 Choose the correct responses.

1. **A:** Could you lend me some money?

   B: _Sure._ _____

   • Sure.

   • Oh, sorry.

   • No, thanks.

2. **A:** Would you mind helping me?

   B: _____

   • Sorry, I can't right now.

   • No, thanks.

   • I forgot.

3. **A:** Excuse me, but you're sitting in my seat.

   B: _____

   • I'll close it.

   • Not right now.

   • Oh, I'm sorry. I didn't realize that.

4. **A:** Would you like to come in?

   B: _____

   • That's no excuse.

   • Sorry, I forgot.

   • All right. Thanks.

5. **A:** Would you mind not leaving your clothes on the floor?

   B: _____

   • OK, thanks.

   • Oh, all right. I'll put them away.

   • Excuse me. I'll pay for them.

6. **A:** Can you hand me the remote control?

   B: _____

   • No problem.

   • You could, too.

   • I'll make sure.

8 For each complaint, apologize and either give an excuse, admit a mistake, make an offer, or make a promise.

1. **Roommate 1:** Could you turn the TV down? I'm trying to study, and the noise is bothering me.

   Roommate 2: _Sorry. I didn't realize you_ _were studying._

2. **Benjamin:** You're late! I've been here for half an hour!

   Jen: _____

3. **Customer:** I brought this laptop in last week, but it's still not working right.

   Salesperson: _____

4. **Father:** You didn't take out the garbage this morning.

   Son: _____

5. **Customer:** This steak is very tough. I can't eat it.

   Waiter: _____

6. **Neighbor 1:** Could you do something about your dog? It barks all night and it keeps me awake.

   Neighbor 2: _____

7. **Resident:** Would you mind moving your car? You're parked in my parking space.

   Visitor: _____

8. **Teacher:** Please put away your papers. You left them on your desk yesterday.

   Student: _____

9 Choose the correct words.

1. Throw that old food away. Put it in the _____.
   (trash can / living room / refrigerator)

2. Would you mind picking up some _____? We need coffee, milk, and rice.
   (dry cleaning / groceries / towels)

3. Turn the _____ off. Electricity costs money!
   (lights / oven / stereo)

4. My neighbor made a _____. He said, "I'll be sure to stop my dog from barking."
   (mistake / request / promise)

10 Make requests

A Match the words in columns A and B. Then write the phrases.

A	B
☑ pick up	☐ your bedroom
☐ not criticize	☑ some milk
☐ mail	☐ the groceries
☐ not talk	☐ your sunglasses
☐ put away	☐ these bills
☐ take off	☐ the TV
☐ turn down	☐ so loudly
☐ clean up	☐ my friends

1. pick up some milk
2. _____
3. _____
4. _____
5. _____
6. _____
7. _____
8. _____

B Write requests using the phrases in part A.

1. Would you mind picking up some milk?
2. _____
3. _____
4. _____
5. _____
6. _____
7. _____
8. _____

11 Write six complaints you have about a friend or a relative. Then write a wish for each complaint.

1. My roommate is always using my hair dryer.
    I wish she had her own hair dryer.
2. _____
   _____
3. _____
   _____
4. _____
   _____
5. _____
   _____
6. _____
   _____

7 What do you use this for?

1 **What are these items used for? Write a sentence about each item using *used for* and the information in the box.**

☐ do boring jobs	☐ store and send data	☐ take and delete photos easily
☑ write reports	☐ determine your exact location	

computer | robot | digital camera | flash drive | GPS system

1. A computer is used for writing reports.

2. _____

3. _____

4. _____

5. _____

2 **Check (✓) the technology and its use. Then write sentences using *be used to*.**

1. ☑ text messages   ☑ cell phone   ☐ photocopies

   A cell phone is used to send text messages.

2. ☐ flash drive   ☐ take photos   ☐ back up files

   _____

3. ☐ weather   ☐ GPS system   ☐ places

   _____

4. ☐ videos   ☐ messages   ☐ video camera

   _____

5. ☐ the Internet   ☐ robots   ☐ information

   _____

3 Choose the correct word to complete each sentence. Use the correct form of the word.

1. Robots are used to ___perform___ (find / perform / study) many dangerous jobs.

2. Computers are used to _____ (connect / download / sing) music.

3. The Internet is used for _____ (check / watch / write) streaming TV.

4. Home computers are used to _____ (play / pay / have) bills.

5. External hard drives are used for _____ (back up / email / buy) data.

6. Airport scanners are used to _____ (hide / allow / find) dangerous items.

4 Complete the sentences with *used to*, *is used to*, or *are used to*.

1. My sister _____used to_____ visit me on weekends when I was in college.

2. People _____ write letters, but now they usually send emails instead.

3. A cell phone _____ make calls and send texts.

4. I _____ have a desktop computer, but now I just use a laptop.

5. We download all of our movies. We _____ buy DVDs, but we don't buy them anymore.

6. Wi-Fi networks _____ access the Internet wirelessly.

5 Then and now

A Scan these ads from a sales catalog from 1917 and from a Web store a century later. What is different?

1917 CATALOG

DETROIT ELECTRIC AUTOMOBILE

So quiet because it does not need a gasoline engine. The large, high windows make you feel like you're sitting in your living room! Travels 80 miles without being recharged. $2,700.

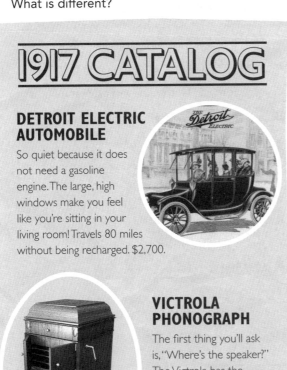

VICTROLA PHONOGRAPH

The first thing you'll ask is, "Where's the speaker?" The Victrola has the speaker inside the cabinet! The beautiful wood of the cabinet makes the sound sweeter! $250.00.

AMERICAN EAGLE TELEPHONE

Allows you to talk easily to family and friends all over the country. Available with a wooden case and weighs less than 5 pounds. $25.00.

2017 WEB STORE

Aethera Electric Car

Has autopilot and automatic steering to allow you to drive safely. Travels 300 miles without recharging the battery. $43,000.

Big Sky Sound System

Allows streaming and plays compact discs so you can listen to all the music you love. Also included is a record player for your grandparents' records and the new ones you just bought! $299.00.

FutureNow Smartphone

Stay connected to everyone you know by telephone and on the Internet. This beautifully slender phone puts the whole world in your pocket. And it takes incredible photos! $799.00.

B Read the ads. Then answer these questions in your own words.

1. Would you buy a Detroit electric car today for use in your town or city? Why or why not?

_____

2. Have you listened to music over the Internet, on CDs, and on records? Which do you think sounds the best? Why?

_____

3. Although the American Eagle telephone is a hundred years old, is there anything about it that you like as much as today's smartphone?

_____

6 Useful types of websites

A Match the types of websites with how people use them.

Types of websites	How people use websites
_d_ question and answer sites	**a.** find out what's happening in the world
_____ blogs	**b.** share information and photos with friends
_____ gaming sites	**c.** buy clothes, electronics, and other items
_____ media sharing sites	**d.** ask and answer questions online
_____ news sites	**e.** find information on the Internet
_____ search engines	**f.** play online games
_____ social media sites	**g.** post online diaries
_____ shopping sites	**h.** upload videos and music

B Do you use any of the types of websites in part A? What do you use them for? Write sentences.

1. _I use question and answer sites to ask and answer questions online._ OR
I use question and answer sites for asking and answering questions online.

2. _____

3. _____

4. _____

7 Put these instructions in order. Number them from 1 to 5.

● ● ● ‹ ›

GETTING STARTED WITH SOCIAL NETWORKING

_____ Next, check what the site has to offer you. Don't worry if you can't understand all its functions.

_____ First of all, join a social networking site. Choose a site where you already know people.

_____ After that, use the site's search features to find friends. Be sure to browse through groups who share your interests.

_____ Finally, invite people to be your friend. Try not to be shy! A lot of people may be waiting to hear from you.

_____ Then customize your profile page. For example, play with the colors to make the page reflect your personality. Now you're ready to start exploring!

8 Write a sentence about each picture using an expression in the box.

☐ Be sure to . . .   ☐ Make sure to . . .   ☐ Try not to . . .
☑ Don't forget to . . .   ☐ Remember to . . .   ☐ Try to . . .

1. _Don't forget to turn off your computer._

2. _____

3. _____

4. _____

5. _____

6. _____

9 Write *a* or *an* in the correct places. (There are nine other places in this paragraph.)

My brother just bought ⌄*a* smartphone. It's really great. It has lot of high-tech features.
In fact, it's amazing handheld computer, not just cell phone. For example, it has Wi-Fi
connectivity, so my brother can connect to the Internet in most places. He can send
message to friend by email or through social networking site. He can also find out
where he is because it has GPS app. That's perfect for my brother because he likes
mountain climbing. He'll never get lost again! His smartphone also has excellent
camera, so he can take photos of his climbing trips. And, of course, it's phone. So he
can talk to his girlfriend anytime he wants!

10 **Rewrite these sentences. Find another way to say each sentence using the words given.**

1. I use my computer for paying bills. (online)

   I pay my bills online.

2. It breaks very easily. (fragile)

   _____

3. Take it out of the outlet. (unplug)

   _____

4. Remember to keep it dry. (spill)

   _____

5. Don't let the battery die. (recharge)

   _____

11 **Look at the pictures and complete this conversation. Choose the correct responses.**

A: What a day! First, my microwave didn't work.

B: What happened?

A: _It burned my lunch._

   • It didn't cook my lunch.

   • It burned my lunch.

   Then I tried to use my computer, but that didn't work either.

B: Why not?

A: _____

   • I couldn't get a Wi-Fi signal.

   • I couldn't turn it on.

   After that, I tried to use the vacuum cleaner.

B: Let me guess. It didn't pick up the dirt.

A: Worse! _____

   • It made a terrible noise.

   • It spread dirt around the room.

B: Did you take the vacuum cleaner to get it fixed?

A: Well, I tried, _____

   • but my car wouldn't start.

   • but I forgot.

B: Oh, no! Do you need a ride to work tomorrow?

8 Time to celebrate!

1 Complete this paragraph with the words in the box.

☐ get together ☐ music ☐ fireworks ☐ decorations
☑ holidays ☐ customs ☐ picnic ☐ celebrate

One of the most important national ___holidays___ in the United States is Independence Day. This is the day when Americans _____ winning their independence from Britain almost 250 years ago. There are many _____ for Independence Day. Most towns, big and small, mark this holiday with parades and _____. They put up a lot of _____, usually in red, white, and blue, the colors of the U.S. flag. Bands play patriotic _____. It's also a day when many Americans _____ with family and friends to celebrate with a barbecue or a _____.

2 Complete the sentences with the clauses in the box.

☐ when I feel sad and depressed ☐ when people have to pay their taxes
☐ when school starts ☐ when summer vacation begins

1. I hate April 15! In the United States, it's the day
_____.
I always owe the government money.

2. June is my favorite month. It's the month
_____.
I always go straight to the beach.

3. September is my least favorite month. It's the month _____.
Good-bye, summer!

4. I've never liked winter. It's a season
_____. The cold weather always affects my mood negatively.

3 Special days

A Use words from the box to complete the sentences.

☐ February	☐ tricks
☑ June	☐ wedding
☐ anniversary	☐ presents
☐ party	☐ fireworks

1. _June_____ is the time of year when there are a lot of weddings in the U.S.

2. We always have a _____ at our house on New Year's Eve.

3. Janice and Nick are getting married soon. They plan to have a small _____ with just a few family members.

4. Valentine's Day is on _____ 14th every year.

5. My friends and family gave me some very nice _____ on my birthday.

6. People like to play _____ on each other on April Fools' Day.

7. On the Fourth of July, many people shoot _____ into the sky at night.

8. Tomorrow is my parents' 25th wedding _____.

B Use the cues in parentheses to create sentences with relative clauses of time.

1. (Thanksgiving / a day / people spend time with their families)
   Thanksgiving is a day when people spend time with their families.

2. (Spring / the season / flowers start to bloom)
   _____

3. (New Year's Eve / a night / people celebrate new beginnings)
   _____

4. (The weekend / a time / people relax)
   _____

5. (Father's Day / a day / children spend time with their fathers)
   _____

6. (Winter / the season / we go skiing)
   _____

4 A lot to celebrate!

A Read about these special days in the United States. Do you celebrate any of them in your country?

EVENT	DAY	HOW PEOPLE CELEBRATE IT
Martin Luther King Jr. Day	3rd Monday in January	People honor the life and work of the civil rights leader Martin Luther King Jr.
Valentine's Day	February 14th	People give chocolates, flowers, and gifts to the ones they love.
April Fools' Day	April 1st	This is a day when people play tricks on friends. Websites sometimes post funny stories or advertise fake products.
Mother's Day	2nd Sunday in May	People honor their mothers by giving cards and gifts. They may also have a family gathering.
Father's Day	3rd Sunday in June	People honor their fathers by giving them cards and presents. They may also have a family gathering.
Independence Day	July 4th	Americans celebrate their country's independence from Britain. There are parades and fireworks.
Labor Day	1st Monday in September	People honor workers and celebrate the end of summer. Many people have barbecues with friends and family.
Thanksgiving	4th Thursday in November	People celebrate the fall season by eating a big dinner, often with turkey, with family members and friends.

B Complete the chart. Check (✓) the correct answers.

	Americans give gifts on:	Americans don't give gifts on:
Martin Luther King Jr. Day	☐	☐
Valentine's Day	☐	☐
April Fools' Day	☐	☐
Mother's Day	☐	☐
Father's Day	☐	☐
Independence Day	☐	☐
Labor Day	☐	☐
Thanksgiving	☐	☐

5 What happens at these times in your country? Complete the sentences.

1. Before a man and woman get married, _they_ _usually date each other._

2. When someone has a birthday, _____

3. After a couple moves into a new home, _____

4. After a student graduates, _____

5. When a woman gets engaged, _____

6. When a couple has their first child, _____

6 Complete the paragraph with the information in the box. Add a comma where necessary.

> **Grammar note: Adverbial clauses of time**
>
> **The adverbial clause can come <u>before</u> or <u>after</u> the main clause.**
>
> **If it comes <u>before</u> the main clause, add a comma.**
>
> *When a couple gets married, they often receive gifts.*
>
> **Do not add a comma <u>after</u> the main clause.**
>
> *A couple often receives gifts when they get married.*

- ☐ before the wedding reception ends
- ☐ many newlyweds have to live with relatives
- ☐ most couples like to be alone
- ☐ when they have enough money to pay for it

Newly married couples often leave on their honeymoon _____ .
When they go on their honeymoon _____ . After they come back
from their honeymoon _____ . They can only live in their
own place _____ .

7 Write three paragraphs about marriage customs in your country.
In the first paragraph, write about what happens before the wedding.
In the second paragraph, write about the wedding ceremony. In the final
paragraph, write about what happens after the wedding.

_____

_____

_____

_____

_____

_____

_____

_____

Japan

Morocco

Scotland

India

8 Choose the correct word or phrase.

1. Wedding _____ (celebrations / flowers / birthdays) are often held in a restaurant
   or hotel.

2. Children's Day is a day when people in many countries _____ (meet / honor / find)
   their children.

3. Fall is the _____ (custom / tradition / season) when people in the U.S.
   celebrate Thanksgiving.

4. In Indonesia, on Nyepi Day, Balinese people _____ (last / stop / observe) a day of
   silence to begin the new year.

9 **Rewrite these sentences. Find another way to say each sentence using the words given.**

1. Everyone in the family comes to my parents' home on Thanksgiving. (get together)
   Everyone in the family gets together at my parents' home on Thanksgiving.

2. Many people have parties on New Year's Eve. (New Year's Eve / when)

   _____

3. At the end of the year, Japanese people give and receive *oseibo* presents to show their appreciation for the people in their lives. (exchange)

   _____

4. June is the month when many Brazilians celebrate the Festa Junina. (in June)

   _____

5. In Sweden, people observe Midsummer's Day around June 21. (occur)

   _____

10 **Imagine you are in a foreign country and someone has invited you to a New Year's Eve party. Ask questions about the party using the words in the box or your own ideas.**

| ☐ clothes | ☐ midnight | ☐ sing and dance |
| ☐ fireworks | ✓ present | ☐ special food |

1. _Should I bring a New Year's present?_ _____

2. _____

3. _____

4. _____

5. _____

6. _____

9 Only time will tell.

1 Complete this passage with the verbs in the box. Use the past, present, or future tense.

☐ buy	☐ drive	☐ do	☐ leave	☐ sell
☐ change	☑ go	☐ have to	☐ sell	☐ use

In many countries nowadays, food shopping takes very little time. In the past, people _____*used to go*_____ to a different shop for each type of item. For example, you _____ meat at a butcher's shop and fish at a fish market. A fruit market _____ fruits and vegetables. For dry goods, like rice or beans, you _____ go to grocery stores. Today, the supermarket or superstore _____ all these things. Once every week or two, people _____ in their cars to these huge stores to buy everything – not only food, but also clothes, electronic goods, furniture, and medicine. But in the future, the way we shop _____ again. Nowadays, people _____ a lot of their shopping online. Soon, maybe, no one _____ home to go shopping. Everyone _____ their computers to order everything online.

2 Choose the correct responses.

1. **A:** When did people travel by horse and carriage?
   B: _____
   • In the next few years.   • About 100 years ago.   • These days.

2. **A:** When might doctors find a cure for the flu?
   B: _____
   • Nowadays.   • In the next 50 years.   • A few years ago.

3. **A:** When did the first man go to the moon?
   B: _____
   • Sometime in the future.   • Today.   • About 50 years ago.

4. **A:** When is everyone going to buy everything online?
   B: _____
   • In the past.   • Right now.   • Soon.

3 **Complete the sentences. Use the words given and ideas from the pictures.**

1. These days, _people go to the beach for vacation._ (beach)
   In the future, _they might go to space for vacation._ (space)

2. In the past, _____
   _____ (collect CDs)
   Nowadays, _____
   _____ (listen to music online)

3. A few years ago, _____
   _____ (desktop computers)
   Today, _____
   _____ (tablets)

4. Fifty years ago, _____
   _____ (business suits)
   These days, _____
   _____ (casual clothes)

5. Nowadays, _____
   _____ (drive their own cars)
   Sometime in the future, _____
   _____ (cars that drive themselves)

4 Music is change

A Read the article. How did popular music change?

Music Is Change

Popular music has changed a lot in the last one hundred years in the United States. From jazz to rock to hip-hop, music is always moving forward.

Jazz music began to make its appearance about a century ago in the United States as a fusion of European and African musical forms that people could immediately identify as something very new. Musicians all over the world began to play jazz and to make important contributions from their own musical cultures. An example of this is bossa nova (new beat), which began to emerge in Brazil in the 1950s.

Jazz evolved into Swing in the 1930s and 1940s, with large orchestras playing music that people would dance to. The big bands of Count Basie, Duke Ellington, Benny Goodman, and Artie Shaw were very popular. However, the expense of maintaining large orchestras and changing tastes led to a quite different kind of popular music in the 1950s.

In the 1950s, the rock 'n' roll electric guitar began to replace the jazz horn. Bands with only a guitarist or two, a drummer, and a singer became popular. Of course, the most important singer of this music in the U.S. was Elvis Presley. Like jazz, rock 'n' roll inspired musicians from all over the world, such as the Beatles from England, to make some of the best and most popular songs.

In the 1970s, alternatives to rock 'n' roll began to appear. Three of the most important new sounds were disco, punk, and hip-hop. Disco was famous for the rich sound created by studio musicians and the flashy clothes of the dancers. Punk was a return to small bands that played their own instruments very loud and fast and criticized society in their songs. Hip-hop began as a way to use record players to make music for parties without the need for musicians playing traditional instruments.

Some people say that these musical forms are the "children" of jazz. In any case, they are now played throughout the world with each country contributing its own very particular sound.

B What about you? Answer these questions about your own country's music.

1. What kind of music do you think your grandparents listened to? Do you like this kind of music?

_____

2. Was rock 'n' roll important to your parents? Was there someone like Elvis Presley or the Beatles in your country? Who?

_____

3. What kind of popular music do you listen to? Is it influenced by any of the musical forms discussed in the article? Which ones?

_____

5 Choose the correct responses.

1. A: What if I get in shape this summer?

   B: _____

   - You might be able to come rock climbing with me.
   - You won't be able to come rock climbing with me.

2. A: What will happen if I stop exercising?

   B: _____

   - Well, you won't gain weight.
   - Well, you might gain weight.

3. A: What if I get a better job?

   B: _____

   - You won't be able to buy new clothes.
   - You'll be able to buy some new clothes.

4. A: What will happen if I don't get a summer job?

   B: _____

   - You'll probably have enough money for your school expenses.
   - You probably won't have enough money for your school expenses.

6 Verb pairs

A Which words go with which verbs? Complete the chart.

☐	a cold	☐	money
☑	energetic	☐	relaxed
☐	a group	☐	time
☐	married	☐	a gym

feel	get	join	spend
energetic			

B Write sentences with *if*. Use some of the words in part A.

1. _If I feel energetic, I might go for a walk._ _____

2. _____

3. _____

4. _____

5. _____

6. _____

7 Complete these sentences with your own information. Add a comma where necessary.

1. If I go shopping on Saturday, _I might spend too much money._ _____

2. I'll feel healthier _____
   _____

3. If I get more exercise _____
   _____

4. If I don't get good grades in school _____
   _____

5. I might get more sleep _____
   _____

6. I'll be happy _____
   _____

8 Nouns and adjectives

A Complete the chart with another form of the word given.

Noun	Adjective	Noun	Adjective
energy	_____	_____	medical
_____	environmental	success	_____
health	_____		

B Complete the sentences. Use the words in part A.

1. There have been a lot of ___ medical ___ advances in the past half century, but there is still no cure for the common cold.

2. There are a lot of _____ problems in my country. There's too much air pollution, and the rivers are dirty.

3. My _____ is not as good as it used to be. So, I've decided to eat better food and go swimming every day.

4. My party was a great _____. I think I might have another one soon!

5. If I start exercising more often, I might have more _____.

9 **Rewrite these sentences. Find another way to say each sentence using the words given.**

1. Today, people ride bicycles less often than before. (used to)

   People used to ride bicycles more often than they do today. ____ OR

   In the past, people used to ride bicycles more often than they do today.

2. If I stop eating junk food, I may be able to lose weight. (diet)

   _____

3. In the future, not many people will use cash to buy things. (few)

   _____

4. If I get a better job, I can buy an apartment. (be able to)

   _____

5. I'm going to arrive at noon. (will)

   _____

10 **Write three paragraphs about yourself. In the first paragraph, describe something about your past. In the second paragraph, write about your life now. In the third paragraph, write about your future.**

I used to live in a very quiet place . . .

Now, I live in a big city. My job is . . .

If my English improves, I may be able to get a job with an international company . . .

Next year, I'm going to . . . I might . . .

_____

_____

_____

_____

_____

_____

_____

_____

_____

_____

_____

_____

_____

_____

10 I like working with people.

1 Choose the correct responses.

1. **A:** I enjoy working in sales.

   B: _____

   • Well, I can.   • Neither do I.   • So do I.

2. **A:** I like working the night shift.

   B: _____

   • Well, I don't.   • Neither do I.   • Neither am I.

3. **A:** I can't stand getting to work late.

   B: _____

   • I can't.   • Neither can I.   • Well, I do.

4. **A:** I'm interested in using my language skills.

   B: _____

   • So am I.   • Oh, I don't.   • Oh, I don't mind.

2 Complete the sentences with the words and phrases in the box. Use gerunds.

| ☐ commute | ☐ start her own business | ☑ work under pressure |
| ☐ learn languages | ☐ use a laptop | ☐ work with a team |

1. Elena enjoys being a journalist. She has to write a news story by 4:00 P.M. every day, but she doesn't mind _working under pressure_ .

2. Takiko is a novelist. He writes all his books by hand because he hates _____.

3. Sarah usually works alone all day, but she enjoys _____, too.

4. Jennifer works for a large company, but she's interested in _____.

5. Pablo has to use Portuguese and Japanese at work, but he's not very good at _____.

6. Annie has to drive to work every day, but she doesn't like _____.

3 **Rewrite these sentences. Find another way to say each sentence using the words given.**

1. I'm happy to answer the phone. (mind)

   I don't mind answering the phone.

2. I can't make decisions quickly. (not good at)

   _____

3. I hate making mistakes. (stand)

   _____

4. I don't enjoy working alone. (with a team)

   _____

4 **Complete these sentences about yourself. Use gerunds.**

On the job or at school

1. I like *meeting people, but I'm a little shy.*
2. I can't stand _____
3. I don't mind _____

In my free time

4. I'm interested in _____
5. I'm not interested in _____

At parties or in social situations

6. I'm good at _____
7. I'm not very good at _____

5 **Choose the correct words.**

1. Eric hates waiting in line. He's a very _____ person.
   (impatient / disorganized / punctual)

2. You can trust Marta. If she says she's going to do something, she'll do it.
   She's very _____ .
   (hardworking / level-headed / reliable)

3. Kevin isn't good at remembering things. Last week, he missed another
   important business meeting. He's so _____ .
   (efficient / forgetful / moody)

6 Job ads on the Internet

A Read these job listings. Match the job titles in the box with the listings below.

_____ flight attendant   _____ journalist   _____ language teacher   _____ stockbroker

JOBSEARCH

find a job

1. Are you hardworking? Do you enjoy using computers? Do you like learning about world news? This job is for you. Must be good at working under pressure. Some evening and weekend work.

2. Must be well organized, energetic, able to make decisions quickly, and good with numbers. Applicants must be level-headed and able to take responsibility for handling other people's money. No weekend work, but some evening work required.

3. No previous experience necessary, but applicant must be willing to work long hours. Successful applicant will also be punctual and reliable. Excellent position for someone who enjoys traveling.

4. Have you studied a foreign language? You may be the right person for this position. Applicants should be comfortable speaking in front of a group and they should be able to communicate well with others.

B What key word(s) in each job ad helped you find the answers in part A?

1. _____
2. _____
3. _____
4. _____

C Which job would be the best for you? The worst? Number them from 1 (the best) to 4 (the worst) and give reasons. List your special experience, preferences, or personal traits.

Job	Reason
_____ language teacher	_____
_____ journalist	_____
_____ flight attendant	_____
_____ stockbroker	_____

7 **Read what these people say about themselves. Then look at the jobs in the box. Choose a job each person should do and a job each person should avoid. Write sentences using *because*.**

☐ accountant	☐ detective	☐ lawyer	✓ nurse	☐ salesperson
☐ carpenter	☐ factory worker	☐ marine biologist	☐ model	✓ social worker

> I enjoy helping people, but I can't stand working nights and weekends.

Alan

1. (make a good / could never) _Alan would probably make a good social_
   worker because he enjoys helping people. He could never be a nurse
   because he can't stand working nights and weekends.

> I really like doing things with my hands. I also enjoy working with wood. I don't enjoy working in the same place every day, and I hate being in noisy places.

Olivia

2. (could / couldn't) _____
   _____
   _____

> I'm really interested in meeting people, and I enjoy wearing different clothes every day. I'm not so good at organizing my time, and I don't like to argue.

Margo

3. (would make a good / would make a bad) _____
   _____
   _____

> I'm really good at selling things. I also love helping people. But I'm not so good at solving problems.

Ha-joon

4. (could be / wouldn't make a good) _____
   _____
   _____

> I love the outdoors and I'm very interested in the sea. I don't like sitting in an office all day, and I'm not good with numbers.

Eddie

5. (would make a good / wouldn't want to be) _____
   _____
   _____

8 | Add *a* or *an* in the correct places.

1. Mike could never be $\overset{a}{\wedge}$ nurse or teacher because he is very short-tempered and impatient with people. On the other hand, he's efficient and reliable person. So he would make good bookkeeper or accountant.

2. Scott would make terrible lawyer or executive. He isn't good at making decisions. On the other hand, he'd make excellent actor or artist because he's very creative and funny.

9 | Opposites

A Write the opposites. Use the words in the box.

☐ boring	☐ forgetful	☐ late	☐ outgoing
✓ disorganized	☐ impatient	☐ moody	☐ unfriendly

1. efficient / _disorganized_

2. friendly / _____

3. punctual / _____

4. interesting / _____

5. level-headed / _____

6. patient / _____

7. quiet / _____

8. reliable / _____

B Complete the sentences with the words in part A.

1. Mingyu is an _____ person. She really enjoys meeting new people.

2. Hannah is very _____. One day she's happy, and the next day she's sad.

3. I can't stand working with _____ people. I like having reliable co-workers.

4. Charles is an _____ person. I'm never bored when I talk to him.

A Choose the correct word to complete each sentence.

☐ critical	☐ efficient	☐ forgetful	☐ generous
☐ impatient	☐ level-headed	☑ reliable	☐ strict

1. I always do my job well. My boss never has to worry because I'm ____reliable____.

2. Ed would make a great nurse because he's so _____. He never gets anxious or upset when things go wrong.

3. A good lawyer has to remember facts. Nathan is a terrible lawyer because he's very _____.

4. My favorite teacher at school was Mrs. Wilson. She was pretty _____, so no one misbehaved in her class.

5. My boss is very _____. She gave me a big holiday bonus.

6. June's assistant is very _____. She works fast and never wastes time.

7. My boss complains about everything I do. He's so _____.

8. Julie is so _____. She can't stand waiting for anything.

B Complete the conversations. Use the phrases in the box.

☐ Neither do	☐ Neither am	☐ Neither is	☐ I don't mind
☐ So is	☐ I am	☐ Neither can	☐ So am

1. **A:** I'm not very good at video games. How about you?

   B: Oh, _____. I play video games every weekend.

2. **A:** Jake is not punctual.

   B: _____ Karen. She's always late.

3. **A:** I'm so disorganized!

   B: _____ I. My desk is a mess. I can never find anything.

4. **A:** I don't mind traveling for work.

   B: _____ I. I think it's kind of fun.

5. **A:** I can't stand working in the evening.

   B: _____ I. I prefer to work during the day.

6. **A:** I'm not very outgoing at parties.

   B: _____ I. I'm usually pretty quiet at social events.

7. **A:** I hate taking the train to work.

   B: _____. I usually read or listen to music when I'm on the train.

8. **A:** Stella is really creative.

   B: _____ Robert. He always has great ideas.

11 It's really worth seeing!

1 Complete these sentences. Use the passive form of the verbs in the box.

□ compose	□ discover	□ paint
☑ design	□ invent	□ write

1. The Niterói Contemporary Art Museum in Brazil
   _____was designed_____ by the architect
   Oscar Niemeyer.

2. The play *Romeo and Juliet* _____
   by William Shakespeare in the 1590s.

3. The microwave oven _____
   by Percy Spencer in 1947.

4. The picture *Sunflowers* _____
   by Vincent van Gogh in 1888.

5. In 1960, a 1,000-year-old Viking settlement in Canada
   _____ by Norwegian explorer
   Helge Ingstad.

6. The song "Let It Go" from the movie *Frozen*
   _____ by a married couple,
   Robert Lopez and Kristen Anderson-Lopez.

2 Change these active sentences into the passive.

1. Scientists first identified the Ebola virus in 1976.
   The Ebola virus was first identified by scientists in 1976.

2. J. J. Abrams directed the box-office hit *Star Wars: The Force Awakens.*
   _____

3. The Soviet Union launched the first satellite into space in 1957.
   _____

4. E. B. White wrote the children's novel *Charlotte's Web.*
   _____

5. Frank Lloyd Wright designed the Guggenheim Museum in New York City.
   _____

3 Write sentences. Use the simple past form of the passive with *by*.

1. Angkor Wat

builder: Suryavarman II
year: 1150

2. the Blue Mosque

designer: Mehmet Aga
year: 1616

3. Buckingham Palace

builder: the Duke of Buckingham
year: 1705

4. Canberra, Australia

planner: Walter Burley Griffin
year: 1913

5. the Vasco da Gama Bridge

designer: Armando Rito
year: 1998

6. the Burj Khalifa

builders: 12,000 workers
year: 2010

1. _Angkor Wat was built by Suryavarman II in 1150._

2. _____

3. _____

4. _____

5. _____

6. _____

4 Which city?

A Read about these cities. Write the cities in the box next to the correct descriptions below.

☐ Cusco, Peru   ☐ Bogotá, Columbia   ☐ Valparaíso, Chile

☐ Rio de Janeiro, Brazil   ☐ Montevideo, Uruguay   ☐ Ottawa, Canada

_____ This capital city's name is taken from the word *adawa* in the Algonquin language, which probably means "to trade."

_____ The Spanish explorer Juan de Saavedra named this city after his village in Spain. The name means "Valley of Paradise."

_____ The name of this city, which means "River of January" in English, comes from the fact that it was discovered by the Portuguese on January 1, 1502. However, there's no river in the city, just the bay!

_____ The name of this city comes from the expression *Qusqu Wanka* (Rock of the Owl) in Quechua, the language of the Incas. The myth was that a hero who grew wings discovered the place and then became a rock to mark the spot.

_____ The most popular belief about the name of this city is that it comes from the Portuguese expression *monte vid eu* (I saw a hill), spoken by a sailor who first saw this spot in January of 1520.

_____ The name of this city comes from the indigenous Muisca language, but the original word was *bacatá* (planted fields).

B Check (✓) True or False. For statements that are false, write the correct information.

	True	False
1. Both Bogotá and Ottawa were named after a person.	☐	☐
_____		
2. Montevideo and Valparaíso were named by explorers.	☐	☐
_____		
3. Cusco was named after the mythological story of a bird.	☐	☐
_____		
4. Rio de Janeiro was named because of the month of the year it was discovered.	☐	☐
_____		

5 **Add *is* or *are* where necessary.**

Ecuador ˅is situated on the equator in the northwest of
South America. It made up of a coastal plain in the west
and a tropical rain forest in the east. These two areas
separated by the Andes mountains in the center of
the country.

The economy based on oil and agricultural products.
More oil produced in Ecuador than any other South
American country except Venezuela. Bananas,
coffee, and cocoa grown there. Many of these
products exported. Hardwood also produced
and exported.

Many people in Ecuador are of Incan origin. Several
native languages spoken there, such as Quechua.
Spanish spoken in Ecuador, too.

6 **Complete the sentences. Use the words in the box.**

✓ handicrafts	☐ electronics	☐ peso	☐ wheat
☐ beef	☐ mining	☐ tourism	

1. In many countries, __handicrafts__ are sold by people who make them
   as well as sell them.

2. The _____ is the currency that is used in Chile.

3. Millions of people visit Italy every year. _____ is a very
   important industry there.

4. A lot of meat, especially _____, is exported by Argentina.

5. Gold _____ is an important industry in South Africa.

6. Much of the world's _____ is grown in the Canadian prairies.
   It's used to make foods like bread and pasta.

7. A lot of computers are exported by Taiwan. In fact, the _____
   industry is an important part of many East Asian economies.

7 Complete this paragraph with *is* or *are* and the past participle of the verbs in the box. Some words may be used more than once.

border	divide	find	locate
call	fill	know	visit

Every year, millions of tourists visit California. California _____ for its beautiful scenery, warm climate, and excellent food. There are many national parks in California. They _____ by over 30 million people every year. Many world-famous museums _____ there, including the Getty Center in Los Angeles and the San Francisco Museum of Modern Art.

The state _____ into two parts, called Northern California and Southern California. San Francisco and Yosemite National Park _____ in Northern California.

San Francisco _____ by water on three sides. It is a city with a beautiful bay and two famous bridges. San Francisco's streets _____ always _____ with tourists. On the north end of the bay is the world-famous Napa Valley. South of San Francisco, there is an area that is famous for its computer industries; it _____ Silicon Valley. Many computer industries _____ there. Los Angeles, Hollywood, and Disneyland _____ in Southern California. Southern California _____ for its desert areas, which are sometimes next to snowcapped mountains.

8 Rewrite these sentences. Find another way to say each sentence using the words given.

1. The designer of the Montjuic Tower in Barcelona was Santiago Calatrava. (designed)

   _____

2. Switzerland has four official languages. (spoken)

   _____

3. In South Korea, a lot of people work in the automobile industry. (employed)

   _____

4. Malaysia has a prime minister. (governed)

   _____

9 Wh- questions and indirect questions

A Look at the answers. Write Wh- questions.

1. What _____

The telephone was invented by Alexander Graham Bell.

2. Where _____

Acapulco is located in southern Mexico.

3. When _____

Santiago, Chile, was founded in 1541.

4. What _____

Rice is grown in Thailand.

B Look at the answers. Write indirect questions.

1. Do you know _____

The Golden Gate Bridge is located in San Francisco.

2. Can you tell me _____

Don Quixote was written by Miguel de Cervantes.

3. Do you know _____

Antibiotics were first used in 1941.

4. Could you tell me _____

The tea bag was invented by Thomas Sullivan in 1908.

10 Complete the sentences. Use the passive of the words given.

1804 The first steam locomotive

_____ was built _____ (build) in Britain.

1829 A speed record of 58 kph (36 mph)

_____ (establish) by a train

in Britain.

1863 The world's first underground railway

_____ (open) in London.

1964 "Bullet train" service _____

(introduce) in Japan.

1990 A speed of 512 kph (320 mph) _____

(reach) by a French high-speed train.

1995 Maglevs _____ (test) in several countries.

These trains use magnets to lift them above the ground.

2006 The Qinghai-Tibet railway _____ (finish).

It is the world's highest railway and reaches 5,072 meters (16,640 feet).

2011 The journey time from Beijing to Shanghai _____ (reduce)

from 10 hours to 5.5 hours by the new maglev train.

12 It's a long story.

1 **Describe what these people were doing when a fire alarm went off in their apartment building last night. Use the past continuous.**

Carolyn

Peter

the Mitchells

Isabella and Carlos

Mr. Yang

Paula

1. _Carolyn was washing the dishes when the fire alarm went off._

2. _____

3. _____

4. _____

5. _____

6. _____

2 **Describe your activities yesterday. What were you doing at these times?**

At 9:00 A.M.

At 9:00 A.M., I was having
breakfast at a coffee shop
with my friends.

Around noon

_____

_____

_____

About 10:00 last night

_____

_____

_____

At 11:00 in the morning

_____

_____

_____

In the afternoon

_____

_____

_____

At this time yesterday

_____

_____

_____

3 Complete the conversation with the correct word or phrase.

Matt: How did you get your first job, Sonia?

Sonia: Well, I _____*got*_____ a summer job in a department store
(got / was getting)

while I _____ at the university.
(studied / was studying)

Matt: No, I mean your first full-time job.

Sonia: But that *is* how I got my first full-time job. I _____ during the
(worked / was working)

summer when the manager _____ me a job after graduation.
(offered / was offering)

Matt: Wow! That was lucky. Did you like the job?

Sonia: Well, I did at first, but then things changed. I _____ the same
(did / was doing)

thing every day, and they _____ me any new responsibilities.
(didn't give / weren't giving)

I _____ really bored when another company
(got / was getting)

_____ me to work for them.
(asked / was asking)

4 Look at the pictures and complete these sentences.

1. My roommate was studying when
  _she fell asleep!_____

2. I saw an old friend last week while
  _____

3. My car was giving me a lot of trouble, so

4. Coffee arrived while

A Scan the article. Why is Lila Downs famous?

Lila Downs

Lila Downs is a Grammy-award winning singer and songwriter who is famous not only in Mexico and the United States, but throughout the world.

Lila was born in the state of Oaxaca, Mexico in 1968. Her mother belongs to the indigenous Mixtec people who speak both Mixtec and Spanish. Her father, who died when Lila was sixteen, was a professor of art and film from the United States. As a girl living in and traveling between Mexico and the U.S., Lila picked up the musical influences that give her music a very international flavor. She still travels a lot between Mexico and the U.S. because her husband is from Minnesota.

Lila is trilingual. She sings in Mixtec, Spanish, and English. She can sing in other languages, too. She learned to sing as a child by listening to her mother, who was a professional singer of Mexican popular music. Lila's first big success came in 1999 with her album *La Sandunga*, which is the name of a traditional dance in Oaxaca. In 2005 she went on to win the Latin Grammy award for *Una Sangre (One Blood)*.

Lila became known to many people through her singing performance in *Frida*, the 2002 film about the famous Mexican artist Frida Kahlo. She has acted in and contributed music to a number of films, while also writing the music and lyrics with her husband to the musical version of *Como agua para chocolate (Like Water for Chocolate)*, based on the very popular book by Mexican novelist Laura Esquivel.

Although she studied classical voice at college in the United States, Lila has devoted a great part of her career to singing the music of Mexico in Spanish, Mixtec, and Zapotec, which is another indigenous language in the state of Mexico. Many of her songs are concerned with social justice.

B Read the article and check (✓) True or False. For statements that are false, write the correct information.

	True	False
1. Lila Downs' father was a professor of literature in the United States.	☐	☐
2. Her husband is from the United States.	☐	☐
3. She wrote the book *Como agua para chocolate*.	☐	☐
4. She studied classical voice in college in Mexico.	☐	☐
5. She speaks Spanish, Mixtec, and English.	☐	☐

6 How long has it been?

A Write sentences. Use the present perfect continuous and *for* or *since*.

> **Grammar note: *for* and *since***
>
> **Use *for* to describe a period of time.**
> *Linda has been living in Seattle **for three months**.*
> *I haven't been jogging **for very long**.*
> **Use *since* to describe a point of time in the past.**
> *Linda has been living in Seattle **since she changed jobs**.*
> *I haven't been jogging **since I hurt my foot**.*

1. Annie / work / actor / three years

   <u>Annie has been working as an actor for three years.</u>

2. Carrie and Alex / go / graduate school / August

   _____

3. Tom / study / Chinese / a year

   _____

4. Linda / not teach / she had a baby

   _____

5. Lori / not live / Los Angeles / very long

   _____

6. Luis and Silvina / travel / South America / six weeks

   _____

B Write sentences about yourself. Use the phrases and clauses in the box (or your own information) and *for* or *since*.

18 months	**a few weeks**
2006	**I was in high school**
ages	**this morning**

1. <u>I haven't been swimming for ages.</u>
2. _____
3. _____
4. _____
5. _____
6. _____

7 Look at the answers. Write the questions.

Mark: _What have you been doing lately?_

Andrew: I've been working a lot and trying to stay in shape.

Mark: _____

Andrew: No, I haven't been jogging. I've been playing tennis in the evenings with friends.

Mark: Really? _____

Andrew: No, I've been losing most of the games. But it's fun. How about you?

_____

Mark: No, I haven't been getting any exercise. I've been working long hours every day.

Andrew: _____

Mark: Yes, I've even been working on weekends. I've been working Saturday mornings.

Andrew: Well, why don't we play a game of tennis on Saturday afternoon? It's great exercise!

8 Choose the correct responses.

1. A: When I was a kid, I lived on a farm.

   B: _____

- Really? Tell me more.
- Oh, have you?
- So have I.

2. A: I haven't been ice-skating in ages.

   B: _____

- Why were you?
- Wow! I have, too.
- Neither have I.

3. A: I was a teenager when I got my first job.

   B: _____

- Really? Where do you work?
- Really? That's interesting.
- For five years.

4. A: I haven't seen you for a long time.

   B: _____

- I didn't know that.
- Not since we graduated.
- Hmm, I have no idea.

9 Complete the answers to the questions. Use the past continuous or the present perfect continuous of the verbs given.

1. **A:** Have you been working here for long?

   B: No, I <u>haven't been working</u> (work) here for very long –
   only since January.

2. **A:** Were you living in Europe before you moved here?

   B: No, I _____ (live) in South Korea.

3. **A:** How long have you been studying English?

   B: I _____ (study) it for about a year.

4. **A:** What were you doing before you went back to school?

   B: I _____ (sell) real estate.

5. **A:** What have you been doing since I last saw you?

   B: I _____ (travel) around the country.

10 Rewrite these sentences. Find another way to say each sentence using the words given.

1. Terri was about 15 when she started saving up for a world trip. (teenager)

   <u>Terri started saving up for a world trip</u>
   <u>while she was a teenager.</u>

2. I was getting dressed when my friend arrived. (while)

   _____

   _____

3. I've been a fan of that TV show since I was a kid. (a long time)

   _____

   _____

4. I've had a part-time job for a year. (last year)

   _____

   _____

5. I've been spending too much money lately. (not save enough)

   _____

   _____

6. I haven't seen you for a long time. (ages)

   _____

   _____

13 That's entertainment!

1 Choose the correct words to complete these movie reviews.

Classic Movie Review

Login / Register

Home   Reviews   News   Archives   Search

Indiana Jones and the Kingdom of the Crystal Skull

This action movie is dumb. It has ___amazing___ (amazed / amazing) action scenes, but the story is really _____ (bored / boring). I think the other Indiana Jones movies were _____ (excited / exciting), but I think this one is ridiculous.

Brian's Song

This drama is based on a _____ (fascinated / fascinating) true story. It's about Brian Piccolo, a football player who develops a terrible disease, and his friend Gayle Sayers. Maybe it doesn't sound _____ (interested / interesting), but it's a must-see. The film has great acting and a wonderful script. I was very _____ (moved / moving) by the story of the friendship between Piccolo and Sayers.

2 Choose the correct words.

1. Denzel Washington was ___outstanding___ (horrible / ridiculous / outstanding) in his last movie. I think he's a really great actor.

2. I really enjoyed all of the *Hunger Games* movies. In fact, I think they're _____ (terrible / wonderful / boring).

3. The special effects were great in that sci-fi movie we saw last week. They can do such _____ (silly / dumb / incredible) things with 3-D technology these days.

4. The latest *Star Wars* movie was _____ (dumb / disgusting / fantastic), and I'd love to see it again.

3 Choose the correct responses.

1. A: I think that Keira Knightley is very pretty.

B: _Oh, I do, too._

- Oh, I do, too.
- I don't like her either.

2. A: His new movie is the dumbest movie I've ever seen.

B: _____

- Yeah, I liked it, too.
- I didn't like it either.

3. A: It's weird that they don't show more classic movies on TV. I really like them.

B: _____

- I know. It's really wonderful.
- I know. It's strange.

4. A: I think Tina Fey is hilarious.

B: _____

- Yeah, she's horrible.
- Yeah, she's excellent.

5. A: The movie we saw last night was ridiculous.

B: _____

- Yes, I agree. It was exciting.
- Well, I thought it was pretty good.

4 Write two sentences for each of these categories.

1. Things you think are exciting

I think paragliding is exciting.

_____

2. Things you are interested in

_____

_____

3. Things you think are boring

_____

_____

4. Things you are disgusted by

_____

_____

5 Movie classics on the Internet

A Read about these movies available online. Write the number of the movie next to its type.

_____ fantasy   _____ war movie   _____ romantic drama   _____ science fiction

Movie Classics

1. Casablanca (1942)
This is the story of two people in love during World War II who are waiting in Casablanca for a chance to escape from the war. Starring Humphrey Bogart and Ingrid Bergman and directed by Michael Curtiz, this movie is a must!

2. Pan's Labyrinth (2006)
This movie blends a story of the Spanish Civil War with the mythological fantasies of a young girl (Ivana Baquero). It takes place in the mountains of northern Spain where legends of strange creatures are still told. The movie was written and directed by Guillermo del Toro. It is a masterpiece and it is out of this world!

3. 2001: A Space Odyssey (1968)
Directed by Stanley Kubrick, this is a story about two astronauts who are on a fatal mission in outer space. But it's the ship's computer, HAL, who really steals the show.

4. The Bridge on the River Kwai (1957)
You will never forget the music of this film! And you will understand why many people think it is one of the best movies ever made about war. It is the story of British and American soldiers who are prisoners of war. They must build a bridge in Burma during World War II. You will not be disappointed!

B Write the name of the movie described.

1. a movie with an unusual "star": _____

2. two lovers in a difficult situation: _____

3. where dreams and reality meet: _____

4. its music is unforgettable: _____

C Match the expressions in column A with their meanings in column B.

A	B
1. you won't be disappointed _____	**a.** you need to see it
2. out of this world _____	**b.** becomes the center of attention
3. it's a must _____	**c.** you're going to like it
4. steals the show _____	**d.** outstanding

6 Tell me more!

A Rewrite these sentences. Use *who* or *which*.

1. *The Sound of Music* is a movie. It has been very popular for a long time.

   The Sound of Music is a movie which has been very popular for a long time.

2. *The Theory of Everything* is a movie. It is based on a true story about Stephen Hawking.

   _____

3. Elizabeth Taylor was an actress. She won two Academy Awards.

   _____

4. Akira Kurosawa was a director. He was one of the most influential filmmakers in history.

   _____

5. *The Miracle Worker* is a great movie. It won a lot of awards.

   _____

6. Jennifer Lopez is an actress, a dancer, and a singer. She also appears on TV.

   _____

B Write two sentences like those in part A about movies and entertainers. Use *who* or *which*.

1. _____

2. _____

7 Complete the sentences. Use *that* for things or *who* for people.

Heather: Who is Mark Twain?

Carlos: Oh, you know him. He's an author _____who_____ wrote a lot of novels about life in America in the 1800s.

Heather: Oh, I remember. He wrote several stories _____ people have to read in literature classes, right?

Carlos: Yes, but people love reading them for pleasure, too.

Heather: What's his most popular book?

Carlos: I guess *Adventures of Huckleberry Finn* is the one _____ is most famous. It's a work _____ has been very popular since it was published in 1885.

Heather: Ah, yes, I think I've heard of it. What's it about?

Carlos: It's about a boy _____ has a lot of adventures with his friend Tom Sawyer. It was one of the first American novels _____ was written in the first person. It's Huck Finn himself _____ tells the story.

Heather: Now, that's a story _____ I'd like to read.

8 Different kinds of movies

A Write definitions for these different kinds of movies. Use relative clauses and the phrases in the box.

- [ ] has a love story
- [✓] has cowboys in it
- [ ] has a lot of excitement
- [ ] is about a real person
- [ ] is scary
- [ ] makes you laugh
- [ ] shows real events

1. A western *is a movie that has cowboys in it.*
2. A romance _____
3. A comedy _____
4. An action film _____
5. A horror film _____
6. A biography _____
7. A documentary _____

B What kind of movie in part A is your favorite? Your least favorite?
Write one paragraph about each and give reasons for your opinions.

My Favorite Kind of Movie

I really like action movies. They are movies that make me forget about all my problems. . . .

_____
_____
_____
_____
_____

My Least Favorite Kind of Movie

I don't like horror movies because I think they are really dumb. Usually, the story has characters
who are not very scary. . . .

_____
_____
_____
_____
_____

9 Complete these sentences. Use the words in the box.

☐ character   ☐ composer
☐ cinematography   ☐ special effects

1. I thought the _____ in the *Jurassic Park* movies were cool. It's incredible what they can do with computers.
2. Have you ever seen the 1965 film *Doctor Zhivago*? The _____ is beautiful, especially the lighting.
3. Hermione Granger is my favorite _____ in the *Harry Potter* books.
4. I've forgotten the name of the _____ who wrote *Rhapsody in Blue*. Was it George Gershwin?

10 Rewrite this movie review. Where possible, join sentences with *who*, *that*, or *which*.

THE HUNGER GAMES

The Hunger Games is a series of science fiction films. They started to come out in 2012. The first one was directed by Gary Ross. He also wrote the screenplay. The films include some famous actors. The actors include Jennifer Lawrence and Woody Harrelson. The films are about a young girl. She is called Katniss. She joins a contest to save her community in the near future. The future is very dark and dangerous. Will she save her community?

The Hunger Games is a series of science fiction films that started to come out in 2012.

_____

_____

_____

_____

_____

1 What does that mean?

A What do these gestures mean? Match the phrases in the box with the gestures.

a. Stop!
b. I want to turn.
c. We need a taxi.
d. We need help.
e. I'm angry!

1. _e_
2. ___
3. ___
4. ___
5. ___

B Write a sentence about each situation in part A using the phrases in the box.

It could mean . . .	It might mean . . .	It must mean . . .
Maybe it means . . .	Perhaps it means . . .	It probably means . . .

1. _It must mean he's angry._
2. _____
3. _____
4. _____
5. _____

2 Complete the sentences. Use the correct form of the words in the box.

	annoy		confuse		embarrass		frustrate
	bore	✓	disgust		exhaust		

1. The food in that restaurant is __disgusting__.
   I'll never eat there again!

2. That sign is really _____.
   What does it mean? It's not clear at all.

3. I got stuck behind a really slow bus on a
   narrow mountain road. I felt
   _____ because I couldn't
   pass it.

4. I drove for eight hours on a straight, flat road
   where the scenery never changed. I've never
   been so _____!

5. I couldn't get into the parking space,
   and everyone was looking at me. It was
   pretty _____.

6. I went bicycling all day. Now I'm so
   _____ that I'm going to sleep
   for 12 hours!

7. I asked the taxi driver to turn off his radio
   because the loud music was very
   _____.

3 What would you say in each situation? Use the sentences in the box.

	Come here.		Shh. Be quiet!
	That sounds crazy!		Where's the restroom?

1. Your friend wants to dye his hair green and wear orange contact lenses.

   _____

2. You can't concentrate on the movie because the people in front of you are talking.

   _____

3. You wave to your friend because you want to show her something interesting.

   _____

4. You just ordered a meal and want to wash your hands before you eat.

   _____

4 Proverbs

A Match the proverbs with their meanings.

Proverbs

1. The grass is always greener on the other side of the fence.

2. An ounce of prevention is worth a pound of cure.

3. An apple a day keeps the doctor away.

4. There are plenty of fish in the sea.

5. Better late than never.

6. Birds of a feather flock together.

Meanings

_____ If you eat the right food you will be healthy.

_____ People with the same interests become friends.

__1__ We may think we will be happier in a different situation, but it is not necessarily true.

_____ Don't worry if you love someone who doesn't return your love. You can always find someone else.

_____ It is easier to fix something before there is a problem than after the problem has occurred.

_____ It is preferable to do something with some delay than to never do it at all.

B What would you say? Choose a proverb for each situation.

1. **A:** I really don't understand what Miriam sees in Bill.

   B: Oh, I do. They both love movies from other countries and they like learning languages.

   A: Ah, I see! _____

2. **A:** It's 10 o'clock already! Do you think I can get to the party on time?

   B: That depends on whether you can catch the bus.

   A: But what if I don't?

   B: Well, getting there is the important thing. _____

3. **A:** A penny for your thoughts.

   B: I was just thinking about what it's like to be a movie star.

   A: Do you think they're any happier than you are?

   B: They must be, don't you think?

   A: Oh, I don't know. _____

4. **A:** It's cold outside. Why don't you put on your new coat?

   B: Do you think I need to, dear?

   A: Well, you don't want to catch a cold like the one you had last month, do you?

   B: OK, you're right. Like they say, _____

5 What do you think these proverbs mean?

1. Don't cry over spilled milk.

It could mean _____

2. Don't judge a book by its cover.

Maybe it means _____

3. There's no such thing as a free lunch.

It might mean _____

4. Bad news travels fast.

It probably means _____

6 Complete the conversation. Use each phrase in the box only once.

☐	it might be
☐	it's definitely
☐	you can
☐	you have to
☑	you're not allowed to

Teacher: OK, class. This afternoon, we're going to take the school bus to the science museum.

Student 1: Great! I'm going to take some photos.

Teacher: I'm afraid _you're not allowed to_ take photos.

Student 1: But how can they stop me? I'll use my cell phone, not a camera.

Teacher: _____ check all your things with security.

Student 2: Can I take my jacket into the museum?

Teacher: I'm not sure. _____ best to leave it on the bus.

Student 2: But what about my wallet? It might not be safe on the bus.

Teacher: Oh, _____ a good idea to keep your money with you. Keep it in your pocket.

Student 3: And what about touching things in the museum?

Teacher: There are "Don't touch!" signs next to some of the things. But _____ touch things if there is no sign.

7 **Look at the numbered photos of signs below. Then complete the conversations between a driving instructor and his student. Use each word or phrase in the box only once.**

☐ are allowed to   ☐ can   ☐ don't have to
☑ aren't allowed to   ☐ can't   ☐ have to

1. **Student:** This is great!
   Instructor: Hey, slow down! You _aren't allowed to_ go above the speed limit.

2. **Student:** Uh, what does that sign mean?
   Instructor: It means you _____ turn left.

3. **Instructor:** You look confused.
   Student: What . . . what does that sign mean?
   Instructor: It means you _____ do two things. You _____ turn right or go straight.

4. **Instructor:** Why are you stopping?
   Student: The sign says to stop.
   Instructor: Actually, you _____ stop. Just be prepared to, if necessary.

5. **Instructor:** Hey, stop! Didn't you see that sign? It means you _____ come to a complete stop.
   Student: What sign? I didn't see any sign.

8 **Rewrite these sentences. Find another way to say each sentence using the words given.**

1. Maybe it means you're not allowed to fish here. (may)

It may mean you're not allowed to fish here.

2. You can't light a fire here. (allowed)

_____

3. Perhaps that sign means you're not allowed to swim here. (might)

_____

4. I think that sign means you can get food here. (probably)

_____

5. You need to be quiet after 10:00 P.M. (have got to)

_____

9 **Complete each conversation using the words in the box.**

☐ confusing　☐ embarrassing　☐ exhausting　☐ impatient　☐ irritating

1. A: I went to the movies last night. A couple who sat behind me talked during the entire movie.

　B: That's _____!

2. A: I fell asleep during class this afternoon. The teacher had to wake me up.

　B: Oh, that's _____!

3. A: I drove all night to get there on time.

　B: Oh, that's _____! How can you keep your eyes open?

4. A: Did Sara give you directions to the party?

　B: She did, but they're really _____. Hey, can I get a ride with you?

5. A: This movie is taking forever to download. Why does it have to take so long?

　B: You are so _____! There, look. It's done!

15 I wouldn't have done that.

1 I think I'd . . .

A What would you do in these situations? Check (✓) an answer or write your own suggestion.

1. Your classmate leaves her new smartphone in the classroom.

   ☐ run after her and give it back to her immediately

   ☐ take it home overnight to try it out

   ☐ _____

2. Someone climbs through your neighbor's window.

   ☐ call the police

   ☐ ring the doorbell

   ☐ _____

3. Your boss makes things difficult for you at work.

   ☐ talk to your boss

   ☐ look for another job

   ☐ _____

4. A friend sounds unhappy on the phone.

   ☐ ask your friend if he or she has a problem

   ☐ tell jokes to make your friend laugh

   ☐ _____

B Write about what you would do in the situations in part A. Use the phrases in the box.

I'd . . .	I might . . .	I guess I'd . . .
I'd probably . . .	I think I'd . . .	

1. _If my classmate left her new smartphone in the classroom,_
   I think I'd run after her and give it back to her immediately.

2. _____

_____

3. _____

_____

4. _____

_____

2 Complete these sentences with information about yourself.

1. If a relative asked to borrow some money, I'd _____

2. If I had three wishes, _____

3. If I could have any job I wanted, _____

4. If I had a year of vacation time, _____

5. If I could change one thing about myself, _____

3 Choose the correct word.

1. I'd go ____straight____ to the police if I saw someone breaking into a house.
   (seriously / simply / straight)

2. My friend _____ to cheating on the biology exam, but his teacher still failed him.
   (returned / confessed / said)

3. I'm in a difficult _____ at work. I don't know whether to talk to my boss about it or just quit.
   (divorce / predicament / problem)

4. If I saw someone _____ in a store, I'd tell the store manager immediately.
   (cheating / shoplifting / shopping)

5. My uncle died and left me $20,000. I'm going to _____ most of it.
   (invest / return / sell)

6. When I went back to the parking lot, I tried to get into someone else's car _____ mistake.
   (by / in / with)

7. There is so much great music to download from the Internet. I don't know what to _____.
   (choose / confess / fix)

8. My aunt won't let me use her car because she thinks I'm a terrible driver.
   She has a _____. I had two accidents last year!
   (flat tire / point / reward)

4 What to do?

A Read the article. Match what happened to a possible action.

What happened

1. You bought a camera on sale at a store, but it didn't work right. The salesclerk said, "We can't do anything about it."

2. You checked your bank statement and noticed that there was a deposit of $1,000. You didn't make the deposit. You're sure it was a bank error.

3. You sat on a park bench that had wet paint on it. You ruined your clothes. There was no "Wet Paint" sign.

4. You were not happy with the grade you got in an important class.

5. Your next-door neighbors borrowed your vacuum cleaner. When they returned it, it was damaged.

6. A friend gave you an expensive vase for your birthday, but you didn't really like it.

Possible actions

_____ I guess I'd take it back to the store and exchange it for something else.

_____ I guess I'd write a letter of complaint to the manufacturer.

_____ Maybe I'd ask them to repair it.

_____ I think I'd make an appointment to see the instructor to talk about it.

_____ I'd probably wait until the next month to see if the mistake is corrected.

_____ I'd write a letter to the city council and ask them to pay for the damage.

B What would you do in each situation? Write another possible action.

1. _____

2. _____

3. _____

4. _____

5. _____

6. _____

5 What would you have done in these situations? Use *would have* or *wouldn't have.*

1. Lisa had dinner in a restaurant and then realized she didn't have any money. She offered to wash the dishes.

   I wouldn't have washed the dishes. I would have
   called a friend to bring me some money.

2. Alex was on a bus when the woman next to him started talking loudly on a cell phone. He asked her to speak more quietly.

   _____

   _____

3. Ryan invited two friends to dinner on Friday, but they came on Thursday by mistake. He told them to come back the next day.

   _____

   _____

4. Luke's neighbors had their TV on very loud late at night. Luke called and complained to the police.

   _____

   _____

5. Sharon had a houseguest who was supposed to stay for three days, but the woman was still there three weeks later. Sharon finally gave her a bill for her room and board.

   _____

   _____

6. Margo accidentally broke a glass at a friend's house. She decided not to say anything about it.

   _____

   _____

6 Write two things you should have done or shouldn't have done last week, last month, and last year.

1. Last week: _Last week, I should have . . ._ _____

   _____

2. Last month: _____

   _____

3. Last year: _____

   _____

7 Advice column

A Complete each letter with the correct forms of the verbs in each box.

☐ borrow	☐ disagree	☑ marry	☐ spend
☐ deny	☐ enjoy	☐ save	☐ lose

✉ Ask Harriet

Dear Harriet,

I've never written to an advice columnist before, but I have a big problem. I'm going out with this really nice guy. He's very sweet to me, and I really want to ____marry____ him. In fact, we plan to have our wedding next summer. But he has a problem with money. He _____ money like crazy! Sometimes he _____ money from me, but he never pays it back. I want to _____ money because I want us to buy an apartment when we get married. However, if I tell him he has a problem with money, he _____ it. He says, "I _____ with you. You never want to go out and _____ yourself." I don't want to _____ him, but what can I do? – J. M., Seattle

☐ accept	☐ admit	☑ agree
☐ find	☐ forget	☐ refuse

Dear J. M.,

You and your boyfriend must ____agree____ on how you spend your money *before* you get married. If you both _____ that there is a problem, you could probably _____ an answer. He should _____ your idea of saving some money. And you shouldn't always _____ to go out and have fun. Don't _____ that talking can really help.

Good luck! – Harriet

B What advice would you give J. M.? Write a reply to her letter.

_____

_____

_____

_____

_____

_____

8 To accept or to refuse?

A Complete the conversation with *would* or *should* and the correct tense of the verbs given.

Carly: Guess what, Kristin! A university in New Zealand has offered me a scholarship.

Kristin: Great! When are you going?

Carly: That's just it. I may not go. What ____would____ you ____do____ (do) if your boyfriend asked you not to go?

Kristin: Well, I _____ (try) to convince him that it's a good opportunity for me.

Carly: I've tried that. He said I could study the same thing here.

Kristin: If I were you, I _____ (talk) to him again. You know, I once missed a big opportunity.

Carly: Oh? What happened?

Kristin: I was offered a job in Los Angeles, but my husband disliked the idea of moving, so we didn't go. I _____ (take) the job. I've always regretted my decision. In my situation, what _____ you _____ (do)?

Carly: Oh, I _____ (accept) the offer.

Kristin: Well, there's the answer to your predicament. Accept the scholarship!

B What would you do if you were Carly? Why?

If I were Carly, . . . _____

_____

9 What would you do if you found a diamond ring? Complete these sentences.

1. I would _hide it and come back for it later._
2. I wouldn't _____
3. I could _____
4. I might _____
5. I might not _____

16 Making excuses

1 **People are making many requests of Eric. Write the requests.**
Use *ask*, *tell*, or *say* and reported speech.

1.	**Mark:**	"Eric, take my phone calls."
2.	**Julie:**	"Can you do an Internet search for me, Eric?"
3.	**Andrew:**	"Could you check this flash drive for viruses?"
4.	**Tanya:**	"Eric, put this information on a spreadsheet."
5.	**Carla:**	"Don't forget to add paper to the copier, Eric."
6.	**Alan:**	"Reformat this text file as a PDF file."
7.	**Bruce:**	"Get me some coffee, Eric."
8.	**Cindy:**	"Make five copies of the agenda before the meeting."
9.	**Jack:**	"Could you give me a ride home?"
10.	**Robin:**	"Don't be late to work again."

1. _Mark told Eric to take his phone calls._

2. _____

3. _____

4. _____

5. _____

6. _____

7. _____

8. _____

9. _____

10. _____

2 Nouns and verbs

A Complete the chart.

Noun	Verb	Noun	Verb
acceptance	accept	_____	explain
_____	apologize	_____	invite
_____	complain	_____	offer
_____	excuse	_____	suggest

B Complete these sentences. Use the correct form of the words from part A.

1. This coffee tastes awful. I'm going to ___complain___ to the waiter about it.

2. I _____ an invitation to Billy and Kate's house for dinner.

3. I didn't want to go to Jenny's party, so I made up an _____.

4. I was rude to my teacher. I must _____ to him.

5. Can you _____ the end of the movie? I didn't understand it.

6. Steve said he'd take me to the airport. It was really nice of him to _____.

7. Thank you for your helpful _____ on how to fix my essay. The teacher really liked it!

8. I received an _____ to Mindy's party. I can't wait to go.

3 Choose the correct verb. Use the past tense.

☐ express ☐ give ☐ make ☑ offer ☐ tell

1. Jennifer told me she was graduating from college, so I ___offered___ her my congratulations.

2. I _____ a complaint to the police because our neighbors' party was too noisy.

3. I couldn't go to the meeting, so I _____ my concerns in an email.

4. Jake _____ an excuse for being late for work. He said there had been a traffic jam on the highway.

5. Lori was very funny at the class party. As usual, she _____ a lot of jokes.

4 What a great excuse!

A Read the invitations and excuses in these text messages between Eileen and William. Underline the phrases that are invitations or excuses.

Hi, William. It would be wonderful if you could come to our party next Friday! It's Mick's birthday and I really think that he would appreciate it if you could be there. All of his friends will be there. The best part is that Mick doesn't know everyone is going to be there. It's a surprise birthday party! So please come and be part of the surprise.

Hi, Eileen. Thank you for the invitation. You know I would love to come if I could, but unfortunately I am working late on Friday. I have to study for my examination next week. So, have a great time without me, and of course I will send a present to Mick.

Oh, William, come on! Please come. The best present you can give to Mick is being with him on his birthday. I know everyone would really enjoy seeing you, too.

Eileen, I really should study for the test. I know I will probably regret not going, but I think I should stick to my plan.

William, you are so right when you say you will regret it if you don't come to Mick's birthday party. All of your friends will be there. As a matter of fact, I mentioned you to Penelope and she said she is looking forward to talking to you at the party. We will all be disappointed if you don't come. Especially Penelope!

Eileen, I've given it some thought and you are right! I should go to Mick's party. In fact, wild horses couldn't stop me. See you on Friday!

B Read the phrases that you underlined. Answer these questions.

1. Why did Eileen text William?

2. Why can't William come to the party?

3. Why do you think William decided to accept the invitation after all?

5 Sorry, but . . .

A The teacher wants to have a class picnic on Saturday. Look at the excuses that students gave her. Change each excuse into reported speech using *say*.

English Class Picnic on Saturday

1. Tim: "I'm getting my hair cut."

   Tim said he was getting his hair cut.

2. Teresa: "My sister is having a baby shower."

   _____

3. Bill: "I may have some houseguests on Saturday."

   _____

4. Miyako and Yoshiko: "We're going camping this weekend."

   _____

5. Marco: "I'm sorry, but I'll be busy on Saturday afternoon."

   _____

B Change these excuses into reported speech using *tell*.

1. Abbie: "I signed up for a scuba diving class."

   Abbie told her she had signed up for a scuba diving class.

2. Paul and James: "We'll be moving to our new apartment that day."

   _____

3. Luis: "I watch the football game on TV every Saturday."

   _____

4. Sandra: "I've already made plans to do something else."

   _____

C Write excuses for three more students. Use your own ideas.

1. _____

2. _____

3. _____

6 What did they say?

A Match the reports of what people said in column A with the descriptions in column B.

A	B
1. Sam said that he was talking to Jim in the office for an hour. He's very unhappy about the new company rules. _c_	**a.** giving a reason
2. Brian said that the game was canceled because of bad weather. _____	**b.** refusing an invitation
3. Nina said she would be studying on Saturday night. (But she'll actually be at the movies.) _____	**c.** making a complaint
4. Carl told me he couldn't come for dinner on Friday. He said he had to work late. _____	**d.** telling a lie
5. Max told me that he didn't want to go to the party because Kayla would be there. _____	**e.** making an excuse

B Write each person's original words.

1. Sam: _"I was talking to Jim in the office for an hour. He's very unhappy_
about the new company rules."

2. Brian: _____

_____

3. Nina: _____

_____

4. Carl: _____

_____

5. Max: _____

_____

7 Choose the correct responses.

1. A: We're going to go hiking. Do you want to join us?

B: _____

- Sorry, I won't be able to.   • What's up?

2. A: I'm really sorry. We'll be out of town this weekend.

B: _____

- I've made other plans.   • No problem.

3. A: Meet us at 7:00. OK?

B: _____

- Oh, that's all right.   • OK, sounds like fun.

4. A: I'm sorry. I won't be able to make it.

B: _____

- Well, never mind.   • Great.

8 Yes or no?

A Which expressions would you use to accept an invitation? To refuse an invitation? Check (✓) the correct answer.

	Accept	Refuse
1. I'm really sorry.	☐	☐
2. Great.	☐	☐
3. Sounds like fun.	☐	☐
4. I've made other plans.	☐	☐
5. I won't be able to make it.	☐	☐
6. I'm busy.	☐	☐
7. Thanks a lot.	☐	☐
8. I'd love to.	☐	☐

B Use the expressions in part A to accept or refuse these invitations. Offer an excuse if you refuse.

1. Would you like to come to a soccer match with me tomorrow?

_____

2. That new action movie looks great! Do you want to see it with me?

_____

3. A friend asked me to go to the mall after class. Do you want to join us?

_____